MEMORABLE
FILM
CHARACTERS

Dedicated to the memory of Susan Lieberman,

who originally had the idea for this book

but did not survive to see it in print.

My recollection of her enthusiasm for this project

stayed with me through its completion,

and her excitement for all of life will always

remain a positive influence on me.

MEMORABLE FILM CHARACTERS

An Index to Roles and Performers, 1915–1983

Compiled by

SUSAN LIEBERMAN

and

FRANCES CABLE

Bibliographies and Indexes in the Performing Arts, Number 1

Greenwood Press
Westport, Connecticut • London, England

Library of Congress Cataloging in Publication Data

Lieberman, Susan.
  Memorable film characters.

  (Bibliographies and indexes in the performing arts,
ISSN 0742-6933 ; no. 1)
  Bibliography: p.
  Includes indexes.
  1. Characters and characteristics in moving-pictures—
Indexes. 2. Moving-picture actors and actresses—
Indexes. I. Cable, Frances. II. Title. III. Series.
PN1995.9.C36L5 1984   791.43'09'0927   84-10844
  ISBN 0-313-23977-0 (lib. bdg.)

Library of Congress Catalog Card Number: 84-10844
ISBN: 0-313-23977-0
ISSN: 0742-6933

First published in 1984

Greenwood Press
A division of Congressional Information Service, Inc.
88 Post Road West
Westport, Connecticut 06881

Printed in the United States of America

10 9 8 7 6 5 4 3 2 1

TABLE OF CONTENTS

INTRODUCTION

Do you remember such elusive facts as what actress played Prissy in *Gone With the Wind,* the name of the cowboy portrayed by John Wayne in *True Grit,* or the two characters who traveled *Around the World in Eighty Days?* How often have you been unable to finish a crossword puzzle because you're missing a movie name, or been stumped while playing a film nostalgia game at a party? Are you ever kept awake at night because you cannot remember a film character, the actor or actress who played the part, or the title of the movie in which there was a memorable characterization?

The difficulty of answering such questions in a large university reference library prompted the writing of this book. Susan Lieberman and I wanted to produce a convenient, one-volume reference source that would identify and describe, however tersely, some of the more memorable characters that have appeared on the screen. We have tried to create a work that would assist with answering such questions, as well as provide pleasure for anyone with an interest in film—students, movie devotees, nostalgia buffs, crossword puzzle solvers, or merely collectors of film facts.

Scope

The time span covered is from the very beginning of movies through 1983. Over 1500 characters are drawn from the silents and the talkies, predominantly from American but also from foreign films. All genres—Western, drama, comedy, who-done-it, fantasy, historical, musical, and any other category that might set the stage for a memorable characterization—are included.

Methodology

What makes a character memorable? To identify the outstanding characterizations from cinema is difficult and controversial, demonstrated regularly by different reviewers' reactions to the same role. In very few cases does everyone agree, since enjoyment of a movie or a portrayal is personal—an individual experience.

Susan and I felt that a nomination for a prestigious award received by a movie or an individual would be a public rather than a purely personal vote for an outstanding character or performance. We used as our base the casts of films nominated for best movies of the year, plus nominees for best actor and actress and best supporting actor and actress. We did this for awards given by all of the following: the Academy of Motion Picture Arts and Sciences, the New York Film Critics, National Board of Review, British Academy of Film and Television Arts, and the Cannes Film Festival. We read at least three reviews of each of these films released since 1940, and as many reviews as we could find for those prior to that date.

In addition, a questionnaire was devised and sent to 75 acquaintances around the country known to be movie buffs. This questionnaire asked for a list of their most memorable movie characters, indicating at least two out of three of the following for positive identification: name of the actor, title of the film, and a short description of the character. Surprisingly, all but one of the questionnaires were returned. (People do enjoy recalling and sharing memorable movie experiences.) Not surprisingly, 80 percent of the responses had already been included in our work, but the additional names did add an amateur film buff's dimension to a list otherwise tilted toward the tastes of professional artists and critics.

The award searching and questionnaires combined with copious reading, discussion with other movie enthusiasts, and constant attendance at current films and at the reruns shown at the Pennsylvania State University contributed to our final selection.

The resultant entries may still be criticized for some omissions, but the constraints of time and space make this unavoidable. The author and her editors are still discussing characters that might have been included.

The following ground rules were established to insure consistency:

1. *New York Times* reviews were the prime authority for spelling of characters and actors' names, as well as film titles, unless there were obvious errors. I still find variant spellings when using other reference books. When a movie is released in another country, the title may change when it opens in the United States.

2. *The New York Times* was also used to establish release dates, but again, the serious researcher will find differences. Foreign films may first appear in the United States several years after playing in the country of origin. *Variety* frequently cites a different year than the *Times* even though the movie is produced and released here.

3. Our primary purpose is to identify characters. Therefore, characters in remakes or new issues of movies are not traced unless those portrayals are themselves considered memorable. A series character, such as Nick Charles from *The Thin Man,* will only be mentioned once and not necessarily from the first performance. There has been no attempt to link sequels.

Arrangement

A character may be identified in three different ways: by name, by the title of the movie in which he or she appeared, or by the name of the actor or actress portraying the role.

The main text lists the character names in alphabetical order. Following each name is a short description of the character, the title of the film in which that character appears, the date the film was released, and the actor or actress who played the role. "See" references are included throughout.

A selective bibliography is included.

An alphabetical film index lists the selected character names for each movie.

An actor index identifies the selected characters portrayed by each individual actor or actress.

Acknowledgments

Such a book as this would not be possible without the advice and assistance of many people. I would like to thank Michal Van Dommelen for her constructive guidance, enthusiasm, and painstaking attention to detail while revising and editing; Nancy Struble for her mastery of the computer, and for the skill, patience and cheerfulness with which she accomplished the voluminous task of typing frequently revised data; David Van Dommelen for capably and creatively helping to prepare the book for publication; William O'Donnell, my technical mentor, for support during the many difficult and challenging stages of the book's development; and Frank for his love of film, constant encouragement and patient understanding, which carried me through times when the whole project seemed impossible.

Fran Cable
March 1984

MEMORABLE
FILM
CHARACTERS

FILM CHARACTERS

Abelman, Sam.
Aging, dignified, and idealistic doctor in a depressed Brooklyn neighborhood is more concerned with the welfare of his poor patients than with accumulating a fortune.
The Last Angry Man. 1959. Muni, Paul

Abrahams, Harold.
Tough, abrasive, competitive Jew, an Olympic hopeful and Cambridge student who stands up for his rights with a mixture of extroverted charm and ambition, runs to achieve acceptance and visibility in a prejudiced Anglo-Saxon society.
Chariots of Fire. 1981. Cross, Ben

Abu.
Young thief meets the deposed prince of Bagdad in prison and helps him, through the power of a genie and a magic carpet, to seek the hand of a beautiful princess.
The Thief of Bagdad. 1940. Sabu

Actor.
Conceited, jealous actor concocts an elaborate scheme to test his wife's fidelity, but is never satisfied that his suspicions are unfounded.
The Guardsman. 1931. Lunt, Alfred
The Chocolate Soldier. 1941. Eddy, Nelson

Actress.
Alluring, seductive actress will not tell her husband that she knew that he was masquerading as the guardsman to test her faithfulness.
The Guardsman. 1931. Fontanne, Lynn
The Chocolate Soldier. 1941. Stevens, Rise

Adam.
After this strapping Oregon pioneer farmer marries, he encourages his six rowdy brothers to find wives for themselves.
Seven Brides for Seven Brothers. 1954. Keel, Howard

Adams, Alice.
Lonely daughter of a small-town pre-Depression family economically lagging behind their neighbors, Alice is a social climber. At the same time, she is sharply critical of her own romantic pretensions.
Alice Adams. 1935. Hepburn, Katharine

Adams, Mamie.
This amiable and sentimental woman is the head of a "family" of shanty-town prostitutes.
Primrose Path. 1940. Rambeau, Marjorie

Adams, Roger.
Struggling small-town newspaper publisher adopts a child and lovingly raises her until the age of six, when she dies after a brief illness. He then leaves his wife because he cannot bear to be reminded of the dead child, but they are reconciled after deciding to adopt a little boy.
Penny Serenade. 1941. Grant, Cary

Addams, Frankie.
Lonely, complicated 12-year-old tomboy, caught between childhood and adolescence, waits for her adored elder brother's wedding, naively convinced that she will be included in the honeymoon trip.
The Member of the Wedding. 1952. Harris, Julie

Adrian.
Adrian is painfully shy and inarticulate, yet she is able to capture the heart of a locally prominent South Philadelphia boxer.
Rocky. 1976. Shire, Talia

Agnes.
Cared for by a loving nurse, this Swedish spinster, one of three sisters, is terminally ill with cancer. She endures racking coughing spells, cries bitterly for help and has agonizing pain, but through this suffering finds a peace unknown to the more beautiful and healthy sisters.
Cries and Whispers. 1973. Andersson, Harriett

Aisgill, Alice.
Attractive, passionate middle-aged woman, clutching at her last chance for happiness, has a stormy love affair with an ambitious office worker. She suffers an untimely death after he jilts her in favor of a woman who can improve his social position.
Room at the Top. 1959. Signoret, Simone

Albert.
The ultimate Parisian waiter, Albert seats people tactfully, serves them graciously, and is a genius at soothing ruffled feelings.
Service for Ladies. 1927. Menjou, Adolphe

Aldrich, Henry.
Likeable, extroverted, and irrepressible adolescent is constantly getting into trouble, either at Central High where he is a student, or at home where he is perpetually in disgrace over grades, finances, or dates.
What a Life. 1939. Cooper, Jackie

Alex.
Sinister, violent English teen-ager of the 21st century, completely lacking in any sense of morality, lives in a world that is only slightly less corrupt than he is. It is a world that has found no easy solution to the eradication of evil.
A Clockwork Orange. 1971. McDowell, Malcolm

Alex.
Living in a giant old warehouse lot, this radiant, flirtatious welder by day, avant-garde dancer at Mawby's Bar by night, dreams of becoming a member of the Pittsburgh Repertory Dance Company.
Flashdance. 1983. Beals, Jennifer

Alexander, see Ekdahl, Alexander

Alexandra.
This loving but gently neurotic German-born consort of Nicholas II, like her husband, is so self-engrossed and uninformed that she ultimately contributes to the deaths of millions.
Nicholas And Alexandra. 1971. Suzman, Janet

Alfie.
Carefree, Cockney Don Juan has the ability to charm and use many "birds." When he is finished, he throws them away, reasoning that love makes one vulnerable and ultimately leads to disappointment and rejection.
Alfie. 1966. Caine, Michael

Alfred, Count.
The roguish Sylvanian envoy to France has so many amorous adventures in Paris that he is ordered home. In his new assignment, he ultimately falls in love with the queen.
The Love Parade. 1929. Chevalier, Maurice

Alice.
Prissy, puritanical wife is appalled when her swinger friends talk freely about their affairs. However, after her husband also becomes "liberated" and commits adultery, Alice visits a psychiatrist, and eventually she herself proposes an evening of mate-swapping.
Bob & Carol & Ted & Alice. 1969. Cannon, Dyan

Alice.
A would-be actress, dressed like Jean Harlow, enters a dance marathon hoping to be noticed by a talent scout in the audience. She is devastated when her partner receives an offer of work instead.
They Shoot Horses, Don't They? 1969. York, Susannah

Alice, see Hyatt, Alice

Allen, Barbara.
This ignorant Tennessee mountain girl knows no other existence but that of slaving for the lazy menfolk. Her life is changed by the attention of one boy who respects and wants to protect her.
Stark Love. 1927. Munday, Helen

Allen, James.
An unemployed Army veteran, convicted and imprisoned for an offense he did not commit, escapes from the brutal and barbaric practices of the Georgia chain gang, only to be forced against his will into a life of crime.
I am a Fugitive from a Chain Gang. 1932. Muni, Paul

Allen, Marie.
An innocent 19-year-old is sentenced to prison as an accessory in a gasoline station holdup in which her husband is killed. She delivers her child in prison, tries to fight injustice and start anew; but through her association with murderers and prostitutes, and unfair treatment by prison officials, she becomes an unregenerate criminal.
Caged. 1950. Parker, Eleanor

Allessio, Vicki.
A seductive London divorcee with two children, with clear, no-nonsense ideas of what she expects in a man, has an affair with an American insurance broker.
A Touch of Class. 1973. Jackson, Glenda

Allison.
Wholesome, vital teenager, shocked by the knowledge that she was an illegitimate child, leaves Peyton Place and flees to New York.
Peyton Place. 1957. Varsi, Diane

Allison.
In reality a file clerk but masquerading as a corporate librarian, 34-year-old Allison, who thinks she's 22, has a one-night fling with a successful rock composer appearing on the cover of *Time* magazine.
Who is Harry Kellerman and Why is He Saying Those Terrible Things About Me? 1971. Harris, Barbara

Allnutt, Charlie.
Tough, rum-soaked skipper of a decrepit, steam-driven riverboat changes from an uncouth and uncaring drifter to a man of devotion and courage after becoming involved with a lady missionary in German East Africa during World War I.
The African Queen. 1952. Bogart, Humphrey

Alma.
A decent, warmhearted prostitute, known as Lorene at the New Congress Club in World War II Honolulu, yearns to be respectable and proper. She befriends a lonely soldier when his company and officers turn against him.
From Here to Eternity. 1953. Reed, Donna

Alma.
Wisecracking, tipsy, interior decorator's maid perceives that her employer has more on her mind than an aggravating telephone party line. It's probably the other party.
Pillow Talk. 1959. Ritter, Thelma

Alma.
Worldly-wise but lonely housekeeper for a ranch owner has a tantalizing flirtation with the rancher's amoral son. This leads to his drunken attempt at rape and her eventual decision to leave.
Hud. 1963. Neal, Patricia

Alquist, Paula.
This young woman innocently marries a murderer and is soon terrorized and nearly driven insane by his attempts to get possession of her family's jewelry.
Gaslight. 1944. Bergman, Ingrid

Alyosha.
Charming, innocent young Russian soldier earns a ten-day leave from war and uses the time to make the long journey home to see his mother. Along the way he helps a crippled veteran, a faithless wife, and a young homeless girl, so that when he finally arrives home, he has time simply to embrace his mother and to start back to war again.
Ballad of a Soldier. 1960. Ivashov, Vladimir

Anastasia.
Amnesic young woman is recruited to impersonate the daughter of the murdered Russian Czar so that the conspirators may collect a large inheritance. The situation is confounded, however, when it turns out that she may actually be the real Anastasia.
Anastasia. 1956. Bergman, Ingrid

Andrews, Ellie.
After arguing with her father and hitchhiking from Florida to Pennsylvania, this runaway heiress meets a newspaper reporter, falls in love, and matures into a responsible woman.
It Happened One Night. 1934. Colbert, Claudette

Angela.

When her two brothers go off to war, this girl keeps their lighthouse on the Italian coast. She finds a German spy washed up on the rocks, falls in love and marries him, but cannot forgive him when his service to his country results in the death of her brother.
The Love Light. 1920. Pickford, Mary

Angela.

Young circus performer, unjustly convicted of a crime, falls in love with an artist and is eventually sent to prison. Upon her release, she recognizes her portrait in a church and is reunited with the painter.
Street Angel. 1928. Gaynor, Janet

Angela, Sister.

Marooned on a South Pacific island during World War II, this delightful, mild-mannered nun and a gruff, impious Marine corporal work side by side to survive, and develop a tender affection and deep understanding of each other.
Heaven Knows, Mr. Allison. 1957. Kerr, Deborah

Angelique.

This headstrong but loyal mulatto maid, accompanying her mistress from Paris to New Orleans so that the latter can claim her rights and gain revenge, loudly disapproves of the Texas cowboy who appears on the scene.
Saratoga Trunk. 1946. Robson, Flora

Angie.

As her husband's career blossoms, this famous night-club singer begins losing control, turns to the bottle, and soon becomes a pathetic drunk.
Smash-Up—The Story of a Woman. 1947. Hayward, Susan

Angie.

Spunky abandoned wife and her young son tend an isolated ranch despite warnings of Apache uprisings.
Hondo. 1953. Page, Geraldine

Angie.

Bored, dateless Bronx bachelor, living a dull provincial life in the same city block where he was born, resents his best pal's girl friend because she presents a threat to their friendship.
Marty. 1955. Mantell, Joe

Angie.

Charming, spunky Macy's clerk, daughter of a protective Italian family, becomes pregnant after a one-night fling at a summer resort. She subsequently falls in love with the easygoing musician who is the father of the child.
Love With the Proper Stranger. 1963. Wood, Natalie

Animal, see Stosh

Anita.
Hot-blooded Puerto Rican girl, sweetheart of the leader of the Sharks, constantly warns her best friend of the perils of being in love with a boy from another ethnic group.
West Side Story. 1961. Moreno, Rita

Anna.
A poor and sincere country girl, who was tricked into a fake marriage and bore a child who died, finds work as a maid for wealthy farmers from whom she must conceal her past.
Way Down East. 1920. Gish, Lillian

Anna.
Headstrong, proper British schoolteacher, hired to teach the children of the stubborn Siamese monarch, clashes with the powerful king, but eventually comes to respect and love him.
Anna and the King of Siam. 1946. Dunne, Irene
The King and I. 1956. Kerr, Deborah

Anna.
Although always at the side of her dying charge, tenderly nestling and protective, this loving nurse is treated heartlessly after the patient's death by the sisters of the deceased.
Cries and Whispers. 1973. Sylwan, Kari

Anna, in *The French Lieutenant's Woman,* see Sarah

Anne.
The young second wife of an elderly Danish pastor wishes he were dead because she falls in love with his son. When the old man dies, she is accused of being a witch and is condemned to burn.
Day of Wrath. 1943. Movin, Lisbeth

Anne.
Vivacious, sophisticated fashion editor of *Smith's Weekly,* co-worker of a journalist posing as a Jew, has much more sympathy and understanding for the writer than does his fiancee.
Gentleman's Agreement. 1947. Holm, Celeste

Anne.
Beautiful, lonely princess, bored with protocol and court etiquette, runs away to spend a day in Rome. Here she meets and falls in love with a handsome American newspaperman.
Roman Holiday. 1953. Hepburn, Audrey

Anne of Cleves.
Fourth wife of Henry VIII, Anne is able to save her head because she is a businesswoman and is able to avoid the king's romantic passions.
The Private Life of Henry VIII. 1933. Lanchester, Elsa

Annie.
Troubled, determined but always sympathetic, Annie is the skipper of the West Coast tugboat Narcissus. She is always trying to keep her shiftless but likeable husband dry and sometimes would like to kill him, but she never allows anyone else to speak ill of him.
Tugboat Annie. 1933. Dressler, Marie

Annie, in *Lady for a Day,* see Apple Annie

Anshel, see Yentl

Antinea.
Fascinating, capricious vamp, Queen Antinea traps French Army officers in her Saharan kingdom to serve as her successive husbands. As she tires of each, she imprisons him until he dies of love.
Missing Husbands. 1922. Napierkowska, Stacia

Antipov, Pasha.
Pre-Revolutionary bourgeois intellectual and idealist will not compromise his principles. With the Revolution he is transformed into the cruel and vicious Streinikoff, a fanatic killer of all who oppose his ideas.
Doctor Zhivago. 1965. Courtenay, Tom

Antoinette, Marie.
This capricious, extravagant woman is unable to understand the problems of her time and is deserted by her friends. Held captive by her enemies, in her final hours she becomes the true heroine of the French Revolution.
Marie Antoinette. 1938. Shearer, Norma

Anton, Gregory.
This Victorian villain murders his mistress, seduces her niece into marriage, and then attempts to drive the girl mad in order to get possession of her family's jewels.
Gaslight. 1944. Boyer, Charles

Antonia.
Beautiful, intelligent, suffering wife of a famous symphony conductor generously offers her husband his freedom when he has an affair with a journalist.
Interlude. 1968. Maskell, Virginia

Antonietta.
In 1938 in Rome, during Hitler's visit with Mussolini, a woman with six children, married to an ardent Fascist, regains her womanhood and pride with a suspected homosexual outcast who lives across the courtyard.
A Special Day. 1977. Loren, Sophia

Antonio.
When his bicycle, which is essential to his work, is stolen, this poor, anguished billposter, accompanied by his little son, scours the streets of Rome in a frantic but futile hunt for the bike. He is eventually driven to stealing a replacement.
The Bicycle Thief. 1949. Maggiorani, Lamberto

Antony, Marc.
Revengeful Marc Antony discredits Caesar's assassins in his brilliant, spellbinding funeral oration on the Ides of March.
Julius Caesar. 1953. Brando, Marlon

Apperson, James.
Wealthy, pampered private in the U.S. Army during World War I goes to the French front unaware of the harshness of life, and emerges as a bitter, shocked veteran.
The Big Parade. 1925. Gilbert, John

Apple Annie.
Old New York fruit peddler is helped by gangster friends to pose as Mrs. E. Worthington Manville, an elegant society matron, so that she can continue to deceive her visiting daughter.
Lady for a Day. 1933. Robson, May

Applegate, Sue.
A comic romance ensues when this young woman who is short of funds dresses as a little girl so that she can ride for half fare. She shares a Pullman car with a major from a military school.
The Major and the Minor. 1942. Rogers, Ginger

Arden, John.
A famous musician is bitter because he has become deaf and is no longer able to perform. He begins to enjoy his life again when he decides to become a philanthropist for the stepped-upon street people in the neighborhood park.
The Man Who Played God. 1922. Arliss, George

Armbruster, Wendell.
Wealthy American business executive frenetically and confusedly tangles with love and bureaucracy in Italy, where he comes to claim the body of his father, killed when he drove his car off a high cliff.
Avanti. 1972. Lemmon, Jack

Armstrong, Margaret.
Although she loves her husband dearly, this woman turns her attention to a Prussian officer when her husband neglects her.
Blind Husbands. 1919. Billington, Francelia

Armstrong, Robert.
This surgeon who is completely wrapped up in his work does not realize how much his devoted wife needs his love and attention.
Blind Husbands. 1919. De Grasse, Sam

Arnold.
Wealthy, successful New Yorker, one-time agent for his brother, a former television scriptwriter turned nonconformist, begs his brother to return to work and bring his nephew up properly.
A Thousand Clowns. 1965. Balsam, Martin

Arrowsmith, Leora.
An unsophisticated, devoted wife of a famous medical researcher, Leora cannot convince her husband that his healing skills are a more important contribution to society than his chance to become a renowned scientist.
Arrowsmith. 1931. Hayes, Helen

Arrowsmith, Martin.
After the loss of his wife, Martin realizes that his choice to dedicate himself to research rather than to the treatment of people was ill-advised, and he decides to resume his medical practice.
Arrowsmith. 1931. Colman, Ronald

Artful Dodger.
Cunning, self-confident Dodger introduces Oliver Twist to his first pickpocket job and to the city of London as he sings "Consider Yourself at Home."
Oliver. 1968. Wild, Jack

Arthur.
Cocky, likeable, but belligerent Nottingham factory worker works hard during the week, expecting nothing more than his paycheck. On Saturdays he asserts his independence at the local pub before spending the evening with the wife of a friend.
Saturday Night and Sunday Morning. 1961. Finney, Albert

Arthur, in *Arthur,* see Bach, Arthur

Ashe, Jan.
The daughter of a famous attorney finally heeds his advice and leaves her underworld lover. After her new fiance shoots the gangster, she joins her father in the defense of her betrothed.
A Free Soul. 1931. Shearer, Norma

Ashe, Stephen.
An outstanding, albeit alcoholic, criminal lawyer is unable to keep a promise to his daughter Jan to curb his heavy drinking. In an impassioned courtroom soliloquy he does, however, successfully defend Jan's fiance, who is charged with murdering her ex-lover.
A Free Soul. 1931. Barrymore, Lionel

Ashley, Philip.
In the 19th century a young Englishman marries the widow of his foster father, even though he suspects she might have been responsible for her husband's death. When his suspicion is reawakened, he practically engineers her death, forcing himself to wonder for the rest of his life whether or not she was guilty.
My Cousin Rachel. 1952. Burton, Richard

Augusta.
Septuagenerian English aunt, with modified but still existent passions, tries to revitalize her stuffy, plodding, middle-aged nephew during their trans-European travels.
Travels With My Aunt. 1972. Smith, Maggie

Aunt.
Charming, sympathetic but stalwart spinster aunt of Stevie Smith, British poet and novelist, listens to her niece's reminiscences.
Stevie. 1978. Washbourne, Mona

Aunt Augusta, see Augusta

Aunt Belle, see Belle, Aunt

Aunt Betsey, see Trotwood, Betsey

Aunt March, see March, Aunt

Aunt Rose Comfort, see Comfort, Rose

Aurora.
Well-to-do widow and possessive mother, living in a posh house in Houston, Aurora has successfully sublimated her feelings, even towards her daughter whom she really loves. Her emotional life is revived by her neighbor, a fascinating, eccentric ex-astronaut.
Terms of Endearment. 1983. MacLaine, Shirley

Avigdor.
A brash, attractive rabbinical student is prevented from marrying his lovely fiancee through a technicality of religious code. Unaware that his fellow student, Anshel, is an impersonation by a girl, Yentl, he asks him/her to marry his fiancee in his stead.
Yentl. 1983. Patinkin, Mandy

Babe.

Moody Columbia University graduate and dedicated jogger is pursued, captured and tortured by a former Nazi for reasons he is unable to understand. His vengeance is equally painful to the war criminal.
Marathon Man. 1976. Hoffman, Dustin

Baby Doll.

Infantile, flirtatious "child-bride" of a poor white Southerner is seduced by her husband's business acquaintance.
Baby Doll. 1956. Baker, Carroll

Baby Face, see Martin, Baby Face

Bach, Arthur.

Rich, eccentric, often inebriated young man, mothered by his loyal valet, is trying to delay marriage to a boring wealthy girl his parents have chosen for him. He falls in love with a shoplifter whom he meets in an exclusive New York department store.
Arthur. 1981. Moore, Dudley

Bailey, George.

Frustrated because he is trapped in a small town and is facing financial ruin, this personable young man turns suicidal. He is saved by a heavenly messenger who shows him that his life really is rich, rewarding and wonderful.
It's a Wonderful Life. 1946. Stewart, James

Bains, Lulu.

Blonde Lulu, a girl friend of a corrupt, small-time evangelist, becomes a prostitute after she is defiled and abandoned by him. She returns to haunt his expanded reputation.
Elmer Gantry. 1960. Jones, Shirley

Baker.

This tragicomic hero is a bread baker in a French village who has no idea of the harshness and insensitivity of the world. He finds he no longer has the heart to bake after his wife runs off with another man.
The Baker's Wife. 1940. Raimu

Baker, Mrs.

Pushy, overprotective but selfless woman is the mother of a blind young man trying to make a life of his own in a San Franciso garret.
Butterflies are Free. 1972. Heckart, Eileen

Ballard.
Mr. Ballard, an unassuming English village stationmaster, grows and cultivates a rose, names it for Mrs. Miniver, and wins first prize at the annual flower show over the traditional victor, a crotchety old noblewoman.
Mrs. Miniver. 1942. Travers, Henry

Balser, Jonathan.
Self-centered, male chauvinist husband has his tastes and opinions dictated by what is fashionable and acceptable to the New York elite, as he desperately seeks their approval.
Diary of a Mad Housewife. 1970. Benjamin, Richard

Balser, Tina.
In fashionable New York City in the 1950s, this long-suffering, bored young housewife is tormented not only by a fastidious and egomaniacal husband but also by a pair of obnoxious daughters. She has a brief affair with an arrogant writer, who surprisingly is very much like her husband.
Diary of a Mad Housewife. 1970. Snodgress, Carrie

Bandit.
Many centuries ago, a wild and brutal bandit admits to a judge that he waylaid a merchant and his wife, ravished her, and killed the merchant in a fair duel. His testimony is one of four conflicting, yet equally credible, accounts of the same crime, the truth concerning which is never uncovered.
Rashomon. 1951. Mifune, Toshiro

Banks, Ethel.
Frequently visiting her newlywed daughter living in a fifth-floor walk-up in Greenwich Village, Mrs. Banks is overwhelmed by the foreign-born bohemian Don Juan residing in the attic.
Barefoot in the Park. 1967. Natwick, Mildred

Banks, Stanley T.
Forced to organize his daughter's elaborate wedding, this devoted but frustrated father is left emotionally and financially devastated.
Father of the Bride. 1950. Tracy, Spencer

Bannon, Homer.
Idealistic, righteous, aging rancher will not deviate from his principles or soften the hate and scorn he has always felt for his son's amoral behavior.
Hud. 1963. Douglas, Melvyn

Bannon, Hud.
When he revolts against his father's conventional principles in his impatience to control the family ranch, the actions of this unscrupulous, arrogant man have a disastrous impact upon three people's lives.
Hud. 1963. Newman, Paul

Barbara Jean.
Exploited for profit by a manipulative husband, this sensitive, truly talented woman can express her feelings only through her ballads. She becomes a famous singer in Nashville, but sinks deeper and deeper into emotional turmoil.
Nashville. 1975. Blakley, Ronee

Barkley, Catherine.
An English nurse during World War I, learning that she is pregnant and not wishing to expose her lieutenant lover, leaves her hospital post for Switzerland. Complications set in, the baby is stillborn and her lover arrives as she lies dying.
A Farewell to Arms. 1932. Hayes, Helen

Barney.
In Southern California this Communist lawyer undertakes the defense of a Mexican boy accused of murder because he wants to use the case for party fund raising. He then plans to let the lad be convicted.
Trial. 1955. Kennedy, Arthur

Baron, see Von Geigern, Baron Felix

Baroness Von Obersdorf, see Von Obersdorf, Baroness

Barrett, Edward Moulton.
A tyrannical, oppressive father especially loves his daughter Elizabeth and tries to keep her as a helpless invalid in his house on Wimpole Street.
The Barretts of Wimpole Street. 1934. Laughton, Charles
The Barretts of Wimpole Street. 1956. Gielgud, John

Barrett, Elizabeth.
A delicate young woman, dominated by her dictatorial father, meets the young poet Robert Browning, eventually marries him, and becomes one of England's most beloved poets.
The Barretts of Wimpole Street. 1934. Shearer, Norma
The Barretts of Wimpole Street. 1956. Jones, Jennifer

Barrett, Mary.
An aspiring young singer falls in love wih her maestro, the most renowned vocal teacher in Italy.
One Night of Love. 1934. Moore, Grace

Barrett, Oliver, IV.
Ollie, a wealthy Ivy League student, accepts his future with sadness, grace and dignity when he discovers that his young wife is dying.
Love Story. 1970. O'Neal, Ryan

Barrie, Diana.
Staying with her husband at the Beverly Hills Hotel prior to the Academy Awards ceremony, this anguished, hard-talking but beautiful actress, an Oscar nominee, pleads with him to make love to her, even though she knows he is a homosexual who really adores her despite his sexual preference.
California Suite. 1978. Smith, Maggie

Barrow, Buck.
Passionately devoted to his flashier brother Clyde, Buck becomes part of his gang of bank robbers and killers roaming Texas and Oklahoma during the Depression years.
Bonnie and Clyde. 1967. Hackman, Gene

Barrow, Clyde.
Weak of character but ferocious, this hoodlum, yearning to be somebody, catapults from one atrocity to another, lives life for the thrills of the moment, and hides his impotence behind the barrel of a gun.
Bonnie and Clyde. 1967. Beatty, Warren

Barry, Father.
Parish priest becomes a tower of strength for a dockworker, and gives him the courage to give testimony before the Crime Commission.
On the Waterfront. 1954. Malden, Karl

Bartlett, David.
An unbiased and reliable farm boy falls in love with a servant girl who has a shady past, and saves her when his puritanical parents drive her out into a blizzard.
Way Down East. 1920. Barthelmess, Richard

Bartlow, Rosemary.
Flighty, frivolous Southern belle, wife of a professor turned author, comes to Hollywood with her husband and falls into a romantic trap engineered by her husband's ruthless producer.
Bad and the Beautiful. 1952. Grahame, Gloria

Bates, Norman.
Young motelkeeper, claiming a cantankerous old mother, who in fact lives on only in his mind, is responsible for some very gruesome murders.
Psycho. 1960. Perkins, Anthony

Batiatus.
In ancient, decadent Rome, this rascal, a conniving gladiator and slave dealer, is self-serving, greedy, and full of resentment.
Spartacus. 1960. Ustinov, Peter

Baumer, Paul.
Young German enthusiastically enlists during World War I, but after he experiences the horror of battle, the terror of being seriously wounded, and the heartbreak of killing another human being, he realizes that there is no glory in war.
All Quiet on the Western Front. 1930. Ayres, Lew

Baxter, C.C.
Lonely, vulnerable young accountant attempts to advance his career by lending his apartment to company executives for their amorous affairs. His chance meeting with one of these paramours leads to his new view of life.
The Apartment. 1960. Lemmon, Jack

Baxter, Ma.
Living in Florida's wild scrub-country at the end of the 19th century, this decent, hard-working woman tries to scrape together a meager living from the land, but is so embittered over the loss of several children that she is unable to love her husband or her remaining son.
The Yearling. 1946. Wyman, Jane

Baxter, Penny.
This warm and gentle frontier farmer, who has a deep love and understanding of his young son, helps the child gently into manhood when the youngster's beloved yearling deer must be destroyed.
The Yearling. 1946. Peck, Gregory

Beale, Howard.
Old-time newscaster in the style of Edward R. Murrow becomes the sensation of television. When told he's to be fired because of poor ratings, he announces on TV that in the following week, in the middle of the seven o'clock news, he will commit suicide.
Network. 1976. Finch, Peter

Bean, Roy.
Tough-skinned but sentimental real-life judge, known as "the law West of the Pecos," holds court in a Texas saloon in the 1880s.
The Westerner. 1940. Brennan, Walter
The Life and Times of Judge Roy Bean. 1972. Newman, Paul

Beasant, Norma.
A small-town Southern flirt causes trouble for the men in her life.
Coquette. 1929. Pickford, Mary

Beatrice.
Embittered, slovenly widow and mother, living in a world abandoned by men, plods through her life in a seedy house in a run-down city. She torments her two young daughters, and dreams of restoring the family's fortunes by opening a tearoom specializing in cheese cake.
The Effect of Gamma Rays on Man-in-the-Moon Marigolds. 1972. Woodward, Joanne

Beau Brummel, see Brummel, George

Beau Geste, see Geste, Michael

Beaumont.
A French science student is heartbroken after his work is belittled in public and his wife is stolen by another man. He becomes a clown in a traveling circus, where he falls for the equestrienne and plans revenge on those who have hurt him.
He Who Gets Slapped. 1924. Chaney, Lon

Becket, Thomas.
Unswerving in his dedication and stern sense of duty to God, Becket is consecrated as Archbishop of Canterbury. He has a turbulent relationship with the king as he takes on the responsibility of defending the church against Henry's endeavors to impose the authority of the crown.
Becket. 1964. Burton, Richard

Beldon, Carol.
In a small English town, this granddaughter of an aged local autocrat falls in love with an RAF pilot, marries him, and is killed in an air raid shortly after their marriage.
Mrs. Miniver. 1942. Wright, Teresa

Beldon, Lady.
A proud old lady in a small English town during World War II is determined to have her rose win the prize in the annual flower show.
Mrs. Miniver. 1942. Whitty, Dame May

Belinda.
A pathetic young deaf-mute is the victim of rape. Her sorry life is brightened by an understanding doctor who tends to her and her illegitimate child.
Johnny Belinda. 1948. Wyman, Jane

Belle.
Plump Jewish grandmother, enroute to see her son in Israel, is trapped in a capsized luxury liner. She makes a long and courageous underwater swim in an attempt to save the other passengers.
The Poseidon Adventure. 1972. Winters, Shelley

Belle, Aunt.
Patient, gentle aunt is supportive of her beautiful, self-indulgent debutante niece, but finally realizes that the girl has a very selfish and shallow character.
Jezebel. 1938. Bainter, Fay

Belvedere, Lynn.
A cool and haughty man, who nonetheless has a sense that his pomposity can get a bit ridiculous, moves in with a typical American family to be a live-in babysitter to some noisy, troublesome children.
Sitting Pretty. 1948. Webb, Clifton

Ben Canaan, Ari.
This young, active, scheming Sabra belongs to the Haganah, a rebel group dedicated to the recruitment of Jews to the Jewish homeland and to the condemnation of the British presence there.
Exodus. 1960. Newman, Paul

Ben-Hur, Judah.
In the time of Christ a young Jewish prince is betrayed by his Roman friend and condemned to the galleys as a slave. He struggles against Roman tyranny and injustice, and finally achieves emotional and spiritual maturity by following the example and the teachings of Jesus.
Ben-Hur. 1926. Novarro, Ramon
Ben-Hur. 1959. Heston, Charlton

Benedict, Bick.
Raw-boned perverse Texan, a part of the old cattle aristocracy, finds it difficult to accept the new oil-rich.
Giant. 1956. Hudson, Rock

Benedict, Luz.
Bitter, spinster sister of the owner of a great Texas ranch finds it impossible to relinquish her hold on the "Big House," and treats her brother's new well-bred Virginian wife as a guest rather than as the new mistress.
Giant. 1956. McCambridge, Mercedes

Benedict, Sister.
A beautiful, warm, incongruously athletic nun in charge of a poor parochial school is helped by the new parish priest in getting a new building.
The Bells of St. Mary's. 1945. Bergman, Ingrid

Benjamin, Judy.
A Philadelphia "Jewish American Princess," whose only ambition is to have a rich husband and a live-in maid, is conned into joining the U.S. Army. She becomes liberated after a riotous training period, and leaves the Army much more knowledgeable about the way authority is exercised.
Private Benjamin. 1980. Hawn, Goldie

Bennet, Elizabeth.
Known as "Lizzie," this lovely, self-assured, witty young woman is one of five daughters in a 19th-century middle-class English family all looking for a husband.
Pride and Prejudice. 1940. Garson, Greer

Berger.
Warm, sensitive, rumpled psychiatrist insightfully coaxes a young teen-ager out of himself, towards truth and a brighter future.
Ordinary People. 1980. Hirsch, Judd

Bernardo.
Proud, heroic leader of the Sharks, betrothed to a Puerto Rican spitfire, has problems with the increasingly aggressive Jets, a rival gang.
West Side Story. 1961. Chakiris, George

Berndle, Lisa.
A beautiful Viennese adolescent falls madly in love with a young pianist, bears his child after he deserts her, but continues to adore him over the years.
Letter From an Unknown Woman. 1948. Fontaine, Joan

Bernstein, Carl.
Competitive, excitable Washington Post reporter, through a series of investigations, midnight liaisons, and much guesswork, discovers the political machinations that ultimately topple President Nixon from office.
All the President's Men. 1976. Hoffman, Dustin

Berthalet, Paul.
Scornful, crippled but poignant puppeteer can speak his love to a 16-year-old orphan girl only through his marionettes.
Lili. 1953. Ferrer, Mel

Bertier, Andre.
Parisian doctor finds himself caught between his unsuspecting young wife and her conniving, romantic girlhood friend.
One Hour With You. 1932. Chevalier, Maurice

Bertier, Colette.
Busily engaged in helping her friend Mitzi solve her love problems, Colette is entirely innocent of the intrigue revolving about her own marriage.
One Hour With You. 1932. MacDonald, Jeanette

Beth.
Beth is unable to express love for her teen-age son because she had lavished all her attention and affection on an older son killed in a boating accident. This apparently cold and unfeeling wife and mother stubbornly refuses to confront her family's emotional crisis.
Ordinary People. 1980. Moore, Mary Tyler

Bevans, Howard.
Dull, mild-mannered bachelor is pushed into marriage by a spinster schoolteacher who is fearful she will remain single forever.
Picnic. 1955. O'Connell, Arthur

Bibbitt, Billy.
Young man with a serious mother complex is doomed when he joins a revolt of the patients against a tyrannical nurse in a state mental hospital.
One Flew Over the Cuckoo's Nest. 1975. Dourif, Brad

Bickle, Travis.
Although obsessed with the filth and smut of the city, this New York City taxi driver chooses to work in the riskiest parts of town. When he cannot promote his relationship with a beautiful blonde, he shows increasing signs of psychosis, resulting in murderous rampages and, ironically, heroic stature.
Taxi Driver. 1976. De Niro, Robert

Biegler, Paul.
Middle-aged, small-town Michigan lawyer delivers a complex courtroom presentation and cleverly defends an Army lieutenant accused of murdering a bartender.
Anatomy of a Murder. 1959. Stewart, James

Biff.
The oldest son of a traveling salesman becomes a shiftless drifter when he is shattered after discovering his father in a hotel room with a prostitute.
Death of a Salesman. 1951. McCarthy, Kevin

Big Daddy.
Overwhelming millionaire plantation owner wants to leave his estate to his son if the latter will only agree to father a child.
Cat on a Hot Tin Roof. 1958. Ives, Burl

Birdie.
Wise maid and Girl Friday to an actress sees many problems in the star's personal and professional life.
All About Eve. 1950. Ritter, Thelma

Birdwell, Josh.
Intense oldest son of a peace-loving Quaker family in Southern Indiana whose lives are disrupted by the Civil War, Josh fears that he may really be avoiding the war because of cowardice and not as a result of his Quaker upbringing.
Friendly Persuasion. 1956. Perkins, Anthony

Birnam, Don.
A chronic boozer goes on a binge, pawning, begging, and stealing for drinks, and reveals not only the torment and shame of a drunk but also the nature of a basically respectable man who is aware of his weakness.
The Lost Weekend. 1945. Milland, Ray

Black Pirate.
This handsome, crafty hero seeks revenge on the sea robbers responsible for his father's death, and is successful in eliminating them in a series of sudden attacks and daring duels.
The Black Pirate. 1926. Fairbanks, Douglas

Blackburn, Steve.
Typical American male living in London with his wife and family often has his fragile ego crushed in his affair with a British dress designer.
A Touch of Class. 1973. Segal, George

Blaine, Lester.
Slick, homicidal actor marries the playwright who fired him because he was unsuitable for her play and makes plans to kill her through an accomplice.
Sudden Fear. 1952. Palance, Jack

Blaine, Rick.
The owner of a Casablanca cafe during World War II, this tough and stubborn American, who is also idealistic and sentimental, helps his former mistress and her husband to escape from the Nazis.
Casablanca. 1942. Bogart, Humphrey

Blake, Merry Noel.
Upon writing a big trashy novel about the lives and loves of her Malibu neighbors, this good-looking housewife and mother becomes the sensation of America, revealing her innermost secrets on television, and appearing at all the important cocktail parties.
Rich and Famous. 1981. Bergen, Candice

Blake, Unity.
Homely and malformed little servant girl becomes devoted to her employer and kills his cruel, alcoholic wife and herself so that he can marry the young woman he loves.
Stella Maris. 1918. Pickford, Mary

Blanche.
In the steamy squalor of New Orleans, this lonely, deteriorating Southern belle tries to hold on to her fading gentility, but suffers a slow, tragic mental collapse because of her brother-in-law's heartless badgering.
A Streetcar Named Desire. 1951. Leigh, Vivien

Blanche.
A pitifully nervous, hysterical preacher's daughter by accident of marriage finds herself an outlaw. Having no proclivity for this profession, she sticks her fingers in her ears during the gunfights.
Bonnie and Clyde. 1967. Parsons, Estelle

Blandings, Jim.
Tired of living in Manhattan this gullible young advertising man decides to move his wife and two daughters to the country and to build the house of his dreams. However, the dream turns into a nightmare as constant problems surface during the construction of the house.
Mr. Blandings Builds His Dream House. 1948. Grant, Cary

Bligh, William.
Brutal captain of an 18th-century British man-of-war bound for Tahiti is cast adrift by his mutinous crew because of his sadistic treatment of them. His skill and indomitable courage in sailing a dinghy 3600 miles across the ocean demonstrate his heroism and seamanship.
Mutiny on the Bounty. 1935. Laughton, Charles
Mutiny on the Bounty. 1962. Howard, Trevor

Blizzard.
The ruler of San Francisco's underworld, Blizzard is a bitter and totally evil cripple with a lasting hatred for the surgeon who needlessly amputated his legs when he was a child. He becomes obsessed with the idea of having someone else's legs grafted to his body.
The Penalty. 1920. Chaney, Lon

Blodgett, Esther.
Little innocent Esther Blodgett becomes the sensational Hollywood star Vicki Lester, but cannot prevent the disintegration of her marriage to an actor whose career is fading.
A Star is Born. 1937. Gaynor, Janet
A Star is Born. 1954. Garland, Judy

Blood, Peter.
In 1685 during the Monmouth uprising, Dr. Peter Blood, a genteel physician, turns amateur pirate because of an unjust conviction. He becomes the most celebrated buccaneer in the Caribbean when he leads slaves in a successful rebellion.
Captain Blood. 1935. Flynn, Errol

Bloom, Leo.
Meek, totally inhibited accountant helps a producer concoct a scheme to get rich by producing a musical which will close after a single performance; however, "Spingtime for Hitler" surprises both audiences and producers.
The Producers. 1968. Wilder, Gene

Bo.
Stupid, stubborn cowboy, on a visit to Phoenix to ride in a rodeo and find a woman to take to his ranch in Montana, abducts a cafe singer, although his intentions are honorable.
Bus Stop. 1956. Murray, Don

Bob.
After participating in an encounter group, this rich, swinging film maker tries to persuade his friends, who are somewhat square, to express genuine emotion and to expand their capacities for love.
Bob & Carol & Ted & Alice. 1969. Culp, Robert

Bobbie.
"The girl in the airline commercial," this beautiful but simple young woman has had a long, miserable affair with a jock who treats her merely as a sex object.
Carnal Knowledge. 1971. Ann-Margret

Bobo.
A vigorous, tough dock worker in California saves a poor slattern from drowning and reveals his soulful and lonely side when he falls in love and marries her.
Moontide. 1942. Gabin, Jean

Bock, Herbert.
In a huge mismanaged big-city hospital, this once brilliant, tense and suicidal chief doctor, suffering from impotence and alienated from his children, is restored to decency and responsibility after a romantic interlude with the daughter of a difficult patient.
The Hospital. 1971. Scott, George C.

Bok, Yakov.
Poor Jewish handyman in anti-Semitic Czarist Russia is falsely accused of a crime and imprisoned. Beaten and tormented, he comes to symbolize all victims of injustice and prejudice when he refuses to confess.
The Fixer. 1968. Bates, Alan

Boleyn, Anne.
Clever, ruthless, beautiful young woman resists King Henry's sexual entreaties for six years, and then has a thousand days of love and marriage with the King before she is sentenced to death on Cromwell's trumped-up charge of adultery.
Anne of the Thousand Days. 1969. Bujold, Genevieve

Bond, James.
Indestructible British Secret Service operative, Agent 007, works to rid the world of threatening fiends. He uses wonderful gadgets, operates out of exotic locations, and is surrounded by some of the world's sexiest and most willing women.
Dr. No. 1963. Connery, Sean
Live and Let Die. 1973. Moore, Roger

Bonnie, see Parker, Bonnie

Bookkeeper.
Bookkeeper who worked for Maurice Stans, Finance Chairman for the Committee to Re-elect the President, loosens up and confirms some of Carl Bernstein's information when he weasels his way into her home.
All the President's Men. 1976. Alexander, Jane

Boone, Josiah.
In the perilous Southwest of the 1870s, this drunken frontier doctor sobers up enough to deliver a baby during an overland stagecoach journey from Tonto through Indian country to Lordsburg.
Stagecoach. 1939. Mitchell, Thomas

Boone, Leola.
Childish but loyal wife of a tyrannical and cruel war hero in a middle-class Southern Californian housing development cannot hide the deep pain of giving up her illegitimate child, nor disguise her desperate yearning for motherhood.
No Down Payment. 1957. Woodward, Joanne

Borden, Mickey.
A cynical, fatalistic young man from the city slums, Mickey smokes constantly, is rude to everybody, and denounces everything. He marries a talented, small town, family-oriented young woman and commits suicide when he realizes he can never make her happy.
Four Daughters. 1938. Garfield, John

Borg, Isak.
This 78-year-old professor, en route to the University at Lund to receive an honorary doctorate, dreams about and recapitulates many phases of his life. He realizes that he has been admired, not loved, and considered cold and egotistical even by his family.
Wild Strawberries. 1957. Seastrom, Victor

Boss.
This older German trapeze performer, having given up his career after breaking both legs, leaves his domestic life when he falls for a lovely aerialist and returns to the carnival. When she betrays him with an English trapeze star, Boss decides to murder the younger man.
Variety. 1926. Jannings, Emil

Bostrom, Swan.
When his best friend Barney goes off to marry the boss's daughter, this eccentric Swedish foreman of a Wisconsin lumber camp stays on to marry Barney's girl friend, a dance hall hostess.
Come and Get It. 1936. Brennan, Walter

Botts, Ezra.
A meek and gentle psychic researcher puts himself in a trance, and when his spirit leaves his body, a new unborn spirit enters and turns Botts into a spunky, ebullient hero.
One Glorious Day. 1922. Rogers, Will

Boult, Evelyn.
Although she was ideally happy during the first years of marriage, Evelyn has become a miserably embittered drinking woman because her unscrupulous husband prospers through shady methods and will not stop until he can make a fortune for their son.
Edward, My Son. 1949. Kerr, Deborah

Bourvier, Lise.
Although engaged to another man, this young winsome French woman falls in love with a brash, happy-go-lucky former GI.
An American in Paris. 1951. Caron, Leslie

Bowles, Sally.
Oddly beautiful, tough-talking, free-living-and-loving American cabaret singer, in a desperate attempt to become liberated, goes after fame and stardom on the eve of World War II in decadent Berlin.
Cabaret. 1972. Minnelli, Liza

Braddock, Ben.
Just graduated from college and unsure of what he wants to do with his life, this rather bungling, comical, inarticulate young man is seduced by an older woman, but later falls in love with her daughter.
The Graduate. 1967. Hoffman, Dustin

Bradlee, Ben.
Tough but goodhearted Managing Editor of the *Washington Post* allows his reporters to proceed with their investigation, but is not wholly convinced that the break-in at the Watergate Building warrants newspaper space, money, and so much of his staff's time.
All the President's Men. 1976. Robards, Jason

Brady, Joseph.
This cheerful, fun-loving sailor, on shore leave in Hollywood, sings and dances his way on a girl-chasing expedition.
Anchors Aweigh. 1945. Kelly, Gene

Brady, Matthew Harrison.
Proud, pompous, silver-tongued orator, reminiscent of William Jennings Bryan in the famous Monkey Trial, is the prosecution attorney eloquently supporting the fundamentalist interpretation of the Bible.
Inherit the Wind. 1960. March, Fredric

Bramson, Mrs.
Wealthy, old, demanding English widow, confined to a wheelchair, trusts and hires a seemingly pleasant young jack-of-all-trades, and unknowingly hastens her own demise.
Night Must Fall. 1937. Whitty, Dame May

Brangwen, Gudrun.
In World War I England, an educated, artistic woman, trying to become free, carries out her own philosophy of love in an unyielding, destructive way.
Women in Love. 1970. Jackson, Glenda

Brat.
A down-and-out chorus girl is rescued from night court by a novelist who wants to study her type. He brings her to his home where she distresses his conventional family, but eventually wins them over with her love and good humor.
The Brat. 1919. Nazimova, Alla

Bree, see Daniel, Bree

Brenda.
During summer vacation, a charming, tennis-playing "Jewish American Princess" from Westchester has an affair with a poor young Jewish boy working in a Bronx library. When she tires of the relationship, she deliberately allows her wealthy, socially conscious parents to learn of the romance, forcing it to end as abruptly as it started.
Goodbye Columbus. 1969. MacGraw, Ali

Brice, Fanny.
Homely, ungainly tragicomedienne, whose great talent is akin to beauty, rises from the poverty-stricken Lower East Side to Ziegfeld stardom.
Funny Girl. 1968. Streisand, Barbra

Brick.
Tortured, bitter young man, under the control of his dying father, soaks up liquor to forget his feelings of inadequacy. He recoils from the sexual advances of his beautiful wife because he suspects that she was unfaithful.
Cat on a Hot Tin Roof. 1958. Newman, Paul

Brittles, Nathan.
Solitary captain, who lost his wife and children in an Indian raid, is nearing retirement from the Seventh Cavalry. During his last weeks in the military, he is able to avert an Indian war and to win a civilian position as Chief of Scouts.
She Wore a Yellow Ribbon. 1949. Wayne, John

Brodie, Jean.
Romantic, unconventional teacher in a conventional school for girls in Edinburgh, no longer very young but very much in her prime, wants to inspire her young students rather than merely teach them.
The Prime of Miss Jean Brodie. 1969. Smith, Maggie

Bromden, Chief.
Towering, catatonic Indian, long thought to be a deaf mute, decides to escape from the mental institution after his friend McMurphy's lobotomy.
One Flew Over the Cuckoo's Nest. 1975. Sampson, Will

Bronco Billy.
Former New Jersey salesman trains to become a sharpshooting, lasso-twirling, stunt-riding cowboy, and uses these skills as the leader of a traveling Wild West show. He comes to believe in his own legend, and is full of concern for the youngsters in his audience, to whom he preaches the importance of a good education and of being a "straight shooter."
Bronco Billy. 1980. Eastwood, Clint

Bronx Bull, see La Motta, Jake

Brown, Ben.
Mentally disturbed ex-soldier is on trial for killing the town's most respected citizen, whom he had discovered in bed with his wife.
Twilight of Honor. 1963. Adams, Nick

Brown, Bernice Sadie.
In a small Georgia town, a warmhearted, understanding black cook is conscious of the fragile feelings of a lonely motherless girl.
The Member of the Wedding. 1952. Waters, Ethel

Brown, Cluny.
A charming, exuberant girl plumber from London is sent to be a maid at a very proper estate and completely disrupts the tranquility of that stuffy household.
Cluny Brown. 1946. Jones, Jennifer

Brown, Emmy.
A romantic and lonely American schoolteacher in Mexico marries a European ladies' man who does not love her but merely wants to get into the United States.
Hold Back the Dawn. 1941. De Havilland, Olivia

Brown, Molly.
Feisty miner's daughter is cruelly snubbed by the elite in Denver when she and her husband become wealthy. But she becomes a heroine during the sinking of the Titanic and quickly attains social prominence.
The Unsinkable Molly Brown. 1964. Reynolds, Debbie

Brown, Mrs.
Having given up her promising career as a swimmer to marry the local butcher, this strong and loving mother creates an atmosphere of warmth and good family feeling while she encourages her daughter to follow her dreams and realize her ambitions.
National Velvet. 1944. Revere, Anne

Brown, Velvet.
A lively, refreshing English girl gently and confidently trains a magnificent but unknown gelding to run in the Grand National Steeplechase, and rides the horse to victory.
National Velvet. 1944. Taylor, Elizabeth

Browning, Robert.
The celebrated poet courts the invalid Elizabeth Barrett against her tyrannical father's opposition.
The Barretts of Wimpole Street. 1934. March, Fredric
The Barretts of Wimpole Street. 1956. Travers, Bill

Brtko, Tono.
In a Nazi-held town in Czechoslovakia, an average little man, a carpenter, is appointed "Aryan controller" of a small button shop owned by an elderly Jewish widow. He develops a warm relationship with her and when the town's Jews begin to be deported, he must decide whether to protect her or to save his own life.
The Shop on Main Street. 1966. Kroner, Josef

Bruce, Honey.
Onetime stripper, faithful wife of Lenny Bruce defeated by her husband's self-destructiveness, leaves him and becomes involved in a drug arrest in Hawaii.
Lenny. 1974. Perrine, Valerie

Bruce, Lenny.
Although harrassed by narcotics police and prosecuted on obscenity charges, this controversial nightclub performer, responding to his own inner visions and rules, tries to rid society of hypocrisy.
Lenny. 1974. Hoffman, Dustin

Brulov, Alex.
Elderly, humorous psychiatrist, who resembles a kindly Freud, helps a female psychiatrist, a former pupil and friend, to cure her patient's amnesia.
Spellbound. 1945. Chekhov, Michael

Brummel, George.
A dignified, exquisite dandy known as Beau meets the Prince of Wales in the Tenth Hussar Regiment. He easily charms the fat prince and holds sway over him as a haughty arbiter of fashion, but his schemes to put himself above royalty lead to his downfall.
Beau Brummel. 1924. Barrymore, John

Bruno.
Bruno changes from a carefree and lighthearted youngster to a serious and somber child as he joins his father on a fruitless daylong search for a stolen bicycle vital to the family's welfare.
The Bicycle Thief. 1949. Staiola, Enzo

Bryant, Frank.
Decaying, cynical, alcoholic English professor is rescued from his mid-life bitterness and frustration by a semiliterate student whom he is guiding into a world of literary appreciation and self-expression.
Educating Rita. 1983. Caine, Michael

Bryant, Louise.
Selfish, troubled, tempestuous wife of a Portland, Oregon, dentist leaves him to follow journalist John Reed to Greenwich Village. She seeks independence and fulfillment as a writer among the bohemians of 1915, but is recognized only through her relationship with the Socialist, Reed.
Reds. 1981. Keaton, Diane

Buck, Joe.
Handsome but inarticulate small-town Texan outfits himself in a flashy cowboy suit and heads for New York City hoping to make a fortune selling his stud services to rich society women. He establishes his first caring relationship with a tubercular con man, only to have the friendship end in tragedy.
Midnight Cowboy. 1969. Voight, Jon

Budd, Billy.
Handsome young British sailor, goodness personified, wrongly accused of inciting the restless crew to mutiny, kills the cruel accusing officer, and accepts the unjustifiable verdict that he must be executed.
Billy Budd. 1962. Stamp, Terence

Buddusky.
Self-assured, tough-talking, heavy-drinking Navy professional, assigned to escort a young kleptomaniac sailor to prison, is put off by the severity of the sentence and the boy's inexperience. He decides to show the young man a good time before he is locked away.
The Last Detail. 1973. Nicholson, Jack

Bulldog Drummond, see Drummond, Hugh

Bullock, Irene.
Scatter-brained but beautiful debutante becomes infatuated with a hobo turned butler whom she has picked up on a scavenger hunt.
My Man Godfrey. 1936. Lombard, Carole

Burden, Jack.
Deadpan newspaper reporter and narrator of this story, Jackie is a devotee of Willie Stark, the future governor, from the time he's pushed around by machine politics, through his emergence on the national scene, to his assassination on the courthouse steps.
All the King's Men. 1949. Ireland, John

Burke, Sadie.
Hard-boiled and cynical, Sadie starts out disliking the Southern politician Willie Stark, but later becomes his secretary and mistress.
All the King's Men. 1949. McCambridge, Mercedes

Burns, Skeet.
This young recruit from Kansas, who has the audacity to tell the Marine barber what kind of haircut he wants, is especially hated by his sergeant, who rigorously browbeats, ridicules, and disciplines him into a hardened soldier.
Tell It to the Marines. 1926. Haines, William

Burns, Walter.
This clever but unscrupulous editor of a Chicago newspaper is arrested as an accessory to a crime when he tries to disclose corruption in local government.
The Front Page. 1931. Menjou, Adolphe

Burrows, Lucy.
Brutally beaten by her prizefighter father, a vulnerable young girl finds refuge with a quiet, reserved Chinese immigrant who idolizes her and surrounds her with beauty, kindness, and pure love.
Broken Blossoms. 1919. Gish, Lillian
Broken Blossoms. 1937. Haas, Dolly

Butch.
Cruel and brutish murderer leads a prison revolt.
The Big House. 1930. Beery, Wallace

Butler, Rhett.
This dashing and opportunistic blockade runner, the personification of a free spirit, admires and marries a Southern belle. He finally deserts her when he tires of her continuing affection for her first love.
Gone With the Wind. 1939. Gable, Clark

Byam.
Young humane midshipman, condemned together with mutinous sailors, Byam is pardoned after his eloquent description of the horrible circumstances leading to the mutiny.
Mutiny on the Bounty. 1935. Tone, Franchot
Mutiny on the Bounty. 1962. Harris, Richard

Cabiria.
Cabiria, a prostitute, is the eternal optimist, never surprised by cruel turns of fortune. When a serious prospect offering reprieve from her lonely life does appear and proves to be a cad, one would expect her to be totally crushed; but she rebounds from this as well.
Cabiria or the Nights of Cabiria. 1957. Masina, Giulietta

Caesar, Julius.
Caesar has the intelligence, shrewdness, and magnanimity of an emperor, but he is torn by Cleopatra's charm, his hopes for his son, and the ambitions that will ultimately destroy him.
Cleopatra. 1963. Harrison, Rex

Cairo, Joel.
In his fanatical desire to acquire a jeweled statuette, this effeminate, gardenia-scented conspirator allies himself alternately with detective Sam Spade and with an international thief, Kasper Gutman.
The Maltese Falcon. 1941. Lorre, Peter

Caligari, Dr.
Wearing a cape and top hat, this evil and quite mad wizard keeps in his cabinet a somnambulist who commits ghastly murders for him at his bidding.
The Cabinet of Dr. Caligari. 1919. Krauss, Werner

Calvin.
Successful, upper-middle-class Chicago tax attorney, a weak but kind and loving husband and father, tries to renew relationships with his family after the accidental drowning of his elder son.
Ordinary People. 1980. Sutherland, Donald

Cameron.
Down-and-out paranoid lover, a fugitive from the police, able to survive only through his inability to trust anyone, accepts refuge from a director and becomes a stunt man. Eventually he becomes suspicious and imagines the director intends to kill him in the film's climactic stunt.
The Stunt Man. 1980. Railsback, Steve

Cameron, Ben.
A Southern colonel commands his troops bravely during the Civil War, and afterwards becomes a leader of the Ku Klux Klan to avenge his sister's death.
The Birth of a Nation. 1915. Walthall, Henry B.

Cameron, Flora.
During the Reconstruction years after the Civil War, the youngest sister in a Southern family dies when she leaps from a high cliff to avoid being raped by a black man.
The Birth of a Nation. 1915. Marsh, Mae

Cameron, Peggy.
A rich and seemingly flighty American girl visits her uncle in a small Scottish village. She shocks her relatives by her unconventionality, but eventually wins their hearts.
Peggy. 1916. Burke, Billie

Cameron, Rachel.
Thirty-five-year-old spinster schoolteacher finds herself loveless and exploited by a demanding mother. After drifting from one fruitless experience to another, her supposed pregnancy having turned out to be an operable tumor, she finally goes off to Oregon with her mother to start a new job.
Rachel, Rachel. 1968. Woodward, Joanne

Camille, see Gautier, Marguerite

Camonte, Tony.
Brutal, vicious hood, with a scar on his cheek, rises from bodyguard to second-in-command to a Prohibition ganglord. He kills the gangland leader and takes over his rackets and his mistress, but is eventually cornered and shot by the police.
Scarface. 1932. Muni, Paul

Capel, Helen.
A psychopathic killer haunts a New England town, and this mute servant girl in an eerie household full of deep family hatreds is unable to communicate her terror.
The Spiral Staircase. 1946. McGuire, Dorothy

Captain.
Neurotic, tyrannical Navy captain is obsessed with a small palm tree awarded to him for having the most efficient cargo ship in the Pacific theater. This efficiency can be credited more to his executive officer, Mr. Roberts, than to this egomaniacal officer.
Mister Roberts. 1955. Cagney, James

Captain Bligh, see Bligh, William

Captain Blood, see Blood, Peter

Cardinal Wolsey, see Wolsey

Carey, Scott.
This scientist is exposed to a radioactive fog, shrinks to minute size, and views the world from this new perspective.
Incredible Shrinking Man. 1957. Williams, Grant

Carlo.
Carlo, whose only talent appears to be his ability to imitate a gorilla, is the sad-eyed protege of a wealthy New York socialite.
My Man Godfrey. 1936. Auer, Mischa

Carlos.
The king of Spain, a frivolous man who is easily flattered by beautiful women, is bedazzled by a vivacious singing guitarist and brings her to his palace, where he showers her with luxury.
Rosita. 1923. Blinn, Holbrook

Carlton, Mary.
An aged woman goes through her diary called "Secrets," and relives her life as a young English girl who eloped with her sweetheart, faithfully fought bandits alongside him in their Wyoming home, and, as an older woman in upper-class London, forgave him his adultery.
Secrets. 1924. Talmadge, Norma

Carmen.
This fiery, calculating factory worker in the South, living near an Army post, is mainly interested in having a good time. As a result, her turbulent love affairs have destroyed men's lives.
Carmen Jones. 1954. Dandridge, Dorothy

Carmody, Ida.
In Australia a bright, vivacious barmaid-innkeeper sets her sights on a learned eligible bachelor adept at evading matrimony.
The Sundowners. 1960. Kerr, Deborah

Carnehan, Peachy.
This former soldier in the British army in India, now a rascally con artist and loudmouthed braggart, goes to primitive Kafiristan in search of wealth and power. His friend becomes king and Peachy becomes chief of the armed forces and the treasure chamber, until the natives revolt.
The Man Who Would Be King. 1975. Caine, Michael

Carol.
Carol has been liberated after attending a California encounter group, and now believes in smoking pot and in sexual freedom.
Bob & Carol & Ted & Alice. 1969. Wood, Natalie

Carrie.
A hula dancer in a traveling tent show becomes miffed when her boyfriend, the barker, breaks off their relationship with the arrival of his son to join the carnival. She seeks revenge by paying another carnival girl to flirt with the boy.
The Barker. 1928. Compson, Betty

Carrie.
Repressed high-school senior, tormented by her classmates, finally uses her power of telekinesis in revenge, and destroys all her tormentors.
Carrie. 1976. Spacek, Sissy

Carter, Gil.
A bitter, disillusioned cowboy rides into a lonely Nevada cattle town for a short reprieve from his range work. For no apparent reason other than boredom, he joins a posse in search of cattle thieves, and eventually finds himself an unwilling member of a lynch mob.
The Ox-Bow Incident. 1943. Fonda, Henry

Carter, Hal.
Virile, handsome drifter comes to a Kansas farming community and his actions have a catalytic effect on the lives of the local residents.
Picnic. 1955. Holden, William

Carton, Sydney.
Lonely, alcoholic British barrister aids victims during the Reign of Terror of the French Revolution, and then sacrifices his life to save another man from the guillotine.
A Tale of Two Cities. 1935. Colman, Ronald

Case, Johnny.
Suave, free-spirited young man is determined to enjoy life rather than make money.
Holiday. 1938. Grant, Cary

Cass.
Mistaken for a Park Avenue lady, this middle-aged call girl spends a busman's holiday when she is picked up by a flashy New York "cowboy."
Midnight Cowboy. 1969. Miles, Sylvia

Cassidy, Butch.
Charming, good-natured bank robber and his gang rob the Union Pacific Railroad once too often, forcing the railroad president to enlist a posse to hound them to Bolivia. Their activities in Bolivia are no more successful, and Butch and the Sundance Kid are killed in a gun fight with the Bolivian Army.
Butch Cassidy and the Sundance Kid. 1969. Newman, Paul

Castevet, Minnie.
Pushy, rouged elderly leader of a coven of witches in New York City has designs on the unborn baby of the young couple next door.
Rosemary's Baby. 1968. Gordon, Ruth

Catherine.
The charming and frivolous queen of a Balkan state spends her time satisfying her whims. Even when her handsome guard tells her that her troops are rebelling, she is more interested in flirting with him than in hearing the details.
Forbidden Paradise. 1924. Negri, Pola

Cathy.
This bright, affectionate girl loves Heathcliff, but marries another man and finds happiness in her marriage.
Wuthering Heights. 1939. Oberon, Merle

Caul, Harry.
Middle-aged wiretap expert is obsessed with the amoral aspects of his work, and with guarding his own privacy and that of his clients. He gradually breaks down when he becomes emotionally involved in an assignment.
The Conversation. 1974. Hackman, Gene

Cavallini.
An opera singer, mistress of a wealthy man, falls in love with a clergyman.
Romance. 1930. Garbo, Greta

Cavendish, Tony.
The only male member of a family of thespians has hilarious escapades in Europe and Hollywood as he manages to elude a former lover intent on suing him for breach of promise.
The Royal Family of Broadway. 1930. March, Fredric

Cavilleri, Jenny.
Poor college student falls in love with and marries a wealthy Ivy Leaguer. For a short time she is deliriously happy, only to find that she has an incurable disease and does not have long to live.
Love Story. 1970. MacGraw, Ali

Cavilleri, Phil.
Widowed Italian pastrymaker from Cranston, R.I., discovers that his beautiful young daughter, recently married, is dying from a blood disease.
Love Story. 1970. Marley, John

Cesar.
A Marseilles waterfront bar proprietor, a dominating but tender and sympathetic father, becomes the godfather to his own grandson after his friend marries a girl left pregnant by his gallivanting son.
Fanny. 1961. Boyer, Charles

Cesare.
This tall, thin, ghostly-looking sleepwalker is completely in the power of a wicked magician, and at his bidding commits terrifying murders.
The Cabinet of Dr. Caligari. 1919. Veidt, Conrad

Cesira.
Passionate, lusty peasant woman is forced to accept the reality of a world turned upside down by war when she and her 13-year-old daughter, returning to Rome from their native village, are attacked by a group of wild Moroccan soldiers.
Two Women. 1961. Loren, Sophia

Challenger, Professor.
Derided by skeptics in London when he reveals he has found a place where prehistoric creatures still roam, this determined professor leads a volunteer expedition to encounter the giant monsters and is successful in bringing one back alive.
The Lost World. 1925. Beery, Wallace

Chambers, Frank.
A crude, weak, clumsy California ne'er-do-well is tempted by a cheap blonde and becomes involved in the murder of her husband.
The Postman Always Rings Twice. 1946. Garfield, John
The Postman Always Rings Twice. 1981. Nicholson, Jack

Champ.
A likeable, slow-witted ex-fighter is addicted to drinking and gambling, but with the help of a loving son, perseveres and wins his last fight.
The Champ. 1931. Beery, Wallace
The Champ. 1979. Voight, Jon

Chan, Charlie.
Inscrutable, amiable Chinese detective, famous for his droll philosophical epigrams, proves himself to be the kingpin of criminologists as he shows great wisdom and insight into human nature in detecting, pursuing, and capturing underworld characters.
Charlie Chan Carries On. 1931. Oland, Warner
Charlie Chan in Honolulu. 1938. Toler, Sidney

Chance.
Childlike gardener, who cannot read or write, is thrust into the world of wealth and power politics, first as a valued adviser to an industrial tycoon, and then to the brink of a Presidential nomination.
Being There. 1979. Sellers, Peter

Chang.
This elderly Chinese, the High Lama's chief disciple, leads the Europeans to Shangri-La, a land where greed, disease, and war are unknown, and where people never grow old.
Lost Horizon. 1937. Warner, H. B.

Chanticleer, Margery.
Weeping, domineering mother of an immature young man with growing pains protests her husband's decision to allow their son to move out of their home into a boarding house.
You're a Big Boy Now. 1966. Page, Geraldine

Charles, Nick.
Nonchalant retired detective, who rarely appears without his cowardly guard dog Asta, is committed to solving impossible crimes and surprising the police.
The Thin Man. 1934. Powell, William

Charles, Nora.
This perfect example of a happily married wife is forever trying to catch up with her elusive detective husband.
The Thin Man. 1934. Loy, Myrna

Charlet, Marie.
In bohemian Paris in the 19th century, after a tempestuous love affair, this streetwalker harshly denounces the artist who loves her, Toulouse-Lautrec.
Moulin Rouge. 1952. Marchand, Colette

Charlie.
This young daughter in a typical California small town becomes suspicious of her moody uncle who visits the family, and discovers that he is wanted for murder.
Shadow of a Doubt. 1943. Wright, Teresa

Charlotte.
Emotionally drained after her lover of many years dies, this internationally famous concert pianist visits her daughter whom she has not seen in many years. Their exchange of small cruelties builds into an array of hostility and recriminations about the past.
Autumn Sonata. 1978. Bergman, Ingrid

Charly, see Gordon, Charly

Charmaine.
The fickle daughter of a French saloon owner causes a boisterous rivalry between two Marine buddies when she gives her attentions to both.
What Price Glory? 1926. Del Rio, Delores

Chavez, Pearl.
A beautiful and passionate half-breed Indian girl is involved with two brothers, one who is noble and one who is a scoundrel, with tragic results.
Duel in the Sun. 1946. Jones, Jennifer

Cheng, Huan.
The quiet, sensitive Buddhist owner of a London curio shop takes in a girl who has been brutally beaten by her father and showers her with a pure love and kindness she had never known before.
Broken Blossoms. 1919. Barthelmess, Richard

Cherie.
Tinseled, voluptuous, untalented cafe singer, hotly pursued by a dimwitted cowboy on his first trip to Phoenix, fights desperately to maintain her self-respect and dignity.
Bus Stop. 1956. Monroe, Marilyn

Chernen, Helen.
Ruthless, conniving woman, having left behind her small mining town roots, schemes and plots her way to success. She achieves it, but at the expense of destroying her talented sister-in-law's happiness and of being indirectly responsible for a suicide.
The Hard Way. 1943. Lupino, Ida

Chet.
Good-natured, overage hippie is picked up by some ladies out on the town. He spends the night with one, saves her from an attempted suicide, and escapes hurriedly as he spies her husband returning home.
Faces. 1968. Cassel, Seymour

Cheyne, Harvey.
Spoiled, disdainful 12-year-old, neglected by his father, becomes a man at sea because of his admiration for a fisherman's wisdom and the hardships of a fishing life.
Captains Courageous. 1937. Bartholomew, Freddie

Chiaromonte, Angela.
After her beloved fiance is reported slain in battle, this hopelessly grieving Italian girl becomes a nun. Her lover, however, is alive, and when he returns and begs her to marry him, she confesses her devotion to him but remains loyal to her commitment to the Church.
The White Sister. 1923. Gish, Lillian

Chief Bromden, see Bromden, Chief

Chipping, Arthur.
Strict, dedicated schoolmaster in an English boys' school has his stuffy lifestyle suddenly changed when at age 40 he goes on vacation in Austria. There he meets and marries a young musical comedy actress, and blossoms into a warm and witty man.
Goodbye Mr. Chips. 1939. Donat, Robert
Goodbye Mr. Chips. 1969. O'Toole, Peter

Chips, see Chipping, Arthur

Chisholm, Francis.
A humble Catholic missionary priest from Scotland is sent to China where he courageously and patiently builds a tiny mission.
The Keys of the Kingdom. 1945. Peck, Gregory

Chris.
Rough, bombastic, good-natured Uncle Chris has a ranch outside San Francisco and often helps his sister's family by taking his small niece to the hospital or bringing proper nourishment to their house. He always leaves his long-time mistress outside waiting in the automobile.
I Remember Mama. 1948. Homolka, Oskar

Christensen, Diana.
In order to attain control of the news department, this sexy, aggressive executive at United Broadcasting System will do anything to increase audience ratings and her prestige.
Network. 1976. Dunaway, Faye

Christian, Fletcher.
Enigmatic first mate suppresses deep psychological motivations which finally surface when he leads the mutinous sailors and seizes the Bounty from Captain Bligh.
Mutiny on the Bounty. 1935. Gable, Clark
Mutiny on the Bounty. 1962. Brando, Marlon

Christie, Anna.
Prostitute tries to keep the secret of her crimson career when she is reunited with her father after 15 years.
Anna Christie. 1930. Garbo, Greta

Christine.
Distraught mother of a little girl who is possessed of evil is faced with the dilemma of how to handle her child.
The Bad Seed. 1956. Kelly, Nancy

Cisco Kid.
This happy-go-lucky Mexican bandit robs from the rich and gives to the poor.
In Old Arizona. 1929. Baxter, Warner

Citizen Kane, see Kane, Charles Foster

Claiborne, Harlee.
Con artist tries to endear himself to a rich middle-aged woman when guests at a dedication ceremony for a San Francisco skyscraper are trapped by a raging fire.
The Towering Inferno. 1974. Astaire, Fred

Clancy.
Butler and devoted friend of a prominent family of Capitol City in the Middle West now runs the house for the widow of the beloved senator.
The Farmer's Daughter. 1947. Bickford, Charles

Clancy.
This nurse from Flatbush, outwardly cynical but actually warm and understanding, meets Jane Froman in a hospital right after her accident and encourages her on the long road to recovery.
With a Song in My Heart. 1952. Ritter, Thelma

Clara.
Shy, plain, kindhearted teacher, lonely and bored with her existence, has exhausted any hope of ever marrying until she meets a gentle butcher at a neighborhood Bronx dance hall.
Marty. 1955. Blair, Betsy

Clare, Angel.
Idealistically rebelling against Victorian attitudes, this weak, priggish minister's son loves and marries proletarian Tess. Undone by his own sexual hypocrisy, he renounces her when she confesses her past.
Tess. 1980. Firth, Peter

Clarence.
A professor of entomology before World War I, this shy but competent young ex-soldier takes a temporary job before returning to his college, and finds himself a peacemaker in an especially tumultuous household.
Clarence. 1922. Reid, Wallace

Clark, Raymond.
Because of his close friendship with the president, this doughty Southern senator, addicted to bourbon, is assigned to investigate the plot of an Air Force general to seize control of the government.
Seven Days in May. 1964. O'Brien, Edmond

Clark, Willy.
A one-night comeback for a TV special continues the love-hate relationship of this cranky, quarrelsome vaudevillian and his partner, who broke up 11 years ago after 45 years together and haven't spoken since.
The Sunshine Boys. 1975. Matthau, Walter

Claudet, Madelon.
Madelon sacrifices everything so that her illegitimate son can become a physician, but never permits him to learn her true identity.
The Sin of Madelon Claudet. 1931. Hayes, Helen

Claudine.

Beautiful but tough 36-year-old husbandless mother of six, currently on welfare but also secretly working as a maid to keep her family above subsistence level, falls in love with an earthy, twice-married garbageman, and their money problems intensify.
Claudine. 1974. Carroll, Diahann

Cleary, John.

Irish-Catholic father living in the Bronx in 1946 does verbal battle with his wife in their competition for the affection of their son, a returning World War II veteran.
The Subject Was Roses. 1968. Albertson, Jack

Cleary, Nettie.

Upon the return of her veteran son, Nettie argues and becomes cold toward her husband, and uses the boy as a weapon against her spouse.
The Subject Was Roses. 1968. Neal, Patricia

Clegg, Freddie.

Disturbed, repressed young bank clerk, a butterfly collector, kidnaps a beautiful art student and attempts to keep her for his own, hoping that in her imprisonment she will get to know and to love him.
The Collector. 1965. Stamp, Terence

Cleopatra.

In 48 B.C. this beautiful, arrogant Egyptian queen behaves cooly and confidently in every situation, whether the concerns are love, hate, or politics. She enchants two great Roman generals, and thereby affects the destiny of man.
Cleopatra. 1917. Bara, Theda
Cleopatra. 1934. Colbert, Claudette
Cleopatra. 1963. Taylor, Elizabeth

Clodagh, Sister.

An overconfident young Sister Superior is sent to the Himalayas to establish a school and a hospital, and learns humility through the many hardships which cause the mission to fail.
Black Narcissus. 1947. Kerr, Deborah

Clyde, see Barrow, Clyde

Cobbler.

When his son is murdered, this old blind cobbler is able to grab a satchel full of money from the escaping killer. He then waits for the man to return, and when he recognizes the sound of his footsteps, he gets revenge by choking the killer to death.
Footfalls. 1921. Power, Tyrone, Sr.

Cochise.
In Arizona after the Civil War, this feared Apache Indian chief shows foresightedness and noble character in his efforts to bring whites and Indians together.
Broken Arrow. 1950. Chandler, Jeff

Cogburn, Rooster.
A paunchy, one-eyed, over-the-hill U.S. marshall helps a 14-year-old girl track down her father's killer.
True Grit. 1969. Wayne, John

Cohan, George M.
The energetic and cocky real-life actor-writer-musician begins his career in his family's vaudeville act and becomes one of America's most famous entertainers.
Yankee Doodle Dandy. 1942. Cagney, James

Cohan, Jerry.
Leader of the traveling vaudeville act, The Four Cohans, this warm-hearted man is the father of George M. Cohan, one of America's most famous song-and-dance men.
Yankee Doodle Dandy. 1942. Huston, Walter

Colonel Dax, see Dax, Colonel

Comfort, Rose.
This pathetic, half-crazed old woman is the aunt of a child bride in Mississippi.
Baby Doll. 1956. Dunnock, Mildred

Concannon, Ed.
Sleek, sarcastic, established attorney is the mastermind of the defense in a malpractice suit against a Roman Catholic Boston hospital. He uses everything money can buy to win his case, with no qualms about the moral issues.
The Verdict. 1982. Mason, James

Conklin, Willie.
Bigoted chief of the New Rochelle Fire Department deeply resents a black who owns a brand-new Model T Ford. His attempt to humiliate the black leads to violence and death.
Ragtime. 1981. McMillan, Kenneth

Connie, James.
Wise, flippant inmate, with an amazing awareness of happenings both inside and outside the prison, is given a chance to leave the penitentiary for a day in exchange for his help in opening a jammed bank vault.
My Six Convicts. 1952. Mitchell, Millard

Connolly, Jerry.
Compassionate, mild-mannered Irish priest tries to convince the neighborhood slum kids not to emulate a criminal, who happens to be Jerry's former close friend.
Angels With Dirty Faces. 1938. O'Brien, Pat

Connor, Macaulay.
A gossip reporter is assigned to cover a Philadelphia society marriage and falls in love with the bride.
The Philadelphia Story. 1940. Stewart, James

Connor, Mike, see Connor, Macaulay

Conrad.
Tormented by the feeling that he was responsible for the death of his older brother, this lonely, introspective teen-ager attempts suicide and is hospitalized for four months. Upon returning home he undergoes psychotherapy and tries in vain to re-establish communication with his parents.
Ordinary People. 1980. Hutton, Timothy

Constance.
Sullen widow comes back to Peyton Place after the death of her husband and rediscovers the joys of love.
Peyton Place. 1957. Turner, Lana

Contessa.
In Rome, this cunning, sinister procurer of young men, a female pimp, finds attractive assignments for her gigolos.
The Roman Spring of Mrs. Stone. 1961. Lenya, Lotte

Conway, Robert.
Courageous, debonair British foreign secretary-designate, the personification of an English gentleman, Conway is one of a small group of Europeans caught in the Chinese Rebellion who find themselves in a strange but serene Tibetan civilization.
Lost Horizon. 1937. Colman, Ronald

Cooper, Miss.
Dignified, strong owner of a British seaside resort adores a reckless, rowdy guest but accepts his attraction to another woman.
Separate Tables. 1958. Hiller, Wendy

Copeland, Boyd.
This nephew of a newspaper publisher is a tipsy playboy who has connections in the underworld.
Come Fill the Cup. 1951. Young, Gig

Copley, Rafe.
Gentle, long-suffering, illegitimate son marries a pretty neighborhood girl even though she is pregnant by another man, and gives the child the father he himself never had.
Home From the Hill. 1960. Peppard, George

Copperfield, David.
Sensitive and trusting orphan is disliked by his cruel stepfather and helped by his eccentric aunt.
David Copperfield. 1935. Bartholomew, Freddie

Corbett, Jim.
In the 1890s when prizefighting was a spectacle rather than a sport, this gentleman boxer, a scientific fighter, dances into the ring and gives a measure of refinement to the fight game.
Gentleman Jim. 1942. Flynn, Errol

Corcoran, Mr.
Pigheaded father of a beautiful blonde magazine cover model is outraged when she falls in love with a New York sporting goods salesman.
The Heartbreak Kid. 1972. Albert, Eddie

Corkle, Max.
Comical, fast-talking manager of a boxer thinks he has a sure winner, but becomes bewildered when the fighter dies and then comes back in another body. (See below)
Here Comes Mr. Jordan. 1941. Gleason, James

Corkle, Max.
Football coach meets what appears to be a reincarnation of one of his players, who had been killed in an automobile accident. Although requiring considerable reassurance, Max continues to be the loyal friend to Joe that he had been in the player's former life. (See above)
Heaven Can Wait. 1978. Warden, Jack

Corleone, Connie.
Spoiled, angry and dependent upon the brother who had her husband killed, Connie behaves in a self-destructive manner, cultivating handsome, ne'er-do-well playboys.
The Godfather, Part II. 1974. Shire, Talia

Corleone, Don Vito.
An aging but shrewd patriarch, head of one of the most ruthless families in the underworld, follows an unusual code of honor as he runs his criminal empire. (See Corleone, Vito, below)
The Godfather. 1972. Brando, Marlon

Corleone, Michael.
The godfather's youngest and favorite son becomes head of the "family business" upon his father's retirement, leads the family to victory, but changes from a gentle young man to a menacing Mafia mobster. (See below)
The Godfather. 1972. Pacino, Al

Corleone, Michael.
After Don Vito's death Michael expands the family's crime empire. He is a powerful but lonely and disconsolate man as he attempts to emulate his father and to maintain the traditional division of home and business. (See above)
The Godfather, Part II. 1974. Pacino, Al

Corleone, Sonny.
Hot-blooded, high-spirited son temporarily takes his father's place as leader of a Mafia family and is viciously assassinated after he loses his temper and assaults his brother-in-law.
The Godfather. 1972. Caan, James

Corleone, Vito.
Mild-mannered, soft-spoken, reserved young Sicilian immigrant arrives in New York in the early 1900s, adapts the mores of the Mafia to the New World, and becomes the family patriarch. (See Corleone, Don Vito, above)
The Godfather, Part II. 1974. De Niro, Robert

Cosick, Robert.
Because of the mental anguish brought on by leaving his girl friend and denouncing his father, Cosick perches on a 14th story window ledge, threatening to jump. He sways back and forth, thrilling the New York crowd that has assembled below.
Fourteen Hours. 1951. Basehart, Richard

Coward, Noel.
Cynical and debonair Noel Coward meets Gertrude Lawrence early in her career and remains her constant friend and confidante.
Star! 1968. Massey, Daniel

Cowardly Lion, see Zeke

Crabb, Jack.
Captured and raised as a Cheyenne, then rescued by whites at the age of 15, Jack survives two marriages, bankruptcy, and careers as both an Indian scout and a con artist. He becomes a drunk and is about to commit suicide when he decides instead to help the Indians defeat General Custer.
Little Big Man. 1970. Hoffman, Dustin

Craig, Sam.
A tough but easy-going and down-to-earth sportswriter marries a celebrated woman journalist and has difficulty getting used to her fame.
Woman of the Year. 1942. Tracy, Spencer

Crainquebille.
Selling from his pushcart, this cheerful old Parisian is wrongly accused of loitering and sent to prison. Upon his release he tries to drown himself because all his customers have abandoned him, but he is saved by a boy to whom he once gave a piece of fruit.
Crainquebille. 1923. De Feraude, Maurice

Crane, Marion.
En route to join her lover after absconding with $40,000 in cash, this young woman, nervous and inexperienced in the thieving trade, stops for the night at an out-of-the-way motel, where she is brutally murdered while taking a shower.
Psycho. 1960. Leigh, Janet

Cravat, Sabra.
After her husband disappears, this courageous, loyal woman takes over the editorship of the *Oklahoma Wigwam* and becomes influential in civic and state-wide activities.
Cimarron. 1931. Dunne, Irene

Cravat, Yancey.
Pioneer, poet, lawyer, and editor of a weekly liberal newspaper, he helps to turn the overnight camp of Osage, Oklahoma, into a respectable town. Secretly infected with wanderlust, however, Yancey deserts his wife and children for a new life in the Cherokee Strip.
Cimarron. 1931. Dix, Richard

Crawford, Joan.
In this portrait of the actress, adapted from the book by her adopted daughter, Joan is a complicated, egotistical, deeply troubled woman.
Mommie Dearest. 1981. Dunaway, Faye

Crocker-Harris, Andrew.
Unhappy, rigid teacher of classical languages, a pedant and a strict disciplinarian, is unpopular with both his students and his wife. He eventually wins the respect of an intelligent student when he retires from a posh English public school.
The Browning Version. 1951. Redgrave, Michael

Crosbie, Leslie.
The unhappy wife of an English rubber plantation owner near Singapore murders her illicit lover. In order to be acquitted of the crime, she must get back an incriminating letter that she wrote to the dead man.
The Letter. 1929. Eagels, Jeanne
The Letter. 1940. Davis, Bette

Crosby, Charles.
After this well-to-do young man, known as Sonny, is killed in the war, his sympathetic buddy, Joe Marden, goes to his home and impersonates him for the sake of Sonny's blind mother.
Sonny. 1922. Barthelmess, Richard

Cross, El.
Egomaniacal, tough, flamboyant director of a film company, willing to do anything to achieve proper effects, puts a fugitive through some highly dangerous paces as a stunt man while shielding him from the police.
The Stunt Man. 1980. O'Toole, Peter

Cross, Lucas.
This drunk steals his stepson's savings to spend on liquor, and rapes and impregnates his stepdaughter.
Peyton Place. 1957. Kennedy, Arthur

Cross, Noah.
In corrupt Los Angeles of the 1930s, this ruthless, sinister multimillionaire who ravished the land and raped his daughter now intends to corrupt the child he's had by her.
Chinatown. 1974. Huston, John

Cross, Selena.
Nice, sweet 17-year-old is brutally raped by her stepfather, becomes pregnant, but suffers a miscarriage. Years later, when he again tries to attack her, she kills him.
Peyton Place. 1957. Lange, Hope

Crow.
This wisecracking bore, one of a group of men downed in the Sahara Desert by a plane crash, must help devise a scheme to find a way out of their dilemma.
The Flight of the Phoenix. 1965. Bannen, Ian

Crusoe, Robinson.
On a deserted island off South America, this lone survivor of a shipwreck lives face-to-face with nature for 20-odd years, lonely, sometimes close to derangement, desperately longing for a ship to carry him back to civilization.
The Adventures of Robinson Crusoe. 1954. O'Herlihy, Dan

Cullen, Noah.
After working together to elude their captors, Noah, a black man, linked at the wrist to a fellow white prisoner, discovers that he is not different but profoundly the same as his companion.
The Defiant Ones. 1958. Poitier, Sidney

Cunningham, Francesca.
After she tries to commit suicide, this sensitive concert pianist has psychotherapy which relieves her of many complexes caused by unfortunate love affairs and her subservience to a Svengali-like mentor.
The Seventh Veil. 1945. Todd, Ann

Cunningham, Virginia.
A young married woman with a deep guilt complex slowly returns to sanity in a repugnant mental institution, a place of incompetence and brutality.
The Snake Pit. 1948. De Havilland, Olivia

Curie, Marie.
A young and charming Polish student studying in Paris marries a dedicated French scientist; working together, they discover radium.
Madame Curie. 1943. Garson, Greer

Curie, Pierre.
A young, modest and dedicated French scientist works with his Polish wife, and together, after years of research and perseverance, they discover radium.
Madame Curie. 1943. Pidgeon, Walter

Curry, Lizzie.
Plain, tomboyish, single girl on a Kansas farm is conned by a fast talker into thinking that she is beautiful.
The Rainmaker. 1956. Hepburn, Katharine

Curtis, Elizabeth.
Prim, guilt-stricken English lady is part of a safari team searching the jungles of darkest Africa to find her missing husband, lost in the fabled diamond mines.
King Solomon's Mines. 1950. Kerr, Deborah

Cyrano, see De Bergerac, Cyrano

Daigle, Mrs.
Grief-torn mother whose son has drowned pleads with her boy's classmate to relinquish a medal he had won for penmanship.
The Bad Seed. 1956. Heckart, Eileen

Dailey, Henry.
Retired racehorse trainer schools a wild Arabian stallion and the boy whose life the horse saved in a shipwreck, to win a match race against the two fastest horses of the day.
The Black Stallion. 1979. Rooney, Mickey

Dallas.
In the early West this dance-hall girl of dubious morals has been asked to leave the town of Tonto and is traveling on the Lordsburg stagecoach which is caught up in a sudden Apache uprising.
Stagecoach. 1939. Trevor, Claire

Dallas, Laurel.
This sweet, quiet, and tasteful girl is devoted to her shamelessly vulgar mother, even though she has been disappointed countless times by her thoughtlessness.
Stella Dallas. 1925. Moran, Lois
Stella Dallas. 1937. Shirley, Anne

Dallas, Stella.
Sleazy, coarse mill-hand s daughter marries a gentleman but cannot herself become cultured. After she and her husband separate, she selflessly succeeds in forcing her daughter to reject her in exchange for a future of money and opportunity.
Stella Dallas. 1925. Bennett, Belle
Stella Dallas. 1937. Stanwyck, Barbara

Danaher, Mary Kate.
A beautiful redheaded colleen, with a fiery temper to match her tresses, refuses to honor her marriage vows until her husband forces her brother to turn over her dowry.
The Quiet Man. 1952. O'Hara, Maureen

Danaher, "Red" Will.
Burly, pigheaded well-to-do farmer refuses to release his sister's dowry, causing a brawl which involves the whole town.
The Quiet Man. 1952. McLaglen, Victor

Dancer, Claude.
Skillful, unrelenting district attorney is assigned to a murder trial because of the peculiar nature of the case.
Anatomy of a Murder. 1959. Scott, George C.

Daniel, Bree.
Although she is afraid of the obscene letters and unexplained phone calls and has tried to get modeling and acting jobs, this sophisticated, high-priced New York call girl stays with her profession because of the power she wields over her customers.
Klute. 1971. Fonda, Jane

Danny.
Charming baby-faced psychopathic murderer carries a severed head in a hatbox, and both charms and terrorizes a girl and an old woman.
Night Must Fall. 1937. Montgomery, Robert

Dantes, Edmond.
After spending intolerable years in prison, Dantes dedicates his life to vengeance as he spins an intricate web around the three evildoers responsible for condemning him.
Monte Cristo. 1922. Gilbert, John
The Count of Monte Cristo. 1934. Donat, Robert

Danvers, Mrs.
Cold and formal housekeeper resents her employer's new wife.
Rebecca. 1940. Anderson, Judith

Daphne, see Jerry in Some Like It Hot

D'Arcey, Rose-Ann.
Mean, sluggish prostitute is enraged when her blind daughter falls in love with a black man.
A Patch of Blue. 1965. Winters, Shelley

D'Arcey, Selina.
Blind, abused 18-year-old falls in love with a black man, and aided by his kindness and friendship, becomes more self-sufficient and learns to overcome her handicap.
A Patch of Blue. 1965. Hartman, Elizabeth

Darrell, Larry.
An idealistic young aviator returns from World War I seeking salvation and harmony, but when he finds his friends living in pleasure and vanity, he goes off to an Eastern retreat and meditates with an ancient philosopher.
The Razor's Edge. 1946. Power, Tyrone

D'Artagnan.
The incomparable, dashing Gascony hero fences his way past villains, leaps walls at a single bound, and rides horses at a furious gallop, all for gallantry and the defense of damsels in distress.
The Three Musketeers. 1921. Fairbanks, Douglas

Dauphin.
The weak and hesitating Lord of Dauphin allows a peasant girl to lead his armies against the British invaders, but after her victories he yields to bad advice and betrays her.
Joan of Arc. 1948. Ferrer, Jose

Daurier, Lili.
Lonely, shy French orphan who becomes part of a crippled puppeteer's act eventually learns to love the deeply sensitive puppeteer who hides behind a cynical facade.
Lili. 1953. Caron, Leslie

Dave.
In a small college town this recent high-school graduate, who idolizes Italian bike champions so much that he pretends to be Italian himself, with a group of friends challenges the snooty college students to a grueling bicycle race.
Breaking Away. 1979. Christopher, Dennis

Dave, the Dude.
Because he is superstitious and fearful of losing a big bet, this petty gangster and gambler helps Apple Annie to pose as an aristocratic socialite.
Lady for a Day. 1933. William, Warren

David.
The youngest son of a large mountain family dreams that one day he will be entrusted to carry the mail, a job of great honor and respect.
Tol'able David. 1921. Barthelmess, Richard

David.
Bright, unassuming high-schooler, with a flair for computers, unwittingly dials into a military computer, cracks its security code, and spends an afternoon tossing it commands. Later he becomes frightened when he realizes that he almost started World War III.
War Games. 1983. Broderick, Matthew

Davis.
An old drunk sea captain hanging around Tahiti is given command of a decrepit ship which he safely brings through a severe storm to an uncharted island. However, the ruler of this paradise swears that no white man who lands there will leave alive.
Ebb Tide. 1922. Fawcett, George

Davis, Charlie.
A young boxer rises from poverty on the Lower East Side to become middleweight champion, but squanders his money, loses his girl and his best friend, and finally is himself cruelly exploited.
Body and Soul. 1947. Garfield, John

Davis, John.
A weary but sensitive newspaper correspondent comes to London during the blitz, and while covering a story about an orphanage becomes attached to two children whom he brings back to America.
Journey for Margaret. 1942. Young, Robert

Dawes, Clara.
In a Nottinghamshire mining village this married woman, separated from her husband, becomes a passing mistress of a talented young man who has sacrificed a chance to study art in London.
Sons and Lovers. 1960. Ure, Mary

Dawn, Billie.
Brassy dumb blonde, with a pronounced New York accent, is the girl friend of a wealthy junk dealer. She falls in love and marries the tutor who has been hired to help her acquire the polish and sophistication necessary for meeting with influential people.
Born Yesterday. 1950. Holliday, Judy

Dax, Colonel.
This French colonel is forced, under pressure from politically motivated generals, to accept an impossible objective for his regiment. Following their rout, he passionately defends his men's courage, only to see several of them executed as cowards for political expediency.
Paths of Glory. 1957. Douglas, Kirk

De Bergerac, Cyrano.
Eloquent, long-nosed romantic writes impassioned poetry so that his more handsome friend may court the girl he himself secretly loves.
Cyrano de Bergerac. 1950. Ferrer, Jose

De Breux, Yoeland.
Married to a quarrelsome duke, this beautiful 16th-century French aristocrat loses her arrogance and vanity when she and her husband's servant fall in love.
Ashes of Vengeance. 1923. Talmadge, Norma

De Carter, Alfred.
Suspecting that his wife has been unfaithful, this charming and satiric symphony conductor lets his thoughts stray during a concert and envisions, to the music of Rossini, Wagner, and Tchaikovsky, three fantastic slapstick ways to take revenge.
Unfaithfully Yours. 1948. Harrison, Rex

De Paul, Vincent.
A humble young priest in 17th-century France takes charge of a long-neglected plague-ridden parish and cares for the sick and poor with endless energy and sensitivity.
Monsieur Vincent. 1948. Fresnay, Pierre

De Praslin, Duc.
Nineteenth-century French nobleman falls in love with his children's governess, murders his nagging, jealous wife and then commits suicide.
All This and Heaven Too. 1940. Boyer, Charles

De Praslin, Duchesse.
Shrewish, jealous wife of a 19th-century French nobleman drives her frustrated husband to turn to the governess for affection.
All This and Heaven Too. 1940. O'Neil, Barbara

De Vries, Jo.
When six R.A.F. airmen crash their plane in the Dutch countryside, this heroic young woman of the underground leads them to safety.
One of Our Aircraft is Missing. 1942. Withers, Googie

De Winter, Maxim.
Moody and mysterious Cornish landowner has a troubled conscience over the death of his first wife.
Rebecca. 1940. Olivier, Laurence

De Winter, Mrs.
A shy and naive young bride lives under the shadow of her husband's glamorous first wife.
Rebecca. 1940. Fontaine, Joan

Deakins, Jim.
Restless, fun-loving Kentuckian leaves St. Louis in the 1830s and joins a keelboat expedition up the Missouri River.
The Big Sky. 1952. Douglas, Kirk

Dealer.
As her teen-age daughter rises to Hollywood stardom practically overnight, this near-demented mother is placed in a mental institution against her will.
Inside Daisy Clover. 1965. Gordon, Ruth

Debbie.
On high-school graduation night 1962 in Modesto, California, this pretty blonde swinger who thrives on excitement is picked up by a graduate in a borrowed Chevy for an evening of dizzy misadventures.
American Graffiti. 1973. Clark, Candy

Deedee.
All sorts of conflicts and buried hurts appear when Deedee, a former ballet dancer, meets her old friend and rival, a star of a ballet company.
The Turning Point. 1977. MacLaine, Shirley

Deeds, Longfellow.
Naive tuba player and poet laureate of Mandrake Falls, Vermont, travels to Manhattan to claim his deceased uncle's fortune. Even though he is ultimately charged with insanity by the lunacy commission and declines to testify at his own trial, Deeds refuses to be swindled out of the huge legacy.
Mr. Deeds Goes to Town. 1936. Cooper, Gary

Deep Throat.
Unidentifiable source, probably an FBI or CIA agent with a grudge against Nixon, knows about the Watergate break-in and can confirm or deny evidence that a *Washington Post* reporter brings to him in their covert meetings.
All the President's Men. 1976. Holbrook, Hal

Del Lago, Alexandra.
In order to ease her panic-stricken sense of failure, this aging and neurotic film star seeks substitute reality in a world of alcohol and narcotics.
Sweet Bird of Youth. 1962. Page, Geraldine

Delaney, Doc.
Angry, frustrated, alcoholic chiropractor cannot forget that 20 years earlier he was a promising Phi Beta Kappa medical student who ruined his career by impregnating a woman and marrying her "to do the right thing."
Come Back, Little Sheba. 1952. Lancaster, Burt

Delaney, Lola.
Inept, gabby, slovenly housewife tries to cope with her alcoholic husband while mourning her losses: youth, love, and Little Sheba, the dog that ran away.
Come Back, Little Sheba. 1952. Booth, Shirley

Delight, Trixie.
This carnival hootchy-kootchy dancer is tricked into a compromising situation by a nine-year-old con artist, and as a result loses her chance for security.
Paper Moon. 1973. Kahn, Madeline

Delilah.
This black housekeeper dies of a broken heart when her daughter, who has been passing as white, refuses to acknowledge her mother.
Imitation of Life. 1934. Beavers, Louise

Della Rovere.
Shameless black marketeer and gambler is in financial trouble and agrees, in exchange for a reward, to enter prison disguised as General della Rovere, a resistance leader. While in prison he is so moved by the resistance fighters' loyalty to Italy and their growing respect of him as their supposed leader that he decides not to betray them to the Nazis.
Generale della Rovere. 1959. De Sica, Vittorio

Delle Rose, Rosa.
Sensitive, nubile teenage girl, with an eccentric Italian-born mother, becomes infatuated with a sailor whom she meets at a school dance.
The Rose Tattoo. 1955. Pavan, Marisa

Delle Rose, Serafina.
Robust Italian-born widow of a truck driver, endlessly mourning her dead husband's perfection, finds love again when she meets a cheerful, rough-and-tumble trucker.
The Rose Tattoo. 1955. Magnani, Anna

Deluzy-Desportes, Henriette.
Governess to the children of a 19th-century French nobleman falls in love with her employer, but the affair ends tragically when he kills his wife and commits suicide.
All This and Heaven Too. 1940. Davis, Bette

Denard.
An aging, shabby intellectual, an agent of Loyalist Spain, goes to London to prevent a Fascist business deal; he finds that his English contacts have betrayed him and that he is being pursued by Fascist gunmen.
Confidential Agent. 1945. Boyer, Charles

Desdemona.
Daughter of a senator of Venice, the beautifully vibrant and sensitive wife of Othello protests her innocence but accepts the realization of her doom.
Othello. 1965. Smith, Maggie

Desmond, Norma.
Pathetic, aging, legendary star of the silent screen lives out a fantasy existence in a decaying mansion on Hollywood's Sunset Boulevard, planning her return to films in her own adaptation of "Salome."
Sunset Boulevard. 1950. Swanson, Gloria

Devereaux, Matt.
Always grappling with family conflicts, Matt is a self-made, autocratic patriarch of a fading cattle empire. Ruthless because he has had to compete with nature and callous men, he is passionately devoted to his "Senora" and his half-breed son, despite the ostracism of society.
Broken Lance. 1954. Tracy, Spencer

Devereaux, Senora.
Beautiful, dignified Comanche princess, wife of a cattle baron, is passionately devoted to her husband. Senora tries to keep peace among her husband's eldest sons by a former marriage, their father, and their half-breed brother.
Broken Lance. 1954. Jurado, Katy

DeVriess.
Although lax and sloppy, Captain DeVriess, who preceded Captain Queeg on the Navy destroyer-minesweeper Caine, displays a fitness for command and a close rapport with his crew.
The Caine Mutiny. 1954. Tully, Tom

DeWitt, Addison.
Powerful, acid-tongued drama critic is aware of young star's past, but is willing to help her because of selfish interests.
All About Eve. 1950. Sanders, George

Diane.
This lovely Parisian street waif is rescued from a life of hardship and despair by a confident sewer worker. When he must leave for war, her daily prayers for him bring her absolute confidence in his safe return.
Seventh Heaven. 1927. Gaynor, Janet

Dietrichson, Phyllis.
Wicked blonde seduces an insurance salesman in order to enlist his aid in murdering her unwanted husband for his insurance.
Double Indemnity. 1944. Stanwyck, Barbara

Dilg, Leopold.
Philosophical factory worker and soapbox orator, unjustly accused of arson and manslaughter, breaks out of jail and is hidden by a schoolteacher. He is defended by an eminent law professor who tries to teach him some respect for the law.
The Talk of the Town. 1942. Grant, Cary

Dillon, Abner.
Unfortunate Abner becomes the financier of the Broadway show "Pretty Lady" because he is infatuated with the leading actress.
42nd Street. 1933. Kibbee, Guy

Dingle, Benjamin.
An elderly and delightfully comical gent who calls himself a "well-to-do, retired millionaire" shares a war-time apartment with a young working girl.
The More the Merrier. 1943. Coburn, Charles

Dink.
This young boy's continuing faith, loyalty, and love for his erring father, a one-time prizefighting champ, help his father to make a successful comeback and regain his dignity.
The Champ. 1931. Cooper, Jackie
The Champ. 1979. Schroder, Ricky

Dipesto, Rayette.
Featherbrained waitress who loves country and western music, mistress of a California oil-rigger, Rayette manages to accompany him when he visits his dying father, even though she knows she's not welcome.
Five Easy Pieces. 1970. Black, Karen

Disraeli, Benjamin.
Brilliant prime minister of England outwits the Russians to acquire the Suez Canal.
Disraeli. 1929. Arliss, George

Divot, Min.
A tough, good-hearted innkeeper in Southern California, romancing and fighting with her fisherman friend, Bill, works hard to raise her adopted little girl. She is jailed for murder for killing this foundling's capricious mother.
Min and Bill. 1930. Dressler, Marie

Dobbs, Fred C.
A penniless vagrant in Mexico is able, from his lottery winnings, to grubstake a prospecting trip with two other Americans into the bandit-ridden Sierra Madre mountains. Here his vicious greed for gold corrupts both his morals and his mind.
Treasure of Sierra Madre. 1948. Bogart, Humphrey

Doc Boone, see Boone, Josiah

Doc Riedenschneider, see Riedenschneider, Erwin

Doctor Gillespie, see Gillespie, Leonard

Doctor Jekyll, see Jekyll, Henry

Doctor Kildare, see Kildare, James

Dodger.
Dodger, an aging cowhand, affectionately called "Old Man," is close to the land and understands the problems of his employers, young ranchers trying to stand up to a land baron.
Comes a Horseman. 1978. Farnsworth, Richard

Dodsworth, Samuel.
Loyal, middle-aged retired businessman tries to preserve his marriage of 20 years even though his wife is an insensitive and selfish woman.
Dodsworth. 1936. Huston, Walter

Dolgorucki.
A Russian general, commander of the armies and aristocratic cousin to the Czar, becomes a broken man after the Revolution. He ends up in America working as an extra in a movie studio.
The Last Command. 1928. Jannings, Emil

Dolittle, Dr. John.
This gentle, suave veterinary doctor is patient and kind with young children, but would rather communicate with his animals than have dealings with adults.
Dr. Dolittle. 1967. Harrison, Rex

Dolly, see Levi, Dolly

Donnell, Marion.
Young stenographer elopes with a rich man's son and is forced by her cruel father-in-law to annul the marriage.
The Trespasser. 1929. Swanson, Gloria

Donnetti, Beppo.
A young and handsome gondolier emigrates to New York's Little Italy where he and his wife experience the harsh realities of American life. When their baby becomes ill and dies, he seeks revenge on the local political boss who was in part responsible for the child's death.
The Italian. 1915. Beban, George

Dooley.
Poor, happy-go-lucky GI in Italy loves money, wants to build the most beautiful restaurant in New Jersey, and dreams of a four-day-pass with "Gina, Tina and vino."
The Bold and the Brave. 1956. Rooney, Mickey

Dooley, Biff.
A New York taxi driver goes to San Manana and is hilariously caught up in a revolution. Understanding no Spanish, Biff thinks he is being inducted into the army when he is really being captured; when he is to be executed, he thinks he is being asked to lead the forces.
The Dictator. 1922. Long, Walter

Doolittle, Alfred.
Buoyant Cockney dustman, with a penchant for drink, sells his daughter to a language professor who introduces him to an American millionaire, a founder of moral reform societies. Doolittle becomes a wealthy man when the millionaire provides for him in his will.
My Fair Lady. 1964. Holloway, Stanley

Doolittle, Eliza.
Bedraggled, but assertive, Cockney flower girl, taught by a language professor to be mannerly and to speak properly, is transformed into an elegant lady.
Pygmalion. 1938. Hiller, Wendy
My Fair Lady. 1964. Hepburn, Audrey

Doorman.
An old hotel doorman, proud of his position, especially pleased with his gold-braided uniform, and admired in his neighborhood for his sprightly military bearing, plunges into despair when he is fired because of age and given the lowly job of a white-coated washroom attendant.
The Last Laugh. 1924. Jannings, Emil

Doris.
Just by chance, a young housewife meets an accountant, has a one-night fling, and continues to meet him at the same resort for the next 26 years. During this time Doris gets her high school diploma, becomes a Berkeley hippie, a successful businesswoman and finally a grandmother.
Same Time, Next Year. 1978. Burstyn, Ellen

Dorothy.
In a dream adventure, this wistful innocent girl from Kansas and her dog Toto are spirited via tornado to the magical land of Oz. With some bizarre companions she makes her way to the Emerald City to see the Wizard so that he might help her find her way back home.
The Wizard of Oz. 1939. Garland, Judy

Dorsey, Michael.
An unemployed actor with lots of self-confidence and a good sense of humor disguises himself as a woman, Dorothy Michaels, in order to get a part in a soap opera. He becomes the star of the show, but complications arise when he falls in love with a young actress, and her father falls for him.
Tootsie. 1982. Hoffman, Dustin

Dowd, Elwood P.
Gentle, charming middle-aged alcoholic, accompanied by an invisible white rabbit six feet and three inches tall, is under pressure from his relatives to enter a mental hospital.
Harvey. 1950. Stewart, James

Doyle, Edie.
Murdered dockworker's sister helps her friend, Terry Malloy, through love and understanding, to expose the union racketeers.
On the Waterfront. 1954. Saint, Eva Marie

Doyle, Fay.
Lecherous, neurotic wife deceives the editor when she writes a sad but false letter to his lonely-hearts column, saying that her husband is a cripple and unable to make love to her.
Lonelyhearts. 1958. Stapleton, Maureen

Doyle, Jimmy.
Living in a world without standards, where the chase of criminals and their capture are his only satisfactions, this callous, hardnosed narcotics detective, nicknamed Popeye, risks his life repeatedly in his determination to find the heroin transported from Marseilles to New York City.
The French Connection. 1971. Hackman, Gene

Dr. Jekyll, see Jekyll, Henry

Dracula.
Menacing, demented human vampire from Transylvania, living in London, sustains his life by drinking the blood of his victims.
Dracula. 1931. Lugosi, Bela

Dragline.
Illiterate, well-meaning, unofficial leader of a chain gang particularly dislikes a new inmate, but eventually the drive and rebelliousness of this man win Dragline's respect.
Cool Hand Luke. 1967. Kennedy, George

Drake, Susanna.
Vain, shallow Southern beauty fears that somewhere in her family background there is Negro blood.
Raintree County. 1957. Taylor, Elizabeth

Dravot, Daniel.
Former English soldier, an adventurer and charming scoundrel, goes to small remote Kafiristan and sets himself up as king. Rather than trying to escape with the gold he has amassed, he begins to take his royal responsibilities seriously, which ultimately leads to his downfall.
The Man Who Would Be King. 1975. Connery, Sean

Drayton, Christina.
After the first shock, this liberal, bluestocking mother is very positive about her daughter's decision to marry a black man, and is as excited as if it were her own marriage.
Guess Who's Coming to Dinner. 1967. Hepburn, Katharine

Drayton, Matt.
Elite, crusty, sardonic parent is thrown into some confusion when his beloved daughter brings home a distinguished black gentleman whom she intends to marry.
Guess Who's Coming to Dinner. 1967. Tracy, Spencer

Dreyfus, Alfred.
Captain on French General Staff is framed, tried, dishonorably discharged, and sentenced to the French prison on Devil's Island for thirty years.
The Life of Emile Zola. 1937. Schildkraut, Joseph

Dreyfuss, Dr.
Goodhearted, philosophical doctor uses vigorous resuscitative measures to bring a girl around from an overdose of sleeping pills. He is sarcastic and quick to condemn his next-door neighbor, whom he considers a ladies' man and responsible for the trouble.
The Apartment. 1960. Kruschen, Jack

Drummond, Henry.
An agnostic criminal lawyer, wise, humane, skillful at repartee and patterned after Clarence Darrow, represents a young schoolteacher charged with violating the state law forbidding the teaching of Darwin's theory of evolution.
Inherit the Wind. 1960. Tracy, Spencer

Drummond, Hugh.
Known as "Bulldog," this handsome and wealthy war hero becomes bored after the fighting is over and seeks new adventures and danger.
Bulldog Drummond. 1929. Colman, Ronald

Du Barry, Madame.
A heartless, conniving and charming flirt, this French milliner has many lovers, but captures the heart of King Louis XV and completely dominates him.
Passion. 1920. Negri, Pola

DuBois, Blanche, see Blanche in *A Streetcar Named Desire*

Dubrovna, Irena.
A European girl working in New York City as a dress designer is haunted by an eerie temptation to be feline and actually becomes, under stress, a clawing killer leopard.
Cat People. 1942. Simon, Simone

Duc de Tours.
A brutal 16th-century French nobleman kills a member of his guard, but when the rest of the soldiers decide to slay him in revenge, he hides like a coward and will not defend himself.
Ashes of Vengeance. 1923. Beery, Wallace.

Duchess of Brighton.
En route to Miami but stranded in a London airport because of fog, this eccentric old Duchess, never having flown before, pops pep pills, stuggles with her luggage, fights her seat belt, and cannot understand why she is in this uncomfortable situation.
The V.I.P.s. 1963. Rutherford, Margaret

Duddy.
By appearance confident and pushy, yet somehow insecure, this young Canadian Jewish boy obtains riches, women, and power by emulating the well-to-do around him. He then sells everyone out, including his closest friends and family.
Apprenticeship of Duddy Kravitz. 1974. Dreyfuss, Richard

Duke of Florence.
Hen-pecked husband is fearful that his wife will find out about his love affair.
The Affairs of Cellini. 1934. Morgan, Frank

Dulaine, Clio.
A beautiful and high-spirited Creole adventuress, with a good sense of humor and a hunger for money, goes to fashionable Saratoga Springs where she conquers a Texas gambler.
Saratoga Trunk. 1945. Bergman, Ingrid

Dummar, Lynda.
Lovely, romantic but dense, fed up with the futility of her husband's vague schemes to make money, Lynda leaves him to find work as a go-go dancer, is cajoled into remarriage after the divorce, and finally walks out again.
Melvin and Howard. 1980. Steenburgen, Mary

Dummar, Melvin.
Plain, candid, ever-hopeful gas station owner plots very hard to make easy money, but just about stays ahead of the bill collectors. After picking up an unconscious bum in the desert, Melvin becomes an instant celebrity when he is named a major beneficiary in Howard Hughes' will.
Melvin and Howard. 1980. LeMat, Paul

Duncan, Isadora.
This pioneering modern dancer and revolutionary proponent of free love has several love affairs, establishes dancing schools, suffers through her two children's deaths by drowning, and is herself killed in a bizarre accident.
Isadora. 1968. Redgrave, Vanessa

Dunn, Katherine.
Older pretty sister, favorite of her father, Katherine is now an airline stewardess, a shallow pleasure seeker, flitting from trend to trend and watching her life go down the drain.
Looking for Mr. Goodbar. 1977. Weld, Tuesday

Dunn, Theresa.
In an attempt to free herself from a repressive home environment and find her identity, this quiet and devoted teacher of deaf children by day becomes a sexy but vulnerable swinger as she cruises the singles bars at night.
Looking for Mr. Goodbar. 1977. Keaton, Diane

Dunne, Frank.
Australian track star from the Back Country hitchhikes to Perth to enlist with the Anzac troops headed for the Near East during World War I. As a company runner during the battle for Gallipoli, he is killed while returning with an order to suspend an attack, during which his best friend will be shot.
Gallipoli. 1981. Gibson, Mel

Dunsom, Tom.
This physically and mentally tough individualist pioneers the movement of large herds of cattle from Texas to the railheads in Kansas. His determination and stubbornness help him accomplish the near impossible, but bring on a mutiny during the drive.
Red River. 1948. Wayne, John

Dupea, Robert Eronica.
Rootless, independent former classical pianist turned California oilworker, Dupea returns to his eccentric and musical family home on Puget Sound. While there he tries to explain himself to his dying father, seduces his brother's fiancee, and finally heads back on the road again.
Five Easy Pieces. 1970. Nicholson, Jack

Durant, Albert.
A wealthy Parisian, amusingly clumsy but unabashed, poses as a hotel waiter so that he can win the favor of a fascinating Russian lady.
The Grand Duchess and the Waiter. 1926. Menjou, Adolphe

Dussell.
Mr. Dussell, a comical middle-aged bachelor, must share a room with an adolescent girl when he hides from the Nazis in a factory loft for two years with other Dutch Jews.
The Diary of Anne Frank. 1959. Wynn, Ed

Dyer.
Chauffeur and AWOL Army sergeant, cool, clear-eyed lover of a singer, wants her to ease her frantic schedule before she destroys herself.
The Rose. 1979. Forrest, Frederic

Dyke, James.
James kills a man, surrenders to the police, but refuses to give his right name. When his sister comes to visit him on death row, he convinces her that she is mistaken and that her brother died a hero in the World War.
The Valiant. 1929. Muni, Paul

Dysart, Dr.
While treating a troubled stable boy who has blinded six horses, this intense, tormented psychiatrist begins to question his own vocation, which he believes forces people into unstable social normality.
Equus. 1977. Burton, Richard

Earle, Roy.
After his release from prison, Mad Dog Earle, an aging, ruthless killer and social misfit, can still show some kindness with an offer of marriage and medical aid to a crippled girl. Following a robbery, he is pursued into the Sierras, where he makes his last futile stand.
High Sierra. 1941. Bogart, Humphrey

Eastman, George.
Intelligent but emotionally confused factory worker, groping for acceptance in a higher social set, is exposed to the wealth and love of a beautiful debutante. He shuns his pregnant lower-class girl friend and is found morally guilty of murdering her.
A Place in the Sun. 1951. Clift, Montgomery

Echo.
A ventriloquist in a circus sideshow picks pockets with two cronies. They later hatch an elaborate bird-selling and robbery scheme in which Echo cleverly employs his vocal skills to fool people into buying parrots which they think can talk.
The Unholy Three. 1925. Chaney, Lon

Ed.
When he is thrust into the leadership role on a back-to-nature canoe trip, this mild-mannered, ineffectual suburban business man becomes self-confident and cunning in his efforts to lead his companions out of the wilderness and to deflect suspicion from his group during a police investigation.
Deliverance. 1972. Voight, Jon

Eddie.
Although he's an alcoholic and no longer capable of being a ship's mate, Eddie, nicknamed the Rummy, is employed by his friend on a fishing boat as a reward for his loyalty.
To Have and Have Not. 1944. Brennan, Walter

Edwards, Ethan.
A lonely, unregenerate Confederate officer returns from the war to learn that his niece has been kidnapped during an Indian raid on his ranch. During a five-year search for her, Edwards becomes obsessed with a hatred and savagery that very nearly lead to the murder of his own kin.
The Searchers. 1956. Wayne, John

Ekdahl, Alexander.
Solemn ten-year-old's domestic bliss is shattered when his father dies and his mother marries the local bishop. He and his family go off to live in the clergyman's terrifying, spooky castle, where Alexander dreams about and eventually escapes to the house of an old family friend.
Fanny and Alexander. 1983. Guve, Bertil

Ekdahl, Emilie.
In Uppsala, this frail but beautiful actress is the star of the theater that her husband manages. When he dies of a stroke, she marries the local prelate and takes her children with her to live in the bishop's cold and frightening palace.
Fanny and Alexander. 1983. Frolong, Ewa

Ekdahl, Helena.
Still strikingly attractive, this widowed matriarch and former actress, whose husband built a theater for her in Uppsala, is beginning to feel her age. She worries about various members of her large, now grown-up family.
Fanny and Alexander. 1983. Wallgren, Gunn

Eleanor.
This white woman has an affair with Jack Jefferson, the first black heavyweight boxing champion of the world, an unheard-of occurrence in the early 1900s.
Great White Hope. 1970. Alexander, Jane

Eleanor of Aquitaine.
Briefly freed from her ten-year imprisonment, this estranged, exiled, embittered Queen squares off with Henry II, her husband, to choose a successor to the throne of England.
The Lion in Winter. 1968. Hepburn, Katharine

Elgin, Frank.
On the surface Frank appears to be a charming martyr, but in reality he is a weak-willed, broken-down alcoholic musical comedy actor trying to make a comeback, and blaming all his failures on his "country girl" wife.
The Country Girl. 1954. Crosby, Bing

Elgin, Georgie.
Plain, weary, loyal wife suppresses her own personality to encourage and nurture her weak alcoholic husband.
The Country Girl. 1954. Kelly, Grace

Ellen.
An impoverished girl with two loony sisters becomes companion to an old, spoiled actress. When the sisters disrupt the household and Ellen is faced with dismissal, she decides to murder the old woman.
Ladies in Retirement. 1940. Lupino, Ida

Ellen.
A petulant woman is so possessive of her author-husband's love that she is driven to madness; she drowns his younger brother, kills her unborn child, and finally poisons herself.
Leave Her to Heaven. 1945. Tierney, Gene

Elliot, Margaret.
Fading Hollywood film star tries to revive her career, but will not acknowledge the fact that she is too old to play the glamorous roles that once brought her fame.
The Star. 1952. Davis, Bette

Elliott.
Practical, right-minded ten-year-old discovers a frightened alien in the toolshed and, with the help of his brother and sister, tries to domesticate him while safely hiding him in their bedroom. When E.T. begins to fail, Elliott forms a neighborhood bike squad to enable their friend to return to his spaceship.
E.T. the Extra-Terrestrial. 1982. Thomas, Henry

Elspeth.
Elspeth is worried about her attractive, unhappy, middle-aged friend's affair with an ambitious social climber because she is a caring friend and is afraid of the consequences of their relationship.
Room at the Top. 1959. Baddeley, Hermione

Elvira.
In the late 19th century, this beautiful, delicate 17-year-old tightrope walker falls in love with a handsome young cavalry officer. The two live only for each other, he deserting the army and she the circus. Cut off from society, they decide to die rather than be separated.
Elvira Madigan. 1967. Degermark, Pia

Emilia.
Unmindful of her own safety, Iago's wife dares to defend Desdemona's honor before the jealous Othello.
Othello. 1965. Redman, Joyce

Emilia.
Young aspiring ballerina goes to New York to train with a ballet company, shows great promise, and matures emotionally when she falls in love wih a Russian dancer.
The Turning Point. 1977. Broune, Leslie

Emma.
Successful ballerina, reaching an age at which her position is shaky because of heavy competition from younger dancers, meets a long-time friend and tackles some unresolved problems.
The Turning Point. 1977. Bancroft, Anne

Emma.
This loving young woman, raising her family in the Midwest, is heartbroken because, even though her mother calls her every day, she shows very little affection. She has an affair because her husband is dallying with a student, and finds some love before her life abruptly ends in tragedy.
Terms of Endearment. 1983. Winger, Debra

Emma, in *Emma,* see Thatcher, Emma

Emmerich, Alonzo D.
This crooked lawyer, consumed by his lust for high living and his infatuation with expensive blondes, tries to pull a double-cross. He muffs it and it costs him his life.
Asphalt Jungle. 1950. Calhern, Louis

Empress.
This dignified Grand Duchess tries to determine a young amnesiac's credentials as a Romanov.
Anastasia. 1956. Hayes, Helen

Enders, Mrs.
Comic society matron is the mother of an attractive, rich, blonde bachelor. When he buys an apartment in a black ghetto, she visits his building, becomes drunk with one of the tenants, and is transformed into a soul food enthusiast.
The Landlord. 1970. Grant, Lee

Erhardt.
During the Nazi occupation in Poland, this local buffoonish Gestapo chief is seduced by a member of a Warsaw theatrical troupe.
To Be or Not To Be. 1983. Durning, Charles

Erica.
When her husband of 16 years leaves her for another woman, Erica is dazed, scared, and resentful as she tries to piece her life together and enter a new social scene.
An Unmarried Woman. 1978. Clayburgh, Jill

Esmeralda.
A beautiful gypsy girl, who dances with her pet goat for a living, befriends the ugly hunchbacked bell ringer of Notre Dame, Quasimodo.
The Hunchback of Notre Dame. 1923. Miller, Patsy Ruth

Eufemio.
Emiliano Zapata's older brother, an impetuous woman chaser, allows his new status as "liberator" to transform him into a tyrant.
Viva Zapata. 1952. Quinn, Anthony

Evans, Morgan.
A promising youngster from a Welsh mining town is brought to flower by a dedicated school teacher.
The Corn is Green. 1945. Dall, John

Eve.
Aggressive, unscrupulous young woman wants to become the brightest star on Broadway, and will perpetrate anything from adultery to blackmail to achieve her ends.
All About Eve. 1950. Baxter, Anne

Eve.
Georgia housewife and mother has three separate and divergent personalities: Eve White, when she's good; Eve Black, when she's sexy and bad; and Jane, an attractive, intelligent woman.
The Three Faces of Eve. 1957. Woodward, Joanne

Eve.
Meticulous, disciplined and disturbed interior decorator, who has imposed such strict standards of achievement on her three daughters that they all consider themselves failures, falls apart when her wealthy husband announces he is planning to leave her for another woman.
Interiors. 1978. Page, Geraldine

Eyre, Jane.
A timid young woman becomes a governess to a little girl at dark and foreboding Thornfield Hall, and soon falls under the spell of her mysterious employer.
Jane Eyre. 1944. Fontaine, Joan

Fadden, Chimmie.
A jaunty, easy-going, slang-talking young man from New York's Bowery takes off for Death Valley to find a gold mine, with some hilarious results.
Chimmie Fadden Out West. 1915. Moore, Victor

Fagin.
Wily, unsavory but jolly leader of a den of thieves encourages his young charges to be inventive and to "pick a pocket or two."
Oliver Twist. 1922. Chaney, Lon
Oliver. 1968. Moody, Ron

Fairchild, Sabrina.
Sweetly bewitching chauffeur's daughter returns from cooking school in Paris and becomes involved with both of her employer's sons, one a playboy and the other a serious workaholic.
Sabrina. 1954. Hepburn, Audrey

Fanny.
A vivid example of human survival and endurance, this former Miss Sepia, now a tenant in Bedford-Stuyvesant, becomes sexually and emotionally involved with her new white landlord.
The Landlord. 1970. Sands, Diana

Farmer, Frances.
In the 1930s this beautiful but rebellious young girl achieves notoriety with a high-school essay questioning God, becomes a successfull Hollywood star, supposedly suffers a breakdown, and is confined for many years in a mental institution, more for her politics than her psychological problems.
Frances. 1982. Lange, Jessica

Farmer, Lillian.
Frances Farmer's uncaring, domineering mother, only interested in her daughter's fame and fortune, ignores her anguished pleas for help and understanding.
Frances. 1982. Stanley, Kim

Farnsworth, Julia.
Sexy, frenzied wife of a millionaire murders her husband without realizing that he had already died, and that his body was temporarily occupied by a reincarnated Joe Pendleton. This forces Pendleton's spirit to move on to a third body.
Heaven Can Wait. 1978. Cannon, Dyan

Farrelly, Fanny.
Willful, opinionated woman, devoted to the memory of her dead husband and determined to mold her son in his image, makes outrageous remarks and asks probing questions of her visiting daughter and son-in-law concerning their life for the past 18 years.
Watch on the Rhine. 1943. Watson, Lucille

Farrow, Lois.
Attractive but tough middle-aged mother of the prettiest girl in the small, shabby town of Anarene, Texas, recognizes what life is all about and has come to terms with it.
The Last Picture Show. 1971. Burstyn, Ellen

Father.
This short-tempered, raging husband and father of four sons, living comfortably in New York City in 1883, shows from time to time that he really is a kind and warm individual at heart.
Life With Father. 1947. Powell, William

Father Mullin, see Mullin, Tim

Felicia.
Married to a shyster tycoon, Felicia is having an affair with her hairdresser, even after she discovers that he has also been seeing her daughter.
Shampoo. 1975. Grant, Lee

Fellowes, Judith.
This leader of a group of American schoolteachers on tour in Mexico is bent on destroying the tour guide, a defrocked clergyman, for returning the interest shown by an 18-year-old girl in the group.
The Night of the Iguana. 1964. Hall, Grayson

Felson, Eddie.
Self-assured, cocky pool shark challenges the top man for the championship. He loses, and becomes the tool of a professional gambler who teaches him how to think like a winner and moves him into big-time hustling.
The Hustler. 1961. Newman, Paul

Ferdinando.
Elegant, suave but lecherous Sicilian baron plots to trick his nagging wife into a compromising situation so that he can honorably shoot her and be free to marry his 16-year-old cousin, a desirable young beauty.
Divorce, Italian Style. 1962. Mastroianni, Marcello

Ferrari, Senor.
Fat, fez-wearing owner of the Blue Parrot Cafe in Casablanca during World War II shrewdly deals in the black market.
Casablanca. 1942. Greenstreet, Sydney

Ferretti, Amadeo.
Small-town Italian businessman, slyly remembering what he has read about Swedish girls in the travel brochures, gets the chance to live out his fantasies when he is sent on a long trip to Sweden.
To Bed or Not To Bed. 1963. Sordi, Alberto

Fiedler.
Brilliant East German Jew, acting as a double agent for British intelligence, arranges a secret tribunal, with a British agent as the star witness.
The Spy Who Came in from the Cold. 1965. Werner, Oskar

Fields, Jenny.
At mid-life this simple but strong and independent nurse becomes a celebrity when she publishes her autobiography, *A Sexual Suspect.* Hailed as a feminist, she becomes a model for a radical group known as the Ellen Jamesians, who have cut out their tongues to protest a rape.
The World According to Garp. 1982. Close, Glenn

Finch, Atticus.
In Maycomb, Alabama, in the 1930s, this kind, gentle, soft-spoken widowed lawyer is assigned to defend a black sharecropper falsely accused of raping a white woman.
To Kill a Mockingbird. 1962. Peck, Gregory

Finch, Scott.
Her close relationships with her brother and their widowed father help this beguiling six-year-old tomboy withstand some frightening experiences resulting from racial tension and economic depression.
To Kill a Mockingbird. 1962. Badham, Mary

Finley, Boss.
Crooked political boss in a corrupt Southern town renews an old feud with a returned Hollywood gigolo, whom he considers an undesirable suitor for his daughter.
Sweet Bird of Youth. 1962. Begley, Ed

Finley, Heavenly.
Attractive young Southern girl is in love with a handsome actor-gigolo despite her father's protests that he is not worthy of her.
Sweet Bird of Youth. 1962. Knight, Shirley

Firth, Mrs.
Loyal, rugged but feminine pioneer wife of a migrant Irish-Australian sheep drover yearns for a permanent home and raises the funds necessary to buy a farm, whereupon her husband gambles away their entire savings.
The Sundowners. 1960. Johns, Glynis

Fitzgibbon, Father.
The warm-hearted but weary elderly pastor of a poor parish is skeptical of a young progressive priest who is sent to help him.
Going My Way. 1944. Fitzgerald, Barry

Flaemmchen.
Attractive stenographer accepts her boss's advances as part of her job.
Grand Hotel. 1932. Crawford, Joan

Flagg.
A hearty Marine captain, hard-drinking and a lover of wine and women, has a boisterous rivalry with his sergeant over a fickle French barkeeper's daughter, but when it comes to the battlefield, he is a professional soldier and all differences are put aside.
What Price Glory? 1926. McLaglen, Victor

Flagg, Edwin.
Fat piano player, answering an ad for an accompanist, is invited into the house of two former movie stars and goes along with the job in the hope that he can get enough money to leave his possessive mother.
What Ever Happened to Baby Jane? 1962. Buono, Victor

Flanagan, Father.
A gentle, warm, tireless priest, believing there is no such thing as a bad boy, works among juvenile delinquents and establishes a community for wayward boys near Omaha, Nebraska.
Boys' Town. 1938. Tracy, Spencer

Flo.
Tough-talking blonde waitress, with a heart of gold, becomes a friend of Alice Hyatt when she settles down for a while with a job in a diner.
Alice Doesn't Live Here Anymore. 1974. Ladd, Diane

Florian, Mrs.
One-time dancer, now a faded beauty and a drunk, Mrs. Florian will disclose information about anything for a pint of bourbon and a kind word from a man.
Farewell, My Lovely. 1975. Miles, Sylvia

Floriot, Jacqueline.
This wealthy woman leaves her family and is later defended in a murder trial by her son, who does not remember her.
Madame X. 1929. Chatterton, Ruth

Flynn, Michaleen.
Wily, matchmaking bookie, taxi driver, and village drunk tries to convince the leading landowner of Inisfree to allow his sister to marry a repatriated American.
The Quiet Man. 1952. Fitzgerald, Barry

Fogg, Phileas.
Resolute Victorian British gentleman bets 20,000 pounds that he can circle the globe in 80 days, and overcomes monumental obstacles in order to collect his money.
Around the World in Eighty Days. 1956. Niven, David

Foley, Emil.
Shrewd, sarcastic, unrelenting drill sergeant at a Naval Aviation Officer Candidate School is a decent man whose punishment of the recruits is designed to bring out their best traits. He washes out many cadets so that only the most talented will prevail.
An Officer and a Gentleman. 1982. Gossett, Louis, Jr.

Forst, Maria.
Middle-aged wife, unhappy with the emptiness of her marriage, picks up a male hippie in a discotheque, spends the night with him, attempts suicide, and finally returns to her husband, realizing nothing has changed.
Faces. 1968. Carlin, Lynn

Foyle, Kitty.
Career girl has to choose between a personable young doctor and her first love, a Philadelphia aristocrat.
Kitty Foyle. 1940. Rogers, Ginger

Frafuso, Pasqualino.
Egotistical, compliant, base Neopolitan, nicknamed "Seven Beauties," murders an unarmed man, assaults the helpless, executes his friends, and while in a German concentration camp, seduces the ferocious female commandant in his all-consuming desire to survive.
Seven Beauties. 1976. Giannini, Giancarlo

Frances, see Farmer, Frances

Francey.
Still living in one of the dead-end streets in Manhattan in the East 50s, this old girl friend of Baby Face Martin, a murderer, is now a prostitute, a physical ruin, ravaged with disease.
Dead End. 1937. Trevor, Claire

Frank.
Befuddled, sad-eyed, lower-middle-class Italian, father of the bridegroom, reveals his feelings of love and consideration for his family in clumsy and awkward ways.
Lovers and Other Strangers. 1970. Castellano, Richard

Frank, Anne.
Wistful 13-year-old Jewish girl, with an indestructible sense of optimism and faith in the goodness of mankind, records the ordeal of eight people hidden for two years in a factory loft in Nazi-occupied Amsterdam.
The Diary of Anne Frank. 1959. Perkins, Millie

Frank, Otto.
Anne's father, a gentle and sympathetic man, is the bravely persevering and understanding leader of the small group of Jews hidden from the Nazis in a factory loft.
The Diary of Anne Frank. 1959. Schildkraut, Joseph

Frankenstein.
His joy at the success of his experiment quickly turns to horror and dismay when this high-strung, determined scientist realizes that from assembled corpses, he has created an amoral, hideous monster rather than a true human being.
Frankenstein. 1931. Clive, Colin
Frankenstein Meets the Wolfman. 1943. Lugosi, Bela

Frankie.
In a seedy Chicago underworld of card sharks and drug pushers, a professional dealer for a floating poker game battles to conquer his craving for dope.
The Man with the Golden Arm. 1955. Sinatra, Frank

Franko, Victor.
This tough Chicago hood, condemned to death, becomes a model soldier after he and 11 other military prisoners are hauled out of prison and secretly trained for a critical commando raid behind the German lines prior to D-day.
The Dirty Dozen. 1967. Cassavetes, John

French, Gwen.
An instructor at the local college becomes interested in the work of a novelist who has just returned from overseas.
Some Came Running. 1958. Hyer, Martha

Friendly, Johnny.
Corrupt, ruthless king of the docks is feared by all who must deal with him, until he is challenged by a young dockworker and the Crime Commission.
On the Waterfront. 1954. Cobb, Lee J.

Frog.
A repellent, drunk and disheveled swindler operates in New York's Chinatown with three cohorts. He is reformed by a deaf-blind faith healer whom they have come to exploit.
The Miracle Man. 1919. Chaney, Lon

Froman, Jane.
This real-life singer struggles to continue her career after sustaining crippling injuries in a Lisbon airplane crash in 1943 while en route to entertain servicemen overseas.
With a Song in My Heart. 1952. Hayward, Susan

Fuller, Jim.
Considered cured and freed after three years in prison for an attempted seduction of a little girl, Jim tries to work out his problems with the help of an understanding psychiatrist and a loving woman.
The Mark. 1961. Whitman, Stuart

Gabriele.
In 1938, on a day when all Rome has assembled at a rally for Hitler, this suspected homosexual, dismissed from his position as radio announcer and soon to be interned, is drawn together with a housewife neighbor for a brief day of passion.
A Special Day. 1977. Mastroianni, Marcello

Gaby.
Beautiful Parisian girl falls madly in love with a French criminal exiled to Algiers. She entices him to meet her outside the walls of the Casbah, whereupon he is captured, and she sails home to France alone.
Algiers. 1938. Lamarr, Hedy

Gallagher.
After a newspaper reporter writes a story identifying him as the prime suspect in a major crime because he has Mafia relatives, this outraged, innocent businessman gains revenge by turning the methods of his attackers against them.
Absence of Malice. 1981. Newman, Paul

Gallardo, Juan.
A young bullfighter of humble origins rises to wealth and fame.
Blood and Sand. 1922. Valentino, Rudolph

Gallio, Marcellus.
Arrogant Roman tribune, assigned to the execution of Christ, becomes a passionate convert through an obsession with the Savior's confiscated robe.
The Robe. 1953. Burton, Richard

Galvin, Frank.
Heavy-drinking, pathetic, down-and-out lawyer is given the chance of a lifetime to regain his dignity when he is asked to pursue a malpractice suit against a Roman Catholic hospital in Boston. He shocks everyone when he rejects a settlement and takes the suit to trial.
The Verdict. 1982. Newman, Paul

Gandhi, Mahatma.
Born a Hindu, this great but sometimes fallible Indian political leader, believer in nonviolence, shapes a nation as he tries to win India's freedom from the British Empire.
Gandhi. 1982. Kingsley, Ben

Gantry, Elmer.
In the Bible Belt of the 1920s, this corrupt, hypocritical evangelist preaches fire and brimstone from the pulpit, but is himself lustful, adulterous and a blatant opportunist when he cons his way into Sister Falconer's ministry.
Elmer Gantry. 1960. Lancaster, Burt

Garfield, Elliot.
Intense, struggling actor, job-hunting in New York, is forced to share an apartment with a recently jilted woman and her precocious daughter.
The Goodbye Girl. 1977. Dreyfuss, Richard

Garp.
Eccentric nice guy, a successful writer, struggles against overwhelming odds to live a decent, sane life with his wife and children.
The World According to Garp. 1982. Williams, Robin

Garrett.
Philandering, aging, alcoholic former astronaut, desiring a short fling, pushes his way into the life of his next-door neighbor, a handsome widow. Neither is prepared for the emotional changes that their relationship brings.
Terms of Endearment. 1983. Nicholson, Jack

Garrison, Gene.
Forty-year-old widower who has never been able to love his strong-willed father confronts him with his plans to remarry and move to California, and asks that his father join him.
I Never Sang for My Father. 1970. Hackman, Gene

Garrison, Tom.
Irascible, self-centered, tyrannical old man is a one-time pillar of the community who still lives in the past. He refuses his son's offer to move him to California or to hire a housekeeper to attend to his daily needs if he stays behind.
I Never Sang for My Father. 1970. Douglas, Melvyn

Garth, Hugh.
An old, deformed, bad-tempered man on the run from the police, hiding in a cabin in the Canadian Northwest, finds a delicate young girl who is temporarily blinded and lost in the snow. To impress her, he tells her tales about himself which are not in the least bit true.
Snowblind. 1921. Simpson, Russell

Garth, Matthew.
A stubborn, tough-as-rawhide young cowboy on a cattle drive along the Chisholm Trail audaciously tangles with the boss of the drive, Tom Dunson, who is equally strong-minded.
Red River. 1948. Clift, Montgomery

Gauguin, Paul.
This disorderly, creative painter is Van Gogh's close friend and mentor, but also his ultimate irritant.
Lust for Life. 1956. Quinn, Anthony

Gaunt, Dr.
An aging doctor keeps telling his two old bachelor cronies that they all have to get out of the rut they're in and do something exciting. They find their lives are remarkably changed by the young girl who becomes their ward.
Three Wise Fools. 1923. Francis, Alec

Gauthier, Anne.
Beautiful young movie scriptwriter, whose first marriage had a tragic ending, meets and falls in love with a racing car driver, also widowed, while they are visiting their children at school.
A Man and a Woman. 1966. Aimee, Anouk

Gautier, Marguerite.
Beautiful 1850s French courtesan, Camille loves outside the bonds of matrimony but succumbs to the pressures of society and her own physical frailties.
Camille. 1937. Garbo, Greta

Gaye.
Because he uses her as a plaything, humiliates her by ordering her to sing an old song, and plans to leave her behind at the Key Largo Hotel, Gaye, a former actress, turns to alcohol and decides to get even with her racketeer boyfriend, Johnny Rocco.
Key Largo. 1948. Trevor, Claire

Gehrig, Lou.
This real-life, shy and humble young man becomes a great baseball player, but is forced to leave at the height of his career when he becomes terminally ill.
The Pride of the Yankees. 1942. Cooper, Gary

Gelsomina.
Happy, childlike but simple-minded girl is sold by her mother to assist in the act of a strong-man touring Italy. She is so overcome by the shock of a friend's tragic death and her abandonment by Zampano, the strong-man, that she declines and dies.
La Strada. 1954. Masina, Giulietta

Gemma.
This worldly orphan, having learned to live by her wits, has a liaison with a philandering young composer in Venice, returns to London to marry him, and nearly loses him to his brother's wealthy fiancee.
Escape Me Never. 1935. Bergner, Elisabeth

General Mireau, see Mireau, General

General Yang, see Yang, General

Gennini, Charles.
Seasoned professional burglar caught with $1400 in stolen loot passionately swears that he's never been arrested before.
Detective Story. 1951. Wiseman, Joseph

Geoffrey.
Gentle, homosexual youth is given lodging by a lonely, pregnant, unmarried young woman. He tenderly and affectionately cares for her until her brassy, promiscuous mother returns and drives him away.
A Taste of Honey. 1961. Melvin, Murray

George.
A migrant farm hand travels with and takes care of a dim-witted friend, Lennie. They have a dream that one day they will own their own ranch and "live off the fat of the land," and this dream has the power to sway others.
Of Mice and Men. 1939. Meredith, Burgess

George.

A humanitarian newspaper editor in a British mill town struggles for better housing and sanitation, but must also contend with his greedy, reactionary wife who works against his efforts.
So Well Remembered. 1947. Mills, John

George.

Caustic, frustrated, middle-aged history professor, married to the daughter of the president of a New England college and involved in constant verbal conflict with his wife, publicly destroys a myth about the son they never had after she seduces a young professor visiting with his wife.
Who's Afraid of Virginia Woolf? 1966. Burton, Richard

George.

Warm, generous hairdresser pursued by all his clients is delighted by giving pleasure. He considers making love an aesthetic experience and beautifying a woman an act of love.
Shampoo. 1975. Beatty, Warren

George.

Although this New Jersey accountant is happily married, he makes a pact to meet a young California housewife, also reasonably happy, every year at the same resort where they first met by chance and had an unexpected one-night fling. He changes and grows over the next 26 years of rendezvous.
Same Time, Next Year. 1978. Alda, Alan

Georgia.

Charming, talented, divorced Broadway actress, once an alcoholic, returns from a three-month stint at a rehabilitation center, intent on improving her relationship with her teen-age daughter and on revitalizing her once successful career.
Only When I Laugh. 1981. Mason, Marsha

Georgy.

Awkward young girl, a plain Jane, gives up her kooky lifestyle when she adopts her glamorous friend's unwanted baby and marries a wealthy widower old enough to be her father.
Georgy Girl. 1966. Redgrave, Lynn

Geste, Michael.

Along with his two brothers, this young Englishman known as Beau Geste is in the French Foreign Legion, assigned to a desert fortress where he must contend not only with aggressive Arab raiders but with a brutal commander as well.
Beau Geste. 1926. Colman, Ronald
Beau Geste. 1939. Cooper, Gary

Giddens, Regina.
Conspiring and callous woman badgers her sick husband to give her money to invest in a cotton mill. When he refuses, she neglects him when he has a fatal attack.
The Little Foxes. 1941. Davis, Bette

Gideon, Joe.
This ruthless, self-destructive Broadway choreographer and director cannot maintain a permanent relationship with women because of his obsession with work and his constant infidelities. Alcohol, pills and cigarettes help drive him toward a fatal heart attack.
All That Jazz. 1974. Scheider, Roy

Gigi.
Young French tomboy, being groomed as a successful courtesan, becomes the betrothed of the richest, most handsome young man in Paris.
Gigi. 1958. Caron, Leslie

Gillespie, Bill.
Crude, bigoted Mississippi police chief begins his relationship with a black big-city detective with contemptuous suspicion. Although he continues to address the detective as "boy," Gillespie begins to feel grudging admiration as he learns some professional crime-solving procedures from this colleague.
In the Heat of the Night. 1967. Steiger, Rod

Gillespie, Leonard.
Irascible but brilliant Dr. Gillespie, although crippled and confined to a wheelchair, runs both his staff and his New York general hospital in a highly professional manner.
Young Doctor Kildare. 1938. Barrymore, Lionel

Gillis, Joe.
Cynical, impoverished young Hollywood scriptwriter becomes the kept man of a neurotic aging movie queen when he encourages her false hopes to become a star again. He first exploits her and then becomes trapped by her lavish gifts.
Sunset Boulevard. 1950. Holden, William

Gimp, see Snyder, Martin

Gingrich, Willie.
Avaricious, sly, bullying shyster lawyer, brother-in-law of a TV cameraman who is slightly injured during a football game, schemes to collect outrageous personal injury claims from the insurance company and from anybody else even remotely connected with the incident.
The Fortune Cookie. 1966. Matthau, Walter

Ginny.

This brazen but worn-out girl of the streets knows her way around the tawdry night world of seedy bars and cheap hotels.
Crossfire. 1947. Grahame, Gloria

Gino.

Middle-aged wealthy Italian, owner of a Nevada sheep ranch, sends for his dead wife's sister in Italy in the hope that when they marry she will replicate his beloved former wife.
Wild is the Wind. 1957. Quinn, Anthony

Gioia.

Soon after she comes from Italy to marry her dead sister's husband, Gioia falls in love with a hired ranch hand because her husband has no regard for her feelings or pride.
Wild is the Wind. 1957. Magnani, Anna

Girard, Dr.

A Parisian physician with a bored wife takes up with an old flame and resorts to some comical lies and deception.
So This is Paris. 1926. Blue, Monte

Gitl.

At the turn of the century on the Lower East Side, a big-eyed, innocent Russian Jewish immigrant finds it difficult to break away from Old World customs even though her husband delights in the ways of his new country.
Hester Street. 1975. Kane, Carol

Gittes, J.J.

Cool, wisecracking private eye with a passionate loyalty to truth becomes involved over his head in an intricate web of murder and political corruption, and is punished by his own compulsion to see justice done.
Chinatown. 1974. Nicholson, Jack

Giuseppe.

A bewildered and woeful Italian soldier is captured by a small band of Allied troops making their way across the Libyan desert in World War II.
Sahara. 1943. Naish, J. Carrol

Gladney, Edna.

This woman who feels her life is without purpose after her son is killed takes in orphans and eventually establishes the Texas Children's Home and Aid Society.
Blossoms in the Dust. 1941. Garson, Greer

Glenn, John.
Shy, pious and humorless, John Glenn is one of seven men selected for the Mercury space program. He wants to be the first in space, and comes close to burning up on re-entry when his heat shield becomes loose.
The Right Stuff. 1983. Harris, Ed

Glennon, Cardinal.
Craggy old cardinal of Boston, with a rugged Irish personality, is shrewd, politically acute and dedicated, but annoyed at the exclusion of Americans from the Vatican's inner circle.
The Cardinal. 1963. Huston, John

Glocken.
Cheerful, shrewd dwarf is the philosopher and man-about-deck aboard the German ship "Vera" on its 1933 voyage from Veracruz to Bremerhaven.
Ship of Fools. 1965. Dunn, Michael

Gloria.
Embittered, hard-boiled, sharp-tongued young woman enters a dance contest to win the $1500 prize and a chance for a better life. She is so defeated by the marathon that she asks her partner to put her out of her misery.
They Shoot Horses, Don't They? 1969. Fonda, Jane

Gloria.
Terrific looking, tough-talking ex-chorus girl with a heart of gold, now content to live in retirement, finds herself running around New York with a precocious Puerto Rican boy trying to elude the Mafia.
Gloria. 1980. Rowlands, Gena

Glossop, Mimi.
Mimi is getting a divorce from her wandering geologist husband and mistakes an American dancer for the paid correspondent.
The Gay Divorcee. 1934. Rogers, Ginger

God.
The Lord, in very human form, chooses a Tarzana, Califonia, supermarket manager to spread the message that "what we have down here can work."
Oh God. 1977. Burns, George

Godell, Jack.
After a crisis at the nuclear power plant where he is a supervisor, Jack heeds his conscience, stops being a company man, and decides to tell the truth, even though he's hindered by the company executives and the contracting firm that built the plant.
The China Syndrome. 1979. Lemmon, Jack

Gold Hat.
Animalistic bandit chief attacks a gold mining party in the Sierra Madre mountains, but is repelled. Catching one of the miners in the low country, he murders him for his shoes, mistakes the gold dust on his burro for useless sand, and spills it into the wind.
Treasure of Sierra Madre. 1948. Bedoya, Alfonso

Goldman, Arthur.
After the Second World War, a Nazi concentration camp survivor, harboring deep guilt feelings, comes to the United States and sets himself up to be recognized as a notorious war criminal who has slaughtered thousands of Jews.
The Man in the Glass Booth. 1975. Schell, Maximilian

Goldman, Emma.
Earthy, domineering, humane turn-of-the-century Socialist is a frequent mentor, a sometime critic, and always a friend of radical journalist John Reed.
Reds. 1981. Stapleton, Maureen

Golem.
A legendary, enormous clay monster molded by a rabbi is brought to life by inserting a magic word in the creature's chest. The rabbi only wants the Golem to do good, but it does not remain obedient and causes havoc in the ghetto of Prague.
The Golem. 1921. Wegener, Paul

Golightly, Holly.
Charming, free-spirited call girl meets a reserved young writer and falls in love; each exerts a positive influence on the other.
Breakfast at Tiffany's. 1961. Hepburn, Audrey

Gomez, Feto.
A humorous inmate and cell neighbor of Robert Stroud, the Birdman, Gomez breaks through his embittered aloofness and becomes his companion.
Birdman of Alcatraz. 1962. Savalas, Telly

Gondorff, Henry.
Snappy, suave, fast-talking con artist, living through hard times during the Depression, agrees to instruct and to collaborate with a younger swindler in a try for the "big sting."
The Sting. 1973. Newman, Paul

Gooch, Agnes.
Mousy, myopic secretary makes a mistake of a delicate, biological nature.
Auntie Mame. 1958. Cass, Peggy

Goodwin, Peter.
Strong-minded, excitable old Kentuckian, the best judge of horses in the
state, still remembers a feud that dates back to Civil War days.
Kentucky. 1938. Brennan, Walter

Gordon, Bert.
Steely-eyed amoral gambler sees a beaten pool player's potential, teaches
him the psychology of being a winner, and leads him into big-time hustling.
The Hustler. 1961. Scott, George C.

Gordon, Charly.
Mentally retarded thirtyish janitor in a bakery becomes a genius after
submitting to a new surgical technique, and has a brief love affair with his
teacher. He soon returns to his former feeble-minded state because the
results of the operation were only temporary.
Charly. 1968. Robertson, Cliff

Governor.
Because of pressure from the local churchgoers, the governor orders the
sheriff to close the "Chicken House," a bawdy house which has become a
Texas institution, and to send the girls on to better pursuits.
The Best Little Whorehouse in Texas. 1982. Durning, Charles

Gow, Alexander.
A bearded, pot-bellied, bombastic but comical old Scotsman develops a
loving relationship with his orphaned great-grandson.
The Green Years. 1946. Coburn, Charles

Graham, Barbara.
Tough, 32-year-old party girl is executed in the gas chamber for murder
amid debate over her guilt and the severity of the punishment.
I Want to Live. 1958. Hayward, Susan

Grandma Pearl.
Tender, loving, wise grandmother persuades her granddaughter to share
with others her gift of faith healing, perhaps derived from her brush with
death in an automobile accident.
Resurrection. 1980. LeGallienne, Eva

Granny.
This warm, vibrant black washerwoman, with a vast store of human
understanding and an innate sense of dignity, has been a wealthy Southern
woman's servant for years.
Pinky. 1949. Waters, Ethel

Gratia.
After her parents are killed and her nurse dies, a young girl grows up alone on a South Seas island, her only companions the animals. Brought back to civilization by men who want to exploit her, she reveals what a female Tarzan she really is.
A Virgin Paradise. 1921. White, Pearl

Gray, Dorian.
An enigmatic sensualist remains youthful-looking, but his portrait ages with the corruption of his soul.
The Picture of Dorian Gray. 1945. Hatfield, Hurd

Gray, Johnnie.
During the Civil War, this youthful Southern railway engineer, who drives an old locomotive known as The General, rescues a railroad engine stolen by Federal troops, and saves an entire Confederate army single-handedly.
The General. 1927. Keaton, Buster

Grayne, Olivia.
Olivia, companion and housekeeper living with her cranky, crippled old aunt, betrays the young man who has morbidly excited and fascinated her.
Night Must Fall. 1937. Russell, Rosalind

Great Dictator, see Hynkel, Adenoid

Green, Phil.
A magazine journalist masquerades as a Jew while writing a series of articles on anti-Semitism; he is shocked and hurt when he is snubbed socially and his girl friend appears less loyal.
Gentleman's Agreement. 1947. Peck, Gregory

Greene, Phil.
Morally stricken and concerned about the greed and corruption in American business, Phil objects to his partner's illicit tactics in trying to make their business solvent.
Save the Tiger. 1973. Gilford, Jack

Greville, Alex.
A bright, well-educated divorcee in her early 30s is in love with a boyish kinetic sculptor, who casually divides his time between her and a homosexual doctor.
Sunday Bloody Sunday. 1971. Jackson, Glenda

Grey, Miranda.
Beautiful young art student is kidnapped and locked up in a cellar by an obsessed butterfly collector. Although he never hurts her, this terror-stricken girl feels she will never leave her prison alive.
The Collector. 1965. Eggar, Samantha

Gruffydd, Mr.
A new minister in a Welsh mining town befriends and inspires a young boy but loses his own heart's desire, the boy's beautiful sister, because he thinks he is too poor to marry her.
How Green Was My Valley. 1941. Pidgeon, Walter

Grusinskaya.
Lonely, introverted Russian ballerina falls in love with a debonair, aristocratic jewel thief and becomes an enchanting, magnificent woman.
Grand Hotel. 1932. Garbo, Greta

Gruver.
Capable Southern Air Force pilot, emotionally immature but with a good-humored nature under his stern West Point demeanor, falls in love with a beautiful Japanese entertainer during the Korean War.
Sayonara. 1957. Brando, Marlon

Guerrero, Inez.
Inez is the pitiful wife of a psychotic demolitions expert. He hopes to blow up a plane on which he is a passenger so that she can collect his insurance.
Airport. 1970. Stapleton, Maureen

Guiler, Jillian.
Middle-class working mother, depressed because her young son has been captured by aliens, and disoriented by her constant vision of the monolithic Devil's Tower, sets herself up in a motel, sketching her version of the image.
Close Encounters of the Third Kind. 1977. Dillon, Melinda

Gunn, Joe.
A tough, laconic American sergeant leads a handful of weary soldiers across the Libyan desert, where they make a stand against the Germans who try to capture their water hole.
Sahara. 1943. Bogart, Humphrey

Guthrie, Woody.
During the Depression of the 1930s, this reserved folksinger and composer, concerned with social and political injustices, abandons his poverty-stricken family, attempts to organize California's migrant workers, and begins to gain recognition in his radio career.
Bound for Glory. 1976. Carradine, David

Gutman, Casper.
A fat, fastidious British crook, complete with watchchain, waistcoat and spats, tries to gain possession of a valuable jewel-encrusted statuette.
The Maltese Falcon. 1941. Greenstreet, Sydney

Gwendolyn.
This withdrawn and pensive child, who is not without a mischievous streak, has everything money can buy except the love and attention of her busy parents.
A Poor Little Rich Girl. 1917. Pickford, Mary

Gwyn, Chet.
Because of the maneuvering and cunning of his rich Main Line relatives, Chet has become a spendthrift and an alcoholic and is charged with the murder of his uncle.
The Young Philadelphians. 1959. Vaughn, Robert

H., Adele.
Beautiful, spoiled daughter of Victor Hugo, rejected by a young British officer, continues to feel an obsessive, unrelenting, unrequited love; when this is always rebuffed, it leads to her self-destruction.
The Story of Adele H.. 1975. Adjani, Isabelle

Hadley, Kyle.
Irresponsible, incompetent Texas oil millionaire woos a business acquaintance, marries her, and then suspects that the baby she's carrying might be the child of his best friend.
Written on the Wind. 1956. Stack, Robert

Hadley, Marylee.
Spoiled sister of a Texas oil millionaire tries to attract a one-time childhood playmate who is in love with her brother's wife.
Written on the Wind. 1956. Malone, Dorothy

Hagen, Tom.
The adopted non-Italian son and "consigliere" or adviser oversees the Mafia family activities. His law degree gives an aura of respectability to the criminal dynasty.
The Godfather. 1972. Duvall, Robert

Hall, Annie.
Feeling that she's changed emotionally and outgrown her domineering New York boyfriend, Annie wants to pursue her singing career independently.
Annie Hall. 1977. Keaton, Diane

Hamilton, Haven.
Nashville's greatest, most respected male singing star is interested in attaining public office. Even though he is very rich and has reached stardom, Haven still has temper tantrums when recording because he is so egotistical.
Nashville. 1975. Gibson, Henry

Hamilton, Kaye.
Gentle, aspiring young actress in a theatrical boarding house in New York City, Kaye has waited a long time for "that one role."
Stage Door. 1937. Leeds, Andrea

Hamilton, Liz.
Although Liz, a graduate of Smith College, is a highly acclaimed author, and winner of the prestigious National Writer's Award, she cannot achieve such success in her disordered emotional life.
Rich and Famous. 1981. Bisset, Jacqueline

Hamilton, Melanie.
A woman of endless patience and understanding, fragile, warm and gentle with a naive belief in the good of mankind, Melanie is a loyal friend against all odds to her sister-in-law Scarlett, who never stops coveting Melanie's husband, Ashley Wilkes.
Gone With the Wind. 1939. De Havilland, Olivia

Hamlet.
Deeply troubled by the murder of his father and the treachery of his mother, the melancholy and philosophical Prince of Denmark plans to avenge his father's death.
Hamlet. 1948. Olivier, Laurence

Hammett, Dashiell.
Worldly-wise but sardonic author gives Lillian Hellman blunt advice about her writing and helps her to mature personally and as a playwright.
Julia. 1977. Robards, Jason

Hammond, Margaret.
Torn by her own memories of happiness in a marriage tragically ended, this fading widow succumbs to her rough rugby player tenant, but cannot respond with the affection he so badly needs.
This Sporting Life. 1963. Roberts, Rachel

Handley, Dix.
Brazen, bitter, small-time hoodlum, with a weakness for horses, dreams about returning to his childhood home in Kentucky. His participation in one last big jewel heist will do it for him.
Asphalt Jungle. 1950. Hayden, Sterling

Hank.
After discovering that her boyfriend is in love with her sister, this chorus girl trying to succeed on Broadway abandons her sister, finds a new partner and returns to small-town vaudeville.
Broadway Melody. 1929. Love, Bessie

Hannassey, Rufus.
Gruff, rough-hewn patriarch of one of two embittered families feuding about water rights on adjacent land stages a miniature war which leads to violence.
The Big Country. 1958. Ives, Burl

Hanneh.
The mother of a Russian Jewish immigrant family finally scrapes up enough money to paint her tenement kitchen white. When the job is completed, she runs into problems with the landlord, who wants to raise the rent.
Hungry Hearts. 1922. Rosanova, Rosa

Hanson, George.
Handsome, alcoholic and sensitive small-town lawyer develops a camaraderie with two hippies, and joins them on their motorcycle trip across the Southwest because he has long wanted to visit the House of Blue Lights in New Orleans.
Easy Rider. 1969. Nicholson, Jack

Happy.
In western Germany during the last year of World War II, a sensitive young German medical corpsman, an Allied prisoner, willingly volunteers to become an Allied spy because he believes he can help his country by shortening the war. He is trained by American Intelligence, and dropped behind enemy lines posing as a loyal Luftwaffer on leave.
Decision Before Dawn. 1951. Werner, Oskar

Harding, Tess.
A famous woman journalist covering international affairs marries a sportswriter and discovers the problems of balancing a marriage and a career.
Woman of the Year. 1942. Hepburn, Katharine

Hardy, Andy.
This epitome of pre-World War II 14-year-olds, from a typical American family, is beset by the problems of growing up. He experiences the first signs of young love, but must combine this with his overwhelming interest in cars.
A Family Affair. 1937. Rooney, Mickey

Hardy, Edith.
A socialite loses money on the stock exchange and becomes indebted to a wealthy man from the Orient, then shoots him when he brands her shoulder to prove she is his property.
The Cheat. 1915. Ward, Fannie

Harper, Evelyn.
Vicious, sadistic matron in a state prison for women glories in her power, supplementing her salary with bribes from the inmates.
Caged. 1950. Emerson, Hope

Harry.
After being evicted from his New York City apartment, this cranky, independent 72-year-old retiree, willing to accept other peoples' idiosyncrasies and to expand his horizons, takes his cat Tonto on a cross-country journey.
Harry and Tonto. 1974. Carney, Art

Harry.
Having failed on the stage, this bitter, broken-down vaudevillian, who acts as if the whole world were a theater, peddles his own miracle solvent door to door.
The Day of the Locust. 1975. Meredith, Burgess

Hartnett, Jeff.
An alcoholic intellectual who makes frequent allusions to literature and the arts, Jeff is ambivalent in his feelings toward the gangster who is his friend and his financial support.
Johnny Eager. 1942. Heflin, Van

Hayes, Billy.
In 1970, a young American college student, caught smuggling hashish out of Turkey, is arrested and suffers brutality, degradation and frustration in a Turkish prison.
Midnight Express. 1978. Davis, Brad

Haywood, Dan.
Humane but realistic, unusually insightful and eloquent, this gentle, intelligent judge must make monumental decisions as he presides over the Nazi war crimes trial in Nuremburg in 1948.
Judgment at Nuremburg. 1961. Tracy, Spencer

Haze, Charlotte.
A college professor marries this whining, shrewish, possessive widow because he is infatuated with her daughter. When Charlotte learns the truth about her husband's passions, she threatens to expose him, but dies in an automobile accident before she can pursue her intention.
Lolita. 1962. Winters, Shelley

Heath, Joyce.
Unemployed alcoholic actress has a chance to re-establish her reputation when a wealthy architect falls in love with her, but cannot succeed because of her self-destructive personality.
Dangerous. 1935. Davis, Bette

Heathcliff.
Scowling, passionate man, with the bearing and speech of the demon-possessed, is consumed by an almost inhuman desire for vengeance.
Wuthering Heights. 1939. Olivier, Laurence

Hedda.
Bored, articulate, ruthless woman wrecks the lives of the men who pursue her.
Hedda. 1975. Jackson, Glenda

Heep, Uriah.
"Umble," hypocritical villain, who through conniving and deceit becomes a partner in a firm of solicitors, embezzles a wealthy woman's fortune.
David Copperfield. 1935. Young, Roland

Heisler, George.
An anti-Nazi German escapes from a concentration camp and flees in terror and despair from his ruthless hunters.
The Seventh Cross. 1944. Tracy, Spencer

Held, Anna.
Charming, emotional French singer becomes the toast of the New York stage, marries Florenz Ziegfeld, but leaves him when her suspicions of his infidelities are confirmed.
The Great Ziegfeld. 1936. Rainer, Luise

Helen.
A girl from Indiana meets a New York boy, a heroin addict, and moves into his apartment in Needle Park. She picks up his heroin habit and begins a life of prostitution, drug dealing, imprisonment, and betrayals to help support their addiction.
Panic in Needle Park. 1971. Winn, Kitty

Helen of Troy.
Helen is abducted by Paris on a visit to Sparta. As a result, the Greeks attack Troy, kill the men, enslave the women, and burn the city. While the other women mourn their dead, Helen uses all her courage, guile, and beauty to preserve her life.
The Trojan Women. 1971. Papas, Irene

Hellman, Lillian.
Strong-willed, determined woman, whose only fear is of feeling afraid, helps a girlhood friend to secure freedom for Jews and political prisoners by smuggling money into Nazi Germany.
Julia. 1977. Fonda, Jane

Hendrix, Susy.
Gentle young blind woman allows three diabolical thugs into her apartment. When she realizes that she has been duped and is in grave danger, she displays that combination of helplessness and sense acuity often found in the sightless, and manages to save herself without giving up the sought-after heroin-filled musical doll.
Wait Until Dark. 1967. Hepburn, Audrey

Henriette.
After bringing her sister to Paris in search of a cure for her blindness, this fiery, winsome young woman is abducted by a marquis, but is rescued by another aristocrat. She and her lover are sentenced to the guillotine, but she is once again saved at the last moment.
Orphans of the Storm. 1921. Gish, Lillian

Henry II.
Because he needs Becket's intellectual stimulation and friendship and is unable to understand how the Archbishop can put the honor of God before the supreme power of the king, the sad, insecure, frustrated Henry II is responsible for Becket's death.
Becket. 1964. O'Toole, Peter

Henry II.
Loud, bawdy, brutal king wrangles with Eleanor and their three sons about who will succeed to the throne, who will marry the king's mistress, and what will become of the disputed territories of Vexin and Aquitaine.
The Lion in Winter. 1968. O'Toole, Peter

Henry V.
The King of England, urged by his Bishops to invade France, plans and executes the triumphant Battle of Agincourt.
Henry V. 1946. Olivier, Laurence

Henry VIII.
Fiery, indulgent English monarch, a humorous combination of good and evil, discards his wives as more appealing amorata appear.
The Private Life of Henry VIII. 1933. Laughton, Charles

Henry VIII.
Unbalanced, headstrong, heretical 16th-century king demands that Sir Thomas More sign the Act of Succession, which would approve his divorce from Catherine of Aragon and marriage to Anne Boleyn.
A Man For All Seasons. 1966. Shaw, Robert

Henry VIII.
Amoral, weak monarch has a controversial romance with Anne Boleyn, divorces his wife to marry her, and then has her beheaded when she cannot provide him with a male heir.
Anne of the Thousand Days. 1969. Burton, Richard

Henry, Frederic.
An American lieutenant serving with the Italian Ambulance Corps in World War I falls in love with an English nurse and suffers through a tragic love affair.
A Farewell to Arms. 1932. Cooper, Gary

Henry, John.
The younger, solemn, precocious cousin of a 12-year-old tomboy approaching adolescence becomes her playmate during one hot Georgia summer.
The Member of the Wedding. 1952. De Wilde, Brandon

Hercules.
With two cohorts, a strong man in a circus sideshow picks the pockets of absorbed spectators. Even though he is at heart a coward, he helps them when they concoct a more elaborate robbery scheme.
The Unholy Three. 1925. McLaglen, Victor

Hickock, Bill.
Handsome, brave hero helps to establish law and order in the disorganized West of the 1870s.
Wild Bill Hickock Rides. 1942. Cabot, Bruce

Hickory.
The armor-plated Tin Woodman joins the pilgrimage to the Emerald City and the Wizard because he wants a heart.
The Wizard of Oz. 1939. Haley, Jack

Higgins, Henry.
Phonetics expert, fascinated by language, makes a bet with another linguist that he can mold a lower-class Cockney flowergirl into a mannerly, aristocratic personage.
Pygmalion. 1938. Howard, Leslie
My Fair Lady. 1964. Harrison, Rex

Higgins, Mrs.
Svelte, aristocratic mother of a phonetics wizard who is instructing a Cockney flower girl in manners and pronunciation, Mrs. Higgins never fails to rebuff her son and to correct his social lapses.
My Fair Lady. 1964. Cooper, Gladys

High Lama.
Two-hundred-and-fifty-year-old patriarch is dying and wants an English diplomat to succeed him as ruler, and to continue Shangri-La's mission of preserving peace and order throughout the world.
Lost Horizon. 1937. Jaffe, Sam

Hill, Harold.
The "Professor," a city slicker with a fast line of patter, cons the gullible citizens of River City, Iowa, into organizing a high-school band so he can sell them musical instruments.
The Music Man. 1962. Preston, Robert

Hilton, Anne.
Broken-hearted and despairing when her husband must go off to war, this wife and mother proves herself to be gallant and strong despite the strains of fear and loneliness.
Since You Went Away. 1944. Colbert, Claudette

Hilton, Jane.
A sweet girl on the verge of womanhood falls in love with a bashful soldier who soon goes off to war.
Since You Went Away. 1944. Jones, Jennifer

Hire, Monsieur.
A newcomer in Paris becomes the tormented victim of a sadistic mob after he innocently falls in love with a treacherous woman who frames him for a murder.
Panic. 1946. Simon, Michel

Hirsh, Daniel.
Successful homosexual Jewish doctor in his 40s, urbane, competent and intelligent, is in love with a young male sculptor, who at the same time is having an affair with a divorced woman.
Sunday Bloody Sunday. 1971. Finch, Peter

Hirsh, Frank.
Successful jeweler and pillar of the community has a long-standing bitter relationship with his brother.
Some Came Running. 1958. Kennedy, Arthur

Hirth.
A ruthless and relentless Nazi lieutenant survives the sinking of his submarine and tries to flee with his men across Canada to the United States.
The Invaders. 1942. Portman, Eric

Hobart, Hallie.
A gold-digging hotel manicurist marries a man and then swindles his family out of $50,000.
The Devil's Holiday. 1930. Carroll, Nancy

Hobson.
Snobbish, sharp-tongued valet to a drunken playboy is so devoted to his master's welfare that he helps further his employer's relationship with a shoplifter.
Arthur. 1981. Gielgud, John

Hockstader, Arthur.
Modeled on Harry Truman, this shrewd, imposing former president, mortally ill but still politically astute, stands between the two feuding presidential aspirants, both desperate for his endorsement.
The Best Man. 1964. Tracy, Lee

Hoffman, Irene.
Fat young German wife tells how she was accused of having relations with an elderly Jew when "racial contamination" was forbidden and punishable by death in Nazi Germany.
Judgment at Nuremburg. 1961. Garland, Judy

Holden, Guy.
At a fashionable English seaside resort, a lovesick American dancer pursues a lady who mistakes him for another man.
The Gay Divorcee. 1934. Astaire, Fred

Holiday, Billie.
Billie "Lady Day" Holiday, famous for her melancholic, plaintive voice and her distinctive witty phrasing, born in poverty in 1915, becomes the greatest blues singer America has ever produced, but is ultimately defeated by blind prejudice and dies of drug addiction at age 44.
Lady Sings the Blues. 1972. Ross, Diana

Holland.
Mousy, mild-mannered bank messenger, possessed of a fiendish greed, conceives and carries out a clever scheme to steal a fortune in gold bullion from the Bank of England and smuggle it to France.
Lavender Hill Mob. 1951. Guinness, Alec

Hollmann, Patricia.
In postwar, prefascist Germany, a consumptive daughter of a once well-to-do family commits suicide because she is fearful of becoming a burden to those who are dear to her.
Three Comrades. 1938. Sullavan, Margaret

Holly, Buddy.
This lanky perfectionist and talented composer begins his career as a roller-rink musician in Texas. He eventually gains national recognition after a disastrous recording career in Nashville, and dies an untimely death in a plane crash in 1969.
The Buddy Holly Story. 1978. Busey, Gary

Holly, Catherine.
Sensual, neurotic young woman is driven to insanity because she knows the truth concerning her cousin's death.
Suddenly Last Summer. 1959. Taylor, Elizabeth

Holman, Jake.
On a gunboat patrolling Shanghai Harbor, this basically decent machinist's mate, with nine years of Navy service, quarrels with his superiors as he tries to warn them of the potential pitfalls in dealing with the Chinese warlords. He must finally take a possibly mutinous stand to defend his own beliefs.
The Sand Pebbles. 1966. McQueen, Steve

Holmberg, Marilyn.
A dowdy spinster and nursery school teacher is afraid of emotional entanglements, but simultaneously yearns for something to happen. She finds herself romantically involved with a mild-mannered writer recently liberated from his wife.
Starting Over. 1979. Clayburgh, Jill

Holmes, Karen.
Frustrated by a fruitless marriage to a brutal officer, Karen has an affair with an Army sergeant. She is forced to suffer the consequences inevitable in the closed world of the military.
From Here to Eternity. 1953. Kerr, Deborah

Holmes, Oliver Wendell.
During his 27 happy Washington years, the Associate Justice is a plain but wise and witty man, sincerely devoted to his wife and country.
The Magnificent Yankee. 1950. Calhern, Louis

Holmes, Sherlock.
This brilliant but eccentric detective of 221B Baker Street, London, with his ever-present pipe, hunting cap and cape, takes on a mystery; and, with a minimum of clues and his keen intuition and perception of the significant, he shows how simple it is to solve the case.
Sherlock Holmes. 1922. Barrymore, John
The Hound of the Baskervilles. 1939. Rathbone, Basil

Holstrom, Katrin.
A cheerful, honest farm girl of sturdy Swedish stock goes to the big city to work as a maid in a rich household and soon wins not only her employer's love, but a Congressional candidacy to boot.
The Farmer's Daughter. 1947. Young, Loretta

Hondo.
Civilian scout for the U.S. Cavalry discovers a woman and her son living on an isolated ranch and interrupts his mission to defend them against an Indian attack.
Hondo. 1953. Wayne, John

Honey.
Bland, immature young wife, visiting an older faculty couple, gets drunk, then sick, and finally blurts out her own unhappiness.
Who's Afraid of Virginia Woolf? 1966. Dennis, Sandy

Hooker, Johnny.
Young, bright, exuberant small-time con artist dreams about vengeance through the "big con."
The Sting. 1973. Redford, Robert

Horace.
This sentimental and comical old leprechaun convinces a slick New Yorker to give up his life of fame and fortune and settle down in Ireland.
The Luck of the Irish. 1948. Kellaway, Cecil

Horman, Beth.
Accompanied by her father-in-law, this fresh and natural young wife, searching for her husband in Chile, is hindered not only by the Chilean government, but also by the American embassy and military.
Missing. 1982. Spacek, Sissy

Horman, Ed.
Naive, protected, conservative American businessman is enlightened when he goes to Santiago to search for his son who disappeared after the military coup that overthrew Dr. Salvador Allende, the Chilean president.
Missing. 1982. Lemmon, Jack

Horn, Albert.
Now degraded and ashamed, this once famous Jewish tailor is hiding from the Nazis with his elderly mother and pretty daughter. He is resigned to his fate and cannot bring himself to hate the young French Nazi sympathizer who has moved in with them.
Lacombe, Lucien. 1974. Lowenadler, Holger

Hortense, Madame.
Aging French courtesan, marooned in Crete in a cheap little island hotel, dreams about her previous conquests and hopes that she is still attractive enough to get a man.
Zorba the Greek. 1964. Kedrova, Lila

Hot Lips, see O'Houlihan, Margaret

Howard.
A cantankerous old English misanthrope finds himself the guardian of a whole entourage of children trying to escape Nazi-occupied Europe.
The Pied Piper. 1942. Woolley, Monte

Howard.
A wise, humorous and fatalistic old prospector joins two other Americans looking for gold in the bandit-ridden hills of Mexico. He does not come away with the gold, but finds a job as a respected medicine man for a band of Indians.
Treasure of Sierra Madre. 1948. Huston, Walter

Howard, in *Melvin and Howard,* see Hughes, Howard

Howell, Louise.
When her first lover refuses to marry her, this schizophrenic woman weds another, but she never forgets the man who jilted her, and eventually loses control and kills him.
Possessed. 1947. Crawford, Joan

Hubbard.
Police detective, called in to investigate the case of a man plotting to kill his wife and inherit her fortune, solves the mystery by tricking the husband into giving away the entire scheme.
Dial M for Murder. 1954. Williams, John

Hubbell.
Handsome, athletic Wasp, with considerable writing talent, marries a political activist. Because of his inability to make any commitment, his marriage ultimately fails.
The Way We Were. 1973. Redford, Robert

Huberman, Alicia.
This cynical and seductive daughter of a convicted American traitor is sent to spy on a gang of Nazis exiled in South America.
Notorious. 1946. Bergman, Ingrid

Hud, see Bannon, Hud

Hudson, Jane.
Prim, spirited old maid from Ohio yearning for romance, on her first trip to Venice, has a brief love affair with a handsome Italian antique dealer.
Summertime. 1955. Hepburn, Katharine

Hudson, Jane.
Sadly demented former child vaudeville star, envious and spiteful because her sister became more famous than she, is slowly tormenting her now crippled sister to death.
What Ever Happened to Baby Jane? 1962. Davis, Bette

Hudson, Myra.
Rich, successful playwright-heiress discovers through a conversation on a dictating machine that the actor she wed only married her for money and is planning to murder her.
Sudden Fear. 1952. Crawford, Joan

Huerta.
Ambitious for power, this general is defeated in a bloody battle by Pancho Villa and Zapata.
Viva Zapata. 1952. Silvera, Frank

Hughes, Howard.
Mangy, wild-eyed millionaire eccentric, riding his motorcycle around the Nevada desert, hits a water hole and is sent flying. He is rescued by a local gas station owner in a pick-up truck, and names him one of the beneficiaries of his estate.
Melvin and Howard. 1980. Robards, Jason

Hunk.
The Scarecrow desperately wants a brain so he joins Dorothy and her companions on the long trek to the mighty wizard's castle.
The Wizard of Oz. 1939. Bolger, Ray

Hunnicutt, Wade.
Captain Hunnicutt, a rich Texan, is purported to be the mightiest hunter and biggest womanizer in town.
Home From the Hill. 1960. Mitchum, Robert

Hyatt, Alice.
Thirty-five-year-old gutsy, fast-talking housewife, recently widowed, accompanied by her smart-alecky son, travels cross-country chasing her childhood dream of becoming a vocalist like Alice Faye.
Alice Doesn't Live Here Anymore. 1974. Burstyn, Ellen

Hyde, Edward.
This rampaging ape-like monster, who is Dr. Jekyll's chemically-released alter ego, exemplifies the malevolence and depravity of humanity.
Dr. Jekyll and Mr. Hyde. 1920. Barrymore, John
Dr. Jekyll and Mr. Hyde. 1932. March, Fredric

Hyde, Robert.
Charmless, unsympathetic officer, angered by the war and particularly bitter since he has been sent home from Vietnam with an accidentally self-inflicted leg wound, finds out about his wife's affair. Unable to measure up to his own expectations, he commits suicide.
Coming Home. 1978. Dern, Bruce

Hyde, Sally.
After her reactionary Marine captain husband leaves for Vietnam, Sally volunteers for work in a veterans' hospital, meets a paraplegic, and finds the happiness she had never experienced with her spouse.
Coming Home. 1978. Fonda, Jane

Hynkel, Adenoid.
A small, mustachioed Jewish barber looks like and is mistaken for the Hitler-like dictator, Adenoid Hynkel. Chaplin plays the dual role.
The Great Dictator. 1940. Chaplin, Charles

Iago.
Hungry for power and consumed with a burning hatred for Othello, Iago plots to destroy the lives of the Moorish commander and his wife.
Othello. 1965. Finlay, Frank

Ilderim, Sheik.
Wealthy Arab, training his horses for the chariot races, persuades an aristocratic Jew persecuted by the Romans to drive his team.
Ben-Hur. 1959. Griffith, Hugh

Ilya.
Happy, vivacious, worldly-wise Greek prostitute defeats a well-intentioned tourist's efforts to re-educate her and to have her abandon some of her nonintellectual and professional pursuits.
Never on Sunday. 1960. Mercouri, Melina

Imbrie, Elizabeth.
Softhearted but sharp-tongued photographer for the scandal sheet *Spy* is assigned to cover a Philadelphia society wedding.
The Philadelphia Story. 1940. Hussey, Ruth

Indy.
Rugged, rough-and-ready archaeologist, with a former girl friend as his partner, is fearless in the face of danger in his quest to find the Ark of the Covenant before an archaeological rival in the employ of the Nazis discovers it.
Raiders of the Lost Ark. 1981. Ford, Harrison

Inga.
A poor girl in the inflation-ridden Berlin of 1923 spends her nights mending antique chairs and her days digging up her allotment of potatoes and turnips and waiting on line for horsemeat, but still thinks life is wonderful because she is in love.
Isn't Life Wonderful? 1924. Dempster, Carol

Iris.
Self-assured 12-year-old hustler acquires an unwanted protector, who turns his unleashed fury on her unsavory pimp.
Taxi Driver. 1976. Foster, Jodie

Isabella.
Isabella is infatuated with Heathcliff, but finds nothing but unhappiness in her marriage to him. Her tragedy is not in being weak herself, but simply in being weaker than her demon-possessed husband.
Wuthering Heights. 1939. Fitzgerald, Geraldine

Isaksson, Jenny.
This seemingly serene, successful and self-assured Stockholm psychiatrist suddenly lapses into deep despair, and attempts suicide. She eventually recovers when she finds a new understanding of love and human relationships.
Face to Face. 1976. Ullmann, Liv

Iscovescu, Georges.
A European ladies' man callously marries an American school-teacher in Mexico merely to get into the United States, but grows to love her on their honeymoon.
Hold Back the Dawn. 1941. Boyer, Charles

Jack, 14th Earl of Gurney.
Convinced he is Jesus Christ, this paranoid-schizophrenic is released from a mental institution after his father's untimely death to become 14th Earl of Gurney. After rehabilitation he becomes the sadistic and amoral Jack the Ripper, admired by his peers and considered only mildly eccentric for a man of his station in life.
The Ruling Class. 1972. O'Toole, Peter

Jackson, Duane.
Restless young teen-ager, leaving for Korea, is approaching manhood, lonely, bewildered about sex, confused about his goals in life, and without much in the way of male models.
The Last Picture Show. 1971. Bridges, Jeff

Jackson, John.
Nicknamed Joker, this tough, seasoned convict, chained to a black prisoner, is filled with racial antipathy, but in their common struggle to flee a police dragnet he is stripped of all his vulgar bigotry.
The Defiant Ones. 1958. Curtis, Tony

Jackson, Rachel.
Wife of President Andrew Jackson, about to die of the miseries, charges the wife of his Secretary of War to make sure that her husband minds his manners and remembers not to say "ain't."
The Gorgeous Hussy. 1936. Bondi, Beulah

Jacoby, Bertha.
Sprightly Jewish widow, whose wisdom proves to be as effective in Japan as it was in Brooklyn, heals a breach between her son-in-law and a Japanese industrialist who are involved in trade negotiations. She accepts the courtship of the Japanese gentleman when he arrives in New York as a delegate to the United Nations.
A Majority of One. 1962. Russell, Rosalind

James.
Wealthy, lecherous businessman first propositions, but ultimately proposes marriage to, a girl young enough to be his daughter.
Georgy Girl. 1966. Mason, James

Jane.
After being rescued by Tarzan, this pretty, coy, sophisticated young woman so enjoys their relationship that she decides to abandon civilization in favor of the jungle.
Tarzan, the Apeman. 1932. O'Sullivan, Maureen

Jane.
Poor and pregnant French girl lives in a seedy London tenement where she meets all sorts of interesting characters, including a determined young writer who offers her love and hope until another tenant reveals her secret.
The L-Shaped Room. 1963. Caron, Leslie

Javert.
This stereotype of an insensitive lawman relentlessly pursues a pardoned convict, ultimately ruining the man's life; but in so doing, he hastens his own death.
Les Miserables. 1935. Laughton, Charles

Jefferson, Jack.
First black heavyweight boxing champion suffers pain and humiliation because of white men's fear of the strength and sexuality of blacks, made more intense because of his affair with a white woman.
Great White Hope. 1970. Jones, James Earl

Jekyll, Henry.
Famous Victorian doctor and researcher discovers the secret formula that separates good and evil in man, drinks the potion, and cannot restrain the evil side of his nature. He begins to live a double life as the cultured Dr. Jekyll and the monstrous Mr. Hyde.
Dr. Jekyll and Mr. Hyde. 1920. Barrymore, John
Dr. Jekyll and Mr. Hyde. 1932. March, Fredric

Jenny, see Cavilleri, Jenny

Jensen, Arthur.
Chairman of the Board of the multinational conglomerate controlling the UBS network, who believes that the world is "one vast ecumenical holding company," persuades a news commentator to deny his previous public espousal of the independent man.
Network. 1976. Beatty, Ned

Jerry.
Young liberated woman condones her husband's affairs, but when she has her own extramarital adventure, she realizes that her husband is not equally understanding.
The Divorcee. 1930. Shearer, Norma

Jerry.
In crime-ridden Prohibition Chicago, this seedy, out-of-work musician inadvertently witnesses a gangland murder. In an attempt to avoid the mobsters, he dons women's clothing and masquerades as Daphne, a female bass player in an all-girl band bound for Florida.
Some Like It Hot. 1959. Lemmon, Jack

Jesson, Laura.
An ordinary and conventional English housewife and mother meets a married doctor, and although she is shocked and bewildered by her feelings, their friendship grows rapidly into love and they have a brief affair.
Brief Encounter. 1946. Johnson, Celia

Jill.
Eccentric, flighty actress falls in love with the blind man next door.
Butterflies are Free. 1972. Hawn, Goldie

Jim.
Mixed-up, misunderstood high-school student, archetypical of the younger generation of the 50s, is in conflict with the middle-class values of his parents.
Rebel Without a Cause. 1955. Dean, James

Jimmy.
Happy, warm-hearted actor, who has never achieved success and probably never will, is the closest and most loyal friend of a reformed alcoholic actress who is trying to get on her feet again.
Only When I Laugh. 1981. Coco, James

Jo.
Imaginative, awkward young girl, concerned primarily with the happiness and well-being of her family, becomes an author and falls in love with a professor.
Little Women. 1933. Hepburn, Katharine

Jo.
Lonely teen-age daughter of an impoverished, promiscuous woman meets and makes love with an equally lonely black sailor. After he leaves her, she enjoys her first deep friendship with a penniless homosexual, who helps her to prepare for her unborn child.
A Taste of Honey. 1961. Tushingham, Rita

Jo.
Jealous, insecure mother of several children, finding her third marriage falling apart, requires psychiatric help when she becomes aware of her husband's increasing infidelities.
The Pumpkin Eater. 1964. Bancroft, Anne

Joad, Ma.
Indomitable but sensitive farm woman holds her family together on their difficult trip to California following the Dust Bowl disaster in Oklahoma.
The Grapes of Wrath. 1940. Darwell, Jane

Joad, Tom.
Ex-convict with a social conscience fights against injustice as he and his family make their way from Oklahoma to California following the drought of the 1930s.
The Grapes of Wrath. 1940. Fonda, Henry

Joan.
Willed by God to recover the kingdom of France, this peasant girl convinces the Dauphin to let her lead his army against the British and the Burgundians, realizes stunning victories, but is later betrayed and executed.
The Passion of Joan of Arc. 1928. Falconetti, Mlle.
Joan of Arc. 1948. Bergman, Ingrid

Joe.

Tough but indecisive foreman for a California vineyard makes his employer's fiancee pregnant.
They Knew What They Wanted. 1940. Gargan, William

Joe.

When this advertising executive becomes insecure in his job and turns to drink, he is responsible for both his own and his wife's alcoholism.
Days of Wine and Roses. 1962. Lemmon, Jack

Joe Ben.

A member of a patriarchal logging family in Oregon is involved in a logging accident when the family defies a local strike and continues to run its small operation.
Sometimes a Great Notion. 1971. Jaeckel, Richard

Johann.

Cold, detached zealot convinces Lillian Hellman that, even though smuggling money might be of great danger to her, the funds are desperately needed to rescue suffering Jews from the Nazis.
Julia. 1977. Schell, Maximilian

John, Anthony.

A jealous and mentally distressed actor, playing his most famous role as Othello, becomes so obsessed with the character that he takes on many of its facets.
A Double Life. 1948. Colman, Ronald

Johnson, Annie.

Loyal black servant shares her life with a successful actress and her child, but is heartbroken because her own daughter wants to be accepted as white and will not recognize Annie as her mother.
Imitation of Life. 1959. Moore, Juanita

Johnson, Hildy.

An ace reporter plans to leave his profession to get married, but cinches his future as a newspaperman when he cannot resist the call of a good story. He outsmarts local police and politicians who are searching for an escapee from execution by collaring him first.
The Front Page. 1931. O'Brien, Pat

Johnson, Hildy.

An unscrupulous girl crime reporter with printer's ink in her blood provides a comical portrait of the world of journalism.
His Girl Friday. 1940. Russell, Rosalind

Joker, see Jackson, John

Jolly, Amy.
Seductive and glamorous singer in a North African cafe breaks her engagement to a French Foreign Legionnaire after a marriage proposal from an affluent gentleman. She changes her mind, but when she is rejected by her former suitor, she joins a corps of prostitutes who follow the troops through the desert.
Morocco. 1930. Dietrich, Marlene

Jolson, Al.
Beginning his career in burlesque and encouraged by family and friends, this real-life star of stage and film struts and sings his way through a popular "show-biz" life.
The Jolson Story. 1946. Parks, Larry.

Jones, Clinton.
Gruff, cantankerous father, full of anger and contempt, wants better things for his family than he can afford on his clerk's salary. He cherishes and loves his only daughter, but cannot understand her passionate desire to become an actress.
The Actress. 1953. Tracy, Spencer

Jones, Melody.
A gentle and clumsy out-of-work cowboy rides into town, is mistaken for a feared bandit, and becomes intoxicated with the respect his bandit image commands.
Along Came Jones. 1945. Cooper, Gary

Jones, Ruth Gordon.
Teen-age schoolgirl knows she must become an actress, even though her father, whom she loves dearly, has no sympathy for her youthful ambitions.
The Actress. 1953. Simmons, Jean

Jones, Tom.
Impish, goodhearted, free-spirited foundling leads a carefree life, with willing women playing a prominent part, until he almost loses his life at the gallows.
Tom Jones. 1963. Finney, Albert

Jordan, Robert.
Disillusioned American expatriate, looking for a cause in which to believe, joins a band of Loyalist guerrilla fighters during the Spanish Civil War.
For Whom the Bell Tolls. 1943. Cooper, Gary

Joy Boy.
Glum, cynical right-hand man of the most powerful racketeer in New York tries to convince his boss that he should establish himself as a Public Enemy rather than waste his time helping an apple seller.
Pocketful of Miracles. 1961. Falk, Peter

Joyce, Howard.
Honest and dignified lawyer jeopardizes his reputation with the sordid task of retrieving a letter that incriminates his client, a woman who has murdered her lover.
The Letter. 1940. Stephenson, James

Judd, Steve.
Aging, soft-spoken Westerner, down on his luck, accepts, together with an old crony, the job of protecting a gold shipment. His pal wants to make off with the gold, but, redeemed by Judd's disarming honesty, fights by his side to protect and deliver it as promised.
Ride the High Country. 1962. McCrea, Joel

Judge.
Young government official is appointed as investigating magistrate after a political assassination, on the theory that he will not upset matters. To everyone's surprise, he proves to be incorruptible.
Z. 1969. Trintignant, Jean-Louis

Judy.
Wild adolescent's inarticulate frustration is expressed in foolhardiness and the desire to pal around with surly juveniles.
Rebel Without a Cause. 1955. Wood, Natalie

Julia.
Bright, beautiful, charismatic childhood friend of Lillian Hellman studies medicine in Vienna. During the Nazi take-over, she becomes involved in the fighting and is seriously injured while attempting to help the persecuted leave Germany.
Julia. 1977. Redgrave, Vanessa

Julie.
In New Orleans in 1852, a selfish, willful Southern belle, known for manipulating her suitors, is rejected by her only true love. Knowing that everyone holds her in contempt, Julie regains her reputation by nursing her former lover at a leper colony, where all yellow fever victims have been placed.
Jezebel. 1938. Davis, Bette

Julie.
Beautiful soap opera star thinks her costar is a lesbian, not realizing that "Dorothy" is an unemployed actor impersonating a woman and falling in love with her.
Tootsie. 1982. Lange, Jessica

Juliet.
Beautiful 13-year-old daughter of the Capulets falls in love wih the son of her family's sworn enemies.
Romeo and Juliet. 1936. Shearer, Norma
Romeo and Juliet. 1954. Shentall, Susan
Romeo and Juliet. 1968. Hussey, Olivia

Juror 3.
Vengeful, self-made man, tortured by the memory of his son's defiance of his authority, votes to convict a teen-ager accused of murdering his father.
Twelve Angry Men. 1957. Cobb, Lee J.

Juror 8.
Open-minded, conscientious juror at the trial of a tough teen-ager, accused of killing his brutal father, starts out alone against the majority assumption of guilt. He insists on full discussion of the evidence, implants doubts into the minds of his colleagues, and changes the original decision.
Twelve Angry Men. 1957. Fonda, Henry

Justina.
This chief servant, as strict and sadistic as a prison guard, tends two young children when they move into the bleak, terrifying palace that is a bishop's home.
Fanny and Alexander. 1983. Andersson, Harriet

Kane, Charles Foster.
Poor boy eventually becomes a powerful, egomaniacal newspaper publisher, but remains an enigma even to his closest friends, who try to discover what his dying word, "Rosebud," signifies.
Citizen Kane. 1941. Welles, Orson

Kane, Will.
On the day of his retirement and his marriage to a strict Quaker girl, this brave and stubborn marshall in a small Western town controls his fear and frustration as he waits for a bandit with three cohorts who are coming to kill him.
High Noon. 1952. Cooper, Gary

Karamazov, Fyodor.
The rivalry between this gross, beady-eyed father, a crafty, lecherous man, and his arrogant eldest son stems from their common desire for women and money.
The Brothers Karamazov. 1958. Cobb, Lee J.

Karanzin.
This lecherous, contemptible villain poses as a Russian count in Monte Carlo, where he cruelly and indiscriminately preys on women, taking both their money and their self-respect.
Foolish Wives. 1922. Von Stroheim, Erich

Karen.
This wife of a playwright receives recognition in the theatrical world only through her husband's popularity.
All About Eve. 1950. Holm, Celeste

Karenina, Anna.
Because she hates her cold, passionless husband, when Anna falls in love with a dashing young officer of the guards she gives up everything, including her son, to go to her lover. After a few months of happiness, he leaves her. Realizing now that their love was too fragile to withstand the cruelty of society, Anna commits suicide.
Anna Karenina. 1935. Garbo, Greta

Karras, Father.
Jesuit psychiatrist, tormented by his own lapses of faith, is called on to perform an exorcism of a young girl in an attempt to rid her of evil spirits.
The Exorcist. 1973. Miller, Jason

Kate.
In pre-World War I California, this operator of a brothel meets both her sons again after their father has a stroke.
East of Eden. 1955. Van Fleet, Jo

Katherine.
Beautiful, captivating young wife of an English schoolmaster charms everyone at the Brookfield School for boys, and teaches her husband how to cope with his students in a kind and human way.
Goodbye Mr. Chips. 1939. Garson, Greer

Kathy.
When her journalist boyfriend writes in a newspaper article that he is Jewish, this intelligent girl finds she cannot get over the prejudice and bigotry common to her upper-class upbringing.
Gentleman's Agreement. 1947. McGuire, Dorothy

Katie.
Shrewd, ambitious, frizzy-haired Communist, always in a rush, always sure she's right, marries an apolitical Wasp who cannot embrace her many philosophies and causes.
The Way We Were. 1973. Streisand, Barbra

Katrin.
A youthful author, the oldest daughter in a warm and loving Norwegian-American household, watches the family events from the sidelines because she intends to write about them some day.
I Remember Mama. 1948. Bel Geddes, Barbara

Katsumi.
Japanese girl marries an American flyer during the Korean War, and later carries out a joint suicide pact when she finds she will be unable to accompany him to the United States.
Sayonara. 1957. Umeki, Miyoshi

Keller, Helen.
A blind and deaf girl, beloved and spoiled by her family, runs completely wild and goes undisciplined until a determined young woman teaches her to communicate.
The Miracle Worker. 1962. Duke, Patty

Keller, Joe.
An arrogant, greedy, tough little guy sells defective materials to the Air Force, but does not understand his irresponsibility because he feels he did it for the good of his family.
All My Sons. 1948. Robinson, Edward G.

Kelly.
Although aware that the military frowns upon mixed racial marriages, this Air Force sergeant marries a Japanese girl and suffers the consequences.
Sayonara. 1957. Buttons, Red

Kelly, Connie.
Sensitive crippled brother of a boxer on the way to the top recognizes impending tragedy in the fighter's character breakdown, but is unable to stop it.
Champion. 1949. Kennedy, Arthur

Kelly, Eloise Y.
Tough, swinging international playgirl arrives at a big-game hunter's ranch in the Kenya veld and, in a systematic and calculating way, attempts to make him her man.
Mogambo. 1953. Gardner, Ava

Kelly, Midge.
Miserable, determined young boxer works his vicious way to the championship, alienating his friends and family while becoming a hero to his fans.
Champion. 1949. Douglas, Kirk

Kenny, Elizabeth.
This real-life Australian nurse develops a method for treating polio victims, but has to contend with the doctors who refuse to acknowledge the value of her therapy.
Sister Kenny. 1946. Russell, Rosalind

Kenobi, Ben.
At one time known as Obi-Wan, this last survivor of a band of noble knights uses his mystical powers to aid Luke Skywalker in his attempt to rescue Princess Leah.
Star Wars. 1977. Guinness, Alec

Kersaint.
Doctor Kersaint tells a story about a hurricane and its effects on a South Sea Island. This happened many years ago when he was friendly with both natives and Europeans, and his role was as observer rather than activist.
The Hurricane. 1937. Mitchell, Thomas

Kessler.
Jaded, talentless, maniacal director, pretending he is C.B. DeMille producing spectaculars, manages a small, run-of-the-mill Western movie studio.
Hearts of the West. 1975. Arkin, Alan

Kettle, Ma.
A rambunctious, outspoken middle-aged hillbilly woman with a large brood of children is always getting involved in cornball situations.
The Egg and I. 1947. Main, Marjorie

Kid.
Abandoned by his mother as an infant, the Kid is raised by a comical, slum-dwelling tramp and becomes his assistant by breaking windows which the tramp then repairs.
The Kid. 1921. Coogan, Jackie

Kilbourne, Emily.
Scatter-brained matron, with a penchant for helping useless people, picks up a tramp who begins to bring order into the lives of the irresponsible Kilbourne family.
Merrily We Live. 1938. Burke, Billie

Kildare, James.
Young, small-town doctor, trying to find his proper place in the field of medicine, chooses a large city hospital to prove his talent, courage, and loyalty to the medical profession.
Young Doctor Kildare. 1938. Ayres, Lew

Kilgore.
Gung ho, pompous lieutenant colonel, a surfing enthusiast who has his men riding the waves during diversionary attacks, is responsible for a brutal helicopter raid on a Viet Cong village.
Apocalypse Now. 1979. Duvall, Robert

King.
Quizzical, demanding 19th-century monarch of Siam avidly pursues modern scientific knowledge and comes to admire the English governess hired to teach his children.
Anna and the King of Siam. 1946. Harrison, Rex
The King and I. 1956. Brynner, Yul

King Louis XI, see Louis XI

King Louis XVI, see Louis XVI

Kingsfield.
To sharpen their dedication to learning which will make them first-class lawyers, this arrogantly superior Harvard professor intimidates, humiliates and ridicules his law students.
The Paper Chase. 1973. Houseman, John

Kinnie.
Laconic veteran of the 101st Airborne Division leads his platoon more through example than by command. Following the Battle of the Bulge, he raises their war-weary spirits enough to have them march to the rear in dignity, as rookies move in to replace them.
Battleground. 1949. Whitmore, James

Kino.
A Mexican pearl diver finds a priceless pearl which he believes will lift him and his family out of poverty, but instead it brings him misery, violence, and the death of his son.
The Pearl. 1948. Armendariz, Pedro

Kinross, Captain.
The devoted commander of a British destroyer recalls with great pride the glories of his ship and crew during World War II.
In Which We Serve. 1942. Coward, Noel

Kirkland, Arthur.
Sensitive, scruffy, almost idealistic lawyer, who on a daily basis must deal with the complexities and corruptions of the American legal system, tangles with a tyrannical judge accused of brutally raping a young girl.
And Justice For All. 1979. Pacino, Al

Kirsten.
Originally a nondrinker, this young advertising executive's wife drinks with her husband so he won't feel resentful, becomes an alcoholic, and cannot abstain even though it means the loss of her husband and lonely child.
Days of Wine and Roses. 1962. Remick, Lee

Koop.
Proud, big-talking garbageman, a tangle of contradictions, falls in love with a mother of six and carries on a hectic courtship made more complex by money and family problems.
Claudine. 1974. Jones, James Earl

Kotcher, Joseph P.
Lively, garrulous 72-year-old idolizes his grandson but is a nuisance to his son and daughter-in-law. He sets off on his own, befriends the family's pregnant unwed baby sitter, and helps her straighten out her life by giving her companionship and affection.
Kotch. 1971. Matthau, Walter

Kovack, Sandra.
A dazzling but conceited and sardonic concert pianist has an affair with a married man, bears a child that she does not want, and gives the infant to the man's wife.
The Great Lie. 1941. Astor, Mary

Kowalski, Stanley.
Animal-like, inarticulate, coarse-tongued brute, seeing his sister-in-law Blanche's visit as a threat to his relationship with his wife, shatters Blanche's sanity by forcing her to reveal her shady past.
A Streetcar Named Desire. 1951. Brando, Marlon

Kowalski, Stella.
Having turned her back on her decaying aristocratic background and finding happiness with her crude, coarse, animalistic working-class husband, Stella is torn between love and loyalty for her husband and her sister during the latter's visit.
A Streetcar Named Desire. 1951. Hunter, Kim

Kramer, Billy.
A very normal six-year-old boy, constantly vying for attention, struggles to understand the reasons for his parents' separation, all along blaming himself for his mother's departure.
Kramer vs. Kramer. 1979. Henry, Justin

Kramer, Joanna.
Unhappy woman trying to find her own role in life walks out on her husband and six-year-old son. She returns 18 months later and uses the argument of the traditional mother's prerogative to fight for custody of the child.
Kramer vs. Kramer. 1979. Streep, Meryl

Kramer, Ted.
After his wife abruptly walks out on him, this up-and-coming advertising executive, left with a six-year-old son, begins the difficult job of the single parent. He really gets to know and love the child he rarely had time for before, but must fight off his returned wife's demand to regain custody of the child.
Kramer vs. Kramer. 1979. Hoffman, Dustin

Kringelein, Otto.
Tired, meek bookkeeper, knowing death is imminent, decides to enjoy his remaining days in a magnificent hotel suite and to live like the wealthy folk.
Grand Hotel. 1932. Barrymore, Lionel

Kringle, Kris.
This thoroughly charming and generous old gent, the Santa Claus in Macy's department store, claims he is the real Kris Kringle and gets a chance to prove it in court.
Miracle on 34th Street. 1947. Gwenn, Edmund

Kristine.
Tired of their grim existence in 19th-century Sweden, Kristine, her farmer husband and family try to fulfill a dream and emigrate to Minnesota, only to have their life of hardship, poverty and sadness continue.
The Emigrants. 1972. Ullmann, Liv

Kubelik, Fran.
Attractive elevator operator, a perpetual loser with men, is given a $100 cash gift for Christmas by her current paramour. Feeling branded as a prostitute, she takes an overdose of sleeping pills in the apartment of her secret admirer.
The Apartment. 1960. MacLaine, Shirley

Kurtz.
Egomaniacal and murderous renegade Green Beret colonel is slated for secret execution because he has gone mad in the jungle and often leads unauthorized military raids.
Apocalypse Now. 1979. Brando, Marlon

Kwan, Billy.
Fascinating, idealistic Chinese-Australian dwarf is a press photographer with access to all the confidential sources of news in Jakarta in 1965. He becomes the mentor of an Australian journalist, giving him not only leads and photographs for his stories, but also an introduction to his long-standing, unrequited love, an aide at the British Embassy.
The Year of Living Dangerously. 1983. Hunt, Linda

La Condesa.
Fading, middle-aged, drug-addicted countess becomes the ship doctor's lover, knowing that she must disembark at Tenerife to spend the rest of her life in prison.
Ship of Fools. 1965. Signoret, Simone

La Douce, Irma.
Brash, good-natured Parisian prostitute is managed by an ex-policeman turned pimp who falls in love with her and becomes jealous of her clients.
Irma La Douce. 1963. MacLaine, Shirley

La Motta, Jake.
The Bronx Bull, an inarticulate, insanely jealous and self-destructive boxer, goes through two marriages while becoming middleweight boxing champion of the world. Following his defeat, he buys a Florida nightclub, and deteriorates into a second-rate nightclub performer.
Raging Bull. 1980. De Niro, Robert

La Motta, Joey.
Although their relationship is a wild mixture of affection and hostility, this crude but intelligent, violent but sane brother and manager of Jake La Motta cares for and tries to protect him.
Raging Bull. 1980. Pesci, Joe

La Motta, Vickie.
Sexy, blonde teen-age wife rebels against the constant pressure of having to account for her every move when her husband isn't present, and leaves him, taking the children with her.
Raging Bull. 1980. Moriarty, Cathy

La Noue, Marise.
Thinking that she has been abandoned by her sweetheart when they become separated at the Paris train station, this pretty, naive peasant girl falls into a life of despair and squalor.
The Red Lily. 1924. Bennett, Enid

Lachaille, Honore.
In turn-of-the-century Paris, this mellowing, elderly, elegantly dressed man-about-town considers himself a philosopher, a lover, and a collector of antiques.
Gigi. 1958. Chevalier, Maurice

Lachie.
In a Burmese army hospital, a stubborn, overbearing Scottish soldier with only a few weeks to live, not wanting to be pitied, resists his comrades' friendly overtures until he's convinced they're truly sincere.
The Hasty Heart. 1949. Todd, Richard

Lady Day, see Holiday, Billie

Lady Fingers.
Practiced, polished con artist who has played the circuits substitutes for the regular dealer in an important, high-stakes game between an aspiring youth and an established poker champion.
The Cincinnati Kid. 1965. Blondell, Joan

Lady Lou, see Lou, Lady

Lamb, Harold.
Unaware that people are laughing at him, this gullible, bespectacled young college student will do anything to be popular on campus, including playing football, at which he is hilariously inept.
The Freshman. 1925. Lloyd, Harold

Lammoreaux, Millie.
Lonely, ostracized but thoroughly modern and perfectly groomed Millie, a physical therapist in an old folks' health center, finds herself idolized by another young lady therapist.
Three Women. 1977. Duvall, Shelley

Lamont, Lina.
Silent filmdom's number-one glamour girl, a brassy blonde with a shrill, high-pitched voice, cannot make the transition from the silents to the talkies.
Singin' in the Rain. 1952. Hagen, Jean

Lampton, Joe.
Consumed by a burning ambition to get to the top, this handsome, calculating factory-office worker jilts the woman who loves him, marries the daughter of the factory owner, and forces himself into the ranks of the wealthy and socially privileged.
Room at the Top. 1959. Harvey, Laurence

Landau, Dov.
Having learned to use dynamite at Auschwitz to dig the mass graves of his fellow Jews, this tormented and revengeful young man arrives in Palestine. He immediately joins the Irgun, the radical underground movement dedicated to fighting the occupying British, as their demolition expert.
Exodus. 1960. Mineo, Sal

Langford, Jerry.
Popular television talk show host, who both needs and fears his large, worshipping audience, pretends he is warm and caring, but is unable to deal competently with anything that exists outside his own ego.
The King of Comedy. 1983. Lewis, Jerry

Langham, Clive.
Dying, second-rate 78-year-old English writer, a philanderer who ignored his wife, possibly caused her suicide, and alienated his son, drunkenly constructs a last novel featuring his family.
Providence. 1977. Gielgud, John

Lanser, Colonel.
A cold and contemptuous Nazi colonel in an invaded Norwegian mining town is also a skeptic who knows that brutal measures cannot stifle the will of a determined people.
The Moon is Down. 1943. Hardwicke, Cedric

Larrabee, David.
Wealthy and wanton playboy is too busy with his own set to notice that the family chaffeur's beautiful daughter is in love with him.
Sabrina. 1954. Holden, William

Larrabee, Linus.
Strong-willed business aristocrat romances the family chauffeur's daughter.
Sabrina. 1954. Bogart, Humphrey

Larsen, Wolf.
The obsessed, sadistic captain of a scavenger ship in 1900 is a complex maniac who loves to read Shakespeare but rules his men with ruthless terror.
The Sea Wolf. 1941. Robinson, Edward G.

Lautmann, Rosalie.
Frightened old Jewish widow, with failing eyesight and hearing, goes through the daily ritual of business in her bankrupt button store. She treats the "Aryan controller," sent by the Nazis to manage her shop, as her assistant.
The Shop on Main Street. 1966. Kaminska, Ida

Lawrence.
A man of mystery and keen intelligence, this flamboyant and complex British soldier-adventurer in the Middle East during World War I works toward Arab unity but comes to be a beaten man, unwanted by both the British Army and the Arabs.
Lawrence of Arabia. 1962. O'Toole, Peter

Lawrence, Marjorie.
Beautiful Australian farm girl, happily married to an American doctor, is a rising star with the Metropolitan Opera Company. She contracts polio, becomes paralyzed at the height of her career, and makes a valiant struggle to regain her will to live.
Interrupted Melody. 1955. Parker, Eleanor

Lazar, Vania.
A Russian peasant girl dreams that she has been betrayed by the Grand Duke, and in her reverie becomes a wicked vamp in order to get revenge.
The Serpent. 1916. Bara, Theda

Le Moko, Pepe.
Charming Parisian jewel thief and tough guy, exiled to the Casbah in Algiers, sacrifices his freedom for the love of a woman.
Pepe Le Moko. 1937. Gabin, Jean
Algiers. 1938. Boyer, Charles

Leamas, Alec.
Disenchanted, bitter, moody British intelligence agent is called back into service to go undercover and to trap the East German intelligence chief who is responsible for many of the British counterespionage failures.
The Spy Who Came in from the Cold. 1965. Burton, Richard

Lee, Flower Belle.
The buxom, bawdy, shady lady of Greasewood City, who makes a joke of sex and sin, marries "in name only" a scowling misanthrope.
My Little Chickadee. 1940. West, Mae

Leeson, Daniel.
Wealthy respectable suitor from Oklahoma is thrust into the affairs of a couple who are planning a divorce.
The Awful Truth. 1937. Bellamy, Ralph

Leigh, Jocelyn.
In order to escape from a prearranged marriage to odious Lord Carnal, this English lady flees to the colony of Virginia on a ship carrying volunteer wives to the settlers.
To Have and To Hold. 1922. Compson, Betty

Lejaune.
This brutal sergeant, in command of a French Foreign Legion post in the desert, metes out punishment to his men as ruthlessly as he deals with Arab raiders, and eventually must contend with a mutiny.
Beau Geste. 1926. Beery, Noah

Leland, Jedediah.
Drama critic for two of his newspapers and closest friend of Charles Kane, a multimillionaire newspaper publisher, Leland maintains his inner dignity and allegiance to his beliefs throughout his sometimes bristling relationship with Kane.
Citizen Kane. 1941. Cotten, Joseph

Lennie.
This dim-witted and childlike migrant ranch hand loves to stroke soft, smooth things, and shares a dream with his companion that one day they will own their own ranch and Lennie will tend the soft rabbits. But he is so strong that his touch kills a bird, a mouse, a puppy, the ranch foreman's wife, and ultimately their dream.
Of Mice and Men. 1939. Chaney, Lon, Jr.

Lenny.
Honeymooning New York Jewish boy abruptly abandons his plain bride, who is suffering from sun poisoning, to pursue a beautiful young blonde from Minnesota.
The Heartbreak Kid. 1972. Grodin, Charles

Leon.
Frightened, suicidal homosexual is the "wife" of a self-proclaimed bank robber who is holding hostages in a Brooklyn bank to gain the means to provide Leon with his dream of a sex change operation.
Dog Day Afternoon. 1975. Sarandon, Chris

Leonie.
Beautiful, kooky but sensitive young woman, longing for a less frenetic and wearying life, tries to obtain a divorce from her way-out, unpredictable painter husband.
Morgan. 1966. Redgrave, Vanessa

Leonnec, Jean.
The mayor's son elopes to Paris with his young, naive sweetheart and becomes separated from her when he is falsely arrested for a theft. When he finally finds her again, living in need and squalor, he mistakenly assumes she is a prostitute and treats her with contempt.
The Red Lily. 1924. Novarro, Ramon

Lester.
Successful businessman, a heavy contributor to the Nixon-Agnew campaign, is being asked for money by his wife's hairdresser and lover, who wants to open his own beauty shop.
Shampoo. 1975. Warden, Jack

Lester, Vicki, see Blodgett, Esther

Letty.
Genteel girl from the South, transplanted to a windswept desert, survives a lonely marriage, a dust storm, and the threat of an unscrupulous intruder, whom she shoots in self-defense.
The Wind. 1928. Gish, Lillian

Levi, Dolly.
Even though she herself is a matchmaker, Dolly must connive and campaign to marry the richest but most stingy man in Yonkers.
Hello, Dolly! 1969. Streisand, Barbra

Lewis.
Constantly lecturing about the purity of nature and the corruption of civilization, this rugged, macho outdoorsman coerces, then guides, three less hearty, well-to-do friends on a weekend canoe trip. He is ultimately humbled and degraded by nature's strength and his own weaknesses.
Deliverance. 1972. Reynolds, Burt

Lewis, Al.
Fastidious, long-suffering vaudevillian is reunited with his mean-spirited partner for a TV appearance after an 11-year separation.
The Sunshine Boys. 1975. Burns, George

Lewis, Doreen.
Hard, sexually repressed Army captain, an advocate of old-fashioned training methods, is both attracted by the beauty and repelled by the spoiled nature of a recent recruit.
Private Benjamin. 1980. Brennan, Eileen

Libby, Matt.
Matt is the head of a Hollywood studio publicity department and is always unhappy because he hates the people with whom he works.
A Star is Born. 1937. Stander, Lionel
A Star is Born. 1954. Carson, Jack

Liddell, Eric.
Super runner, dedicated young Church of Scotland preacher, Eric believes that by winning the Olympics he can best honor God. However, he is so dedicated to his religious mission that he turns down the request of the British Olympic Committee to race on Sunday.
Chariots of Fire. 1981. Charleson, Ian

Lieberman, Ezra.
Seemingly hapless yet wise and resourceful old Jewish Nazi hunter, a character based on Simon Wiesenthal, is successful in his struggle to track down and outwit the evil Josef Mengele, who was responsible for the murders of thousands of Jews.
The Boys From Brazil. 1978. Olivier, Laurence

Lightfoot.
While trying to elude two bandits looking for their share of a heist from a couple of years ago, this fast-talking, impish apprentice of an older and wiser thief suggests that they pull the same robbery again, exactly duplicating the previous plan.
Thunderbolt and Lightfoot. 1974. Bridges, Jeff

Lila.
Three days after their wedding, this lumpy-faced, voluptuous middle-class Jewish bride is ditched by her husband, who is in hot pursuit of a cool American dream girl.
The Heartbreak Kid. 1972. Berlin, Jeannie

Lili, see Daurier, Lili

Lily.
Dutiful married woman, after a brief affair, is stunned, frightened, and grief-stricken when she must submit to an abortion.
Alfie. 1966. Merchant, Vivien

Lily, in *Shanghai Express,* see Shanghai Lily

Lime, Harry.
Corrupt black marketeer, for a time thought to be dead, is on the run in the ruins of post-World War II Vienna. He is eventually discovered and destroyed by a friend from his boyhood.
The Third Man. 1949. Welles, Orson

Lincoln, Abraham.
From his birth to his assassination, the President is vividly portrayed as a man of honesty, humility and justice, as a husband scolded by his wife for dressing carelessly, and as a dedicated and sympathetic leader of the country during the Civil War.
The Dramatic Life of Abraham Lincoln. 1924. Billings, George A.

Lincoln, Abraham.
During the prairie years before his presidency, the shy and taciturn Lincoln is a shopkeeper, postmaster, lawyer and legislator, but remains filled with doubt and self-criticism.
Abe Lincoln in Illinois. 1940. Massey, Raymond

Linda.
A proponent of women's liberation and youngest editor of the women's magazine *Gloss,* Linda has transformed herself from a fat and homely to a voluptuous and attractive female.
Once is Not Enough. 1975. Vaccaro, Brenda

Linda.
Beautiful, supportive, but commonplace woman works in the supermarket in Clairton, Pennsylvania, and remains the pillar of sanity amidst the physical and psychic turmoil of her Vietnam soldier friends.
The Deer Hunter. 1978. Streep, Meryl

Little Caesar.
Tough, ruthless killer, driven by an unquenchable desire for power, takes over a gang of criminals and then is cornered and killed by the police.
Little Caesar. 1931. Robinson, Edward G.

Little Colonel, The, see Cameron, Ben

Little Sister, The, see Cameron, Flora

Loggins, Addie.
Precocious, independent, beguiling nine-year-old orphan joins a young Kansas con man who might be her father, hooks him into partnership, and finally wins his affection.
Paper Moon. 1973. O'Neal, Tatum

Loman, Linda.
Loyal, long-suffering salesman's wife is steadfast in her support, although she realizes that her husband is a failure.
Death of a Salesman. 1951. Dunnock, Mildred

Loman, Willy.
Shabby, boastful 63-year-old traveling salesman, who worships success and popularity without facing up to reality, confronts the disappointment of his career when he is fired after 34 years of selling with the same company. *Death of a Salesman.* 1951. March, Fredric

Lone Prospector.
Always the perfect gentleman, even in the wild and wooly Klondike, the lonely little tramp falls pathetically in love with a dance hall girl, and hilariously copes with bears and ruffians. *The Gold Rush.* 1925. Chaplin, Charles

Longhetti, Mabel.
Basically spontaneous and childlike, Mabel is anxious and harried because she wants to be a good mother and to live up to her husband's and society's expectations. Her feeling of inadequacy eventually leads to a breakdown and six months in a mental institution, from which she returns chastened and even more fearful. *A Woman Under the Influence.* 1974. Rowlands, Gena

Lonnegan, Doyle.
Propelled by greed and vengeance, a powerful, menacing ganglord becomes an easy mark in a confidence game. *The Sting.* 1973. Shaw, Robert

Loomis, Wilma Dean.
Tormented young girl in love with her high-school sweetheart, too young to marry and not daring to have sexual relations, does not recover from their split-up until she matures and can profit from her own experiences. *Splendor in the Grass.* 1961. Wood, Natalie

Lord, Tracy.
This snobbish and arrogant society girl, about to marry for the second time, becomes involved with the reporter assigned to cover the social event. *The Philadelphia Story.* 1940. Hepburn, Katharine

Lorene, see Alma, in *From Here to Eternity*

Lorenz, Dr.
A dignified college professor, who is also a spy for the Japanese, is looking for information on the Panama Canal's defenses, and matches wits with an American intelligence agent he meets on a freighter bound for that area. *Across the Pacific.* 1942. Greenstreet, Sydney

Loring, Marie.
Cheery, attractive college student rents a room in a middle-aged couple's home and brightens their existence, until her sexual curiosity precipitates havoc in the household.
Come Back, Little Sheba. 1952. Moore, Terry

Lorrison, Georgia.
Alcoholic, inferiority-complexed Hollywood extra is molded into a glamorous, confident star by a hard-working director who pretends to love her.
Bad and the Beautiful. 1952. Turner, Lana

Lottie.
Tough, estranged wife of a writer, living in a farmhouse that her husband bought for her, is "cultivating a beautiful compost heap" and trying to bring up their eight-year-old son.
Charlie Bubbles. 1968. Whitelaw, Billie

Lou.
Old-timer, survivor of the days when the mobs ran Atlantic City, now a petty numbers runner and valet-companion to the widow of a gangster, at last realizes a moment of glory and self-respect.
Atlantic City. 1981. Lancaster, Burt

Lou, Lady.
Beautiful, gaudy queen of the Bowery belles in the 1890s, and friend to all the local dignitaries, brings about her own downfall because she is really sympathetic and warmhearted.
She Done Him Wrong. 1933. West, Mae

Louis VII.
For political reasons, King Louis refuses to expel Becket from France, and when he does withdraw his protection, he arranges a reconciliatory meeting between King Henry II and Becket.
Becket. 1964. Gielgud, John

Louis XI.
Eccentric, wizened, clever king spars with the poet Villon to get his way.
If I Were King. 1938. Rathbone, Basil

Louis XVI.
Inconsistent, vacillating king is a dull and neurotic misfit, incapable of being a ruler.
Marie Antoinette. 1938. Morley, Robert

Louise.
Taken to Paris during the French Revolution by her adopted sister to find a cure for her blindness, Louise falls into the clutches of a beggar woman who makes her perform for money.
Orphans of the Storm. 1921. Gish, Dorothy

Louise.
Pretty, sensible, big-hearted waitress at Max's bar, which boasts an all-male, all-handicapped constituency, is attracted to a cripple, but is reluctant to become sexually involved despite their mutual desire.
Inside Moves. 1980. Scarwid, Diana

Lovelace, Eva.
Stage-struck young girl from a country town in Vermont tries to pursue an acting career, but finds that she is unprepared to withstand the sophistication and seeming insensitivity of New York and its theatrical crowd.
Morning Glory. 1933. Hepburn, Katharine

Luke.
Guilty of wantonly destroying parking meters when drunk and sentenced to two years at hard labor, Luke stubbornly holds fast to a burning determination to maintain his individuality, despite his compromised situation on a chain gang.
Cool Hand Luke. 1967. Newman, Paul

Lund, Ilsa.
Lovely, warm young woman is torn between her emotions and her sense of duty when she and her Czech patriot husband come to Casablanca to escape the Nazis and are helped to safety by her former lover, Rick Blaine.
Casablanca. 1942. Bergman, Ingrid

Luther, Dr.
Wise, unflappable psychiatrist tries to cure a schizophrenic so that she can lead a normal life.
The Three Faces of Eve. 1957. Cobb, Lee J.

Lydecker, Waldo.
A middle-aged columnist and critic, witty and sophisticated but also prone to jealousy and vainly egotistical, is a suspect in the supposed murder of his closest woman friend. He does not find this an intrusion on his private life but rather flattering, and insists on accompanying the police detective on his investigation.
Laura. 1944. Webb, Clifton

Lyndon, Barry.
Poor, good-natured, unscrupulous Irish rogue, born Redmond Barry and later taking the name of Barry Lyndon, climbs to the top of English aristocratic society, and then loses everything by a twist of fate.
Barry Lyndon. 1975. O'Neal, Ryan

Lynn, Loretta.
Earthy, strong-willed poor mountain girl from Butcher Hollow, Kentucky, married at age 14, mother of four at 18, with her husband's encouragement and promotion becomes a success at the Grand Ole Opry and later earns the title of "Queen of Country Music."
Coal Miner's Daughter. 1980. Spacek, Sissy

Lynn, Theodora.
Prim, sheltered, small-town Connecticut girl produces a best-selling risque novel under a pseudonym. In New York to see her publisher, she meets a liberated artist who helps set her free.
Theodora Goes Wild. 1936. Dunne, Irene

M.
A psychopathic killer, who murders little girls, typifies the terrified, suffering human being who can no longer control his urge to molest and kill.
M. 1931. Lorre, Peter

Macauley, Homer.
Young messenger boy for the telegraph office in a small California town learns about people, life, and death as he delivers telegrams during World War II.
The Human Comedy. 1943. Rooney, Mickey

MacDonald, Sophie.
A once placid, happy young woman becomes a degraded, pathetic drunk when her husband and baby are killed in an automobile accident. Given a chance to return to her old lifestyle, she cannot rise above her agony and confusion.
The Razor's Edge. 1946. Baxter, Anne

Machin, Frank.
Well on the road to success and wealth, this brawny, blustering, insecure rugby league football player has an affair with his widowed landlady in a search for his greatest need of all, the feeling of being loved and wanted.
This Sporting Life. 1963. Harris, Richard

MacKay, Miss.
Dignified but humorless old-maidish headmistress of Edinburgh's exclusive Marcia Blaine School repeatedly attempts to dismiss an eccentric but effective teacher.
The Prime of Miss Jean Brodie. 1969. Johnson, Celia

MacKay, Terry.
Young skeptical woman has a mild flirtation on a boat sailing from Naples to New York with a "man of the world." The two arrange to meet six months later to see if they really care for each other, but on the way Terry is crippled in an automobile accident and does not keep the tryst.
Love Affair. 1939. Dunne, Irene

Mackie, Calla.
Touching old maid schoolteacher uses revivalist religion to allay her loneliness and to suppress a leaning toward lesbianism.
Rachel, Rachel. 1968. Parsons, Estelle

MacLaine, Jennie.
Bright and vivacious actress helps a successful young writer dispel his sense of emotional involvement with and lingering guilt feelings over his late wife. After a whirlwind courtship, she becomes his second wife.
Chapter Two. 1979. Mason, Marsha

MacLean, Juneau.
A bright and funny girl from Alaska, who drinks her whiskey neat and has a great left jab, comes to New York with her successful gold miner father and outswindles the crooks who are out to take advantage of them.
The Wilderness Woman. 1926. Pringle, Aileen

MacNeil, Chris.
This helplessly suffering divorced mother tries to save the life of her demonically possessed daughter through an exorcism performed by two Roman Catholic priests.
The Exorcist. 1973. Burstyn, Ellen

Macomber, Margaret.
A nasty, selfish wife on a hunting trip in Africa cruelly mocks her husband when he fails to kill his first lion, cuckolds him with their guide, and ultimately betrays him with a bullet in his head.
The Macomber Affair. 1947. Bennett, Joan

Macreedy, John T.
A stranger, delivering the war medal of a hero son to his Japanese-American family, encounters hostility in a small California town, and discovers the townspeople to be communally guilty of an old murder.
Bad Day at Black Rock. 1955. Tracy, Spencer

Mad Dog Earle, see Earle, Roy

Madame Rosa.
Elderly French-Jewish one-time prostitute, a prisoner at Auschwitz during World War II, Rosa now runs a broken-down boarding house where working-class Arabs, Jews and Gentiles may live. She is dying, but her major worry concerns what will happen to her last boarder, an abandoned Arab boy whom she especially loves.
Madame Rosa. 1978. Signoret, Simone

Madame X, see Floriot, Jacqueline

Maggie.
Impatient, sex-starved wife is motivated by greed, jealousy, and fear as she needles and begs her husband to make her pregnant.
Cat on a Hot Tin Roof. 1958. Taylor, Elizabeth

Maggio, Angelo.
On the eve of World War II, a good-natured private from the slums of New York is beaten to death in the stockade when he rebels against the Army system.
From Here to Eternity. 1953. Sinatra, Frank

Maine, Norman.
Realizing that he is becoming an alcoholic, this once-talented screen idol takes his own life so as not to jeopardize his wife's career as an actress.
A Star is Born. 1937. March, Fredric
A Star is Born. 1954. Mason, James

Major Pollock, see Pollock

Major Rinaldi, see Rinaldi, Allesandro

Malama.
Queen of Hawaii, with primitive regal dignity, leads her people from happy paganism to an uncertain future under Western domination.
Hawaii. 1966. La Garde, Jocelyne

Malena.
This rude, gum-chewing black maid, hired to serve at the dinner given by the Adams family for their daughter's young man, is a prime contributor to the problems and anxieties of the evening.
Alice Adams. 1935. Daniels, Hattie

Malloy, Charley.
Pliable foil to a corrupt labor leader, Charley finds his life in jeopardy as his brother, Terry, threatens to testify about corrupt union practices.
On the Waterfront. 1954. Steiger, Rod

Malloy, Terry.
Dull-witted but well-intentioned ex-pugilist, hired by the union not knowing he is to set up the murder of a dock worker, has his sense of decency aroused and gives testimony about corruption in the longshoremen's union.
On the Waterfront. 1954. Brando, Marlon

Mama.
This loving and understanding mother of a Norwegian-American family in San Francisco is the strong and cheerful mainstay of a household struggling to make ends meet.
I Remember Mama. 1948. Dunne, Irene

Mame.
This flashily dressed, high-living tireless party giver is surprisingly tender and attentive when her fast-paced social life takes on a new complication, a ten-year-old nephew.
Aunty Mame. 1958. Russell, Rosalind

Mammy.
Scarlett's ever-scolding nurse is loyal to the O'Hara family of the ruined plantation, Tara.
Gone With the Wind. 1939. McDaniel, Hattie

Mandrake, Group Captain Lionel.
When the Russians threaten retaliation for an impending nuclear attack, this RAF officer, assigned to the U.S. base from which the attack has been insubordinately launched, is the only one involved showing common sense. He tries to phone the president of the U.S. with the Stop Code.
Dr. Strangelove: or, How I Learned to Stop Worrying and Love the Bomb. 1964. Sellers, Peter

Manero, Tony.
Inarticulate, goodhearted 19-year-old Brooklyn paint store clerk lives only for Saturday nights when he is the champion dancer of the disco, the only place where he can release his frustrated energy and become himself.
Saturday Night Fever. 1977. Travolta, John

Mannon, Lavinia.
Cold-blooded daughter takes justice in her own hands when she goads her brother into killing their mother's lover. For this action she asks no forgiveness from God or anyone else, but condemns herself to a solitary life in her New England home.
Mourning Becomes Electra. 1947. Russell, Rosalind

Mannon, Orin.
Weak, confused son has an incestuous love for his mother, which he later transfers to his sister. After murdering his mother's lover, his guilt is so great that he shoots himself in order to join his mother.
Mourning Becomes Electra. 1947. Redgrave, Michael

Manson, Andrew.
Young Scottish doctor becomes disillusioned and begins to treat wealthy hypochondriacs until his best friend dies because of an incompetent surgeon. He returns to his real work and devotes his life to eliminating disease in a poor Welsh mining village.
The Citadel. 1938. Donat, Robert

Manuel.
Gruff but tender Portuguese fisherman teaches human values to a pampered millionaire's son whom he rescues during a storm at sea.
Captains Courageous. 1937. Tracy, Spencer

Manville, Mrs. E. Worthington, see Apple Annie

March, Aunt.
Gruff, wealthy woman with great inner strength and kindness becomes a spiritual partner to her niece.
Little Women. 1933. Oliver, Edna May

Marden, Joe.
A young man with no family ties becomes the war buddy of a well-to-do soldier known as Sonny. When Sonny is killed, sympathetic Joe goes to his home and impersonates him for the sake of Sonny's blind mother.
Sonny. 1922. Barthelmess, Richard

Margaret, Sister.
Beautiful, serene French nun seeks support to build a children's hospital in Bethlehem, Connecticut.
Come to the Stable. 1949. Young, Loretta

Margo.
Fading stage actress befriends ingenue and realizes that she must step down to allow the younger star to advance her career.
All About Eve. 1950. Davis, Bette

Maria.
Young and innocent Spanish girl who has been cruelly attacked by Fascist soldiers during the Civil War is given refuge by a group of guerrilla fighters, and falls in love with an American who has joined them.
For Whom the Bell Tolls. 1943. Bergman, Ingrid

Maria.
During the Nazi annexation of Austria, this postulant is sent from the convent to serve as governess to the seven motherless Von Trapp children. She turns them into a happy troupe of singers before marrying their father.
The Sound of Music. 1965. Andrews, Julie

Maria.
Maria, the youngest in the family and extraordinarily beautiful, returns home because her oldest sister is dying of cancer. She would like to resume her love affair with the attending doctor, but he feels that she has become lazy and indolent and remains indifferent.
Cries and Whispers. 1972. Ullmann, Liv

Maria, Mother.
Strong-willed and persuasive Mother Superior of a group of German nuns, refugees from East Germany, leads them in meagre existence in the Arizona desert. She feels that Homer Smith, the handyman, has been sent by God to build them a chapel and need not be paid a wage.
Lilies of the Field. 1963. Skala, Lilia

Marian the Librarian, see Paroo, Marian

Marianne.
This beautiful lawyer and her husband are being interviewed for a women's magazine about their seemingly perfect marriage. After ten years together they divorce and each remarries. They later go away for a weekend together, still operating on a base of love.
Scenes From a Marriage. 1974. Ullmann, Liv

Marie.
Tough, sexy drifter, making her way from place to place by practicing petty larceny and accepting favors from admirers, arrives in Martinique and moves dauntlessly into an independent American fisherman's life. He nicknames her Slim.
To Have and Have Not. 1944. Bacall, Lauren

Maris, Stella.
A bedridden and naive young invalid falls in love with the married man who takes care of her. When she becomes well she is disillusioned by the fact that the man's alcoholic wife is an obstacle to their happiness.
Stella Maris. 1918. Pickford, Mary

Markoff.
Brutally sadistic sergeant in the Foreign Legion beats and even maims his men in order to enforce his iron will.
Beau Geste. 1939. Donlevy, Brian

Marlett, Lally.
Young and charming girl is amorously pursued by her stepmother's son.
Their Own Desire. 1930. Shearer, Norma

Marlowe.
Tough, shrewd, taciturn private detective is hired by an elderly Southern California millionaire to protect his daughters from blackmailers.
The Big Sleep. 1946. Bogart, Humphrey

Marnay, Mme.
Sympathetic grandmother sees her grandson as a tender and sensitive person. As a result she helps him and his girl friend to achieve the spiritual harmony and love she felt for her own late husband.
Love Affair. 1939. Ouspenskaya, Maria

Marryot, Jane.
Wife and mother in an upper-middle-class London family shares her loved ones' sacrifices from the late 19th century through World War I.
Cavalcade. 1933. Wynard, Diana

Marsh, Julian.
Exhausted but tyrannical stage director, having lost his money in the stock market, channels all his energy into making his last Broadway show a success.
42nd Street. 1933. Baxter, Warner

Marsh, Lew.
Ace newspaperman, while trying to cure himself of alcoholism and to get his life back together again, is triumphant in tracking down gangsters and scores a sensational scoop.
Come Fill the Cup. 1951. Cagney, James

Marsh, Whitey.
Incorrigible young tough, befriended by a humane and sympathetic priest, learns positive human values and regains his place in normal society.
Boys' Town. 1938. Rooney, Mickey

Martha.
Slovenly, sluttish faculty wife idolizes her father, president of the college, while she taunts her husband for his ineffectiveness, and finally sleeps with a young professor as an act of vengeance.
Who's Afraid of Virginia Woolf? 1966. Taylor, Elizabeth

Marthe.
An aging mistress, drunk and dissolute, is nonetheless a sympathetic and, at times, humorous character.
Anna Christie. 1930. Dressler, Marie

Marthe.
Bored, lovely blonde in her early 30s, married for 11 years, meets a cousin by marriage at a family wedding. Although friends and relatives immediately assume a sexual liaison, the two first become friends, eventually fall in love, and finally have an affair.
Cousin, Cousine. 1976. Barrault, Marie-Christine

Martin, Baby Face.
Tough killer returns after ten years to the slums of New York's Lower East Side and snarls at life because his mother rejects him and his sweetheart hasn't waited for him.
Dead End. 1937. Bogart, Humphrey

Martin, Luke.
With the help of a sympathetic, caring hospital volunteer who becomes his lover, this former captain of the football team, now a helpless paraplegic from Vietnam injuries, makes the transition from humiliation, rage and frustration to serenity and sensitivity.
Coming Home. 1978. Voight, Jon

Martin, Steve.
Warm but truculent master vaudevillian discovers the young Al Jolson, makes him his partner, and does not impede his rise to stardom when the extent of Jolson's talent is revealed in later years.
The Jolson Story. 1946. Demarest, William

Martini, Charley.
A colorful and hearty old vagrant in a California "paisano" district, shocked that his son has been killed in the war but proud that he has been awarded the Medal of Honor, fights with dignity the prominent citizens who try to use him to promote the town.
A Medal for Benny. 1945. Naish, J. Carrol

Marturano, Filomena.
Mistress of a prosperous middle-class merchant for 22 years, this ex-prostitute tries to trick him into marriage to gain respectability for herself and her three sons, whom she has supported and raised secretly.
Marriage Italian Style. 1964. Loren, Sophia

Marty.
Awkward but gentle 34-year-old Bronx butcher, unmarried and lonely, visits the Stardust Ballroom, finds an unglamorous woman as unhappy as he, and, despite the protestations of mother and friends, persists in pursuing their relationship.
Marty. 1955. Borgnine, Ernest

Marvel, Professor.
The Wizard of Oz turns out to be a Kansas magician, and a fake, at that.
Nevertheless, he is able to grant the wishes of Dorothy's friends.
The Wizard of Oz. 1939. Morgan, Frank

Mary, Queen of Scots.
Tremulous, romantic Queen of Scotland is widowed at the age of 18 and
executed 25 years later, after many battles, by Queen Elizabeth of England.
Mary, Queen of Scots. 1971. Redgrave, Vanessa

Mason, Louise.
This young World War I widow, after losing her own child, becomes a baby
nurse and devotes the rest of her life to caring for other people's children.
The Blue Veil. 1951. Wyman, Jane

Master of Ceremonies.
The sly, mocking, insidious Master of Ceremonies at Berlin's Kit Kat Klub,
a cellar cabaret where "everything is beautiful," is the epitome of the
decadence, immorality and corruption of pre-Nazi Germany.
Cabaret. 1972. Grey, Joel

Masterman, John.
An industrialist tyrant rules a futuristic city where the workers live
underground and the rich live in skyscrapers. He plots with a mad inventor
to create a woman robot which will help him crush the workers'
rebelliousness.
Metropolis. 1926. Abel, Alfred

Matto.
Gentle, cheerful clown invites a simple young woman, a carnival assistant, to
join him on the road. Her master, jealous of Matto and angry at his
goading, beats and kills him.
La Strada. 1954. Basehart, Richard

Maudsley, Mrs.
The mother of an elegant family in turn-of-the-century England considers
propriety more important than love as she tries to keep track of her
beautiful daughter so that nothing will spoil her impending marriage to a
viscount.
The Go-Between. 1971. Leighton, Margaret

Max.
Emaciated, drug-addicted English prisoner is emotionally and intellectually
drained by the vicious treatment and subhuman conditions in a Turkish
prison.
Midnight Express. 1978. Hurt, John

Max.

Massive editor of a London-based gourmet magazine considers his own bulk a carefully created work of art. When told he is eating himself to death, Max becomes childishly unreasonable, because he feels that food fulfills his personality, and provides him with stature and authority.
Who is Killing the Great Chefs of Europe? 1978. Morley, Robert

Maximillian.

This ill-fated but courageous and highly idealistic young Austrian prince, husband of the tragic Carlotta, is led to believe by Napoleon III that the Mexican people want him as their emperor.
Juarez. 1939. Aherne, Brian

Mayo, Zack.

Selfish loner enlists in the Navy to give his life direction and to make something of himself. During the intensive training, he is pushed to the limit by a demanding drill sergeant, falls in love with a local girl, and emerges a better and more mature man.
An Officer and a Gentleman. 1982. Gere, Richard

McCabe, John Q.

Cocky, naive small-time gambler, with the help of an ambitious madam, establishes a bordello and casino in the bleak mining town of Presbyterian Church. He succeeds as a small entrepreneur, only to be forcibly taken over by big business.
McCabe & Mrs. Miller. 1971. Beatty, Warren

McCanles, Laurabelle.

Delicate, faded flower of the South, living unhappily with her greedy cattle baron husband and two sons on a big Texas ranch, allows a half-breed Indian, the daughter of a former fiancee, to work at the family home.
Duel in the Sun. 1946. Gish, Lillian

McCarthy, Parnell.

Downtrodden, disheveled friend of a defense attorney abstains from alcohol during a murder trial and helps win the case.
Anatomy of a Murder. 1959. O'Connell, Arthur

McCaslin, Ned.

Philosophical black with kinship ties to a white family seems to coast through life without a care. An untrained driver, he nevertheless absconds with the family's new 1905 Winton Flyer for a pleasure jaunt through the town of Jefferson, Mississippi.
The Reivers. 1969. Crosse, Rupert

McCauly, Edna.
Simple, forthright widow, crippled in a car accident which leaves her
husband dead, slowly begins to realize that her close brush with death has
given her the power of healing by the laying on of hands.
Resurrection. 1980. Burstyn, Ellen

McDonald, Black.
Kindly, gruff father of a deaf-mute is pushed over a cliff and killed when
he discovers and fights the man who raped his daughter.
Johnny Belinda. 1948. Bickford, Charles

McFadden, Lucy.
Precocious 11-year-old daughter of an unemployed dancer is no help with
the clashing egos and plays for power which ensue when she and her
mother are forced to share their apartment with an aspiring actor.
The Goodbye Girl. 1977. Cummings, Quinn

McFadden, Paula.
Even though she wants to be loved, this former dancer, deserted by her
actor husband and jilted by an actor boyfriend, has become so fearful of
being hurt again that she is hostile toward a new actor who comes to share
her apartment.
The Goodbye Girl. 1977. Mason, Marsha

McGuire, Tessie.
A dainty, diminutive clerk in a department store falls into situations in
which her natural talents for mimicry and the exotic serve her well, such as
posing as a model, acting as a Russian countess, and imitating Charlie
Chaplin.
Manhandled. 1924. Swanson, Gloria

McKee, Sally.
Faded and soiled beauty on a crippled airliner is on her way to San
Francisco to marry a man who has proposed to her through the mails.
The High and the Mighty. 1954. Sterling, Jan

McKlennar, Mrs.
In the Mohawk Valley in upstate New York during Revolutionary times,
this willful, warlike widow has a sharp tongue but a soft spot in her heart
for handsome men.
Drums Along the Mohawk. 1939. Oliver, Edna May

McLaidlaw, Lina.
A shy and sensitive girl marries a charming rake and later begins to suspect
that he is a murderer who plans to kill her, too.
Suspicion. 1941. Fontaine, Joan

McLeod, James.
This dedicated, tough-minded New York City detective, full of hatred for the criminals who parade before him, has lost the distinction between revenge and justice. He brings tragedy upon himself when he is unable to be compassionate in his personal life.
Detective Story. 1951. Douglas, Kirk

McLeod, Mary.
Detective's neglected wife, who once used the services of an illicit doctor, leaves her husband when he is unable to overlook her past or care about salvaging their marriage.
Detective Story. 1951. Parker, Eleanor

McMurphy, R.P.
Imprisoned for observation in a mental institution, this charming, fast-talking nonconformist becomes the spokesman for, and leader of, the less fortunate inmates in a conspiracy to deflate the authoritarian Nurse Ratched.
One Flew Over the Cuckoo's Nest. 1975. Nicholson, Jack

McNulty, Ellen.
The frank, unpolished mother of a suave, ambitious young man trying to break into high society becomes a servant in his home without revealing her identity to his wife.
The Mating Season. 1951. Ritter, Thelma

McTeague.
A sincere and good-natured dentist is driven to violence and murder by his shrewish wife and her insatiable greed for money.
Greed. 1923. Gowland, Gibson

Meadows.
Sentenced to eight years in a Navy prison for pilfering $40 from a polio collection box, this apathetic, inexperienced, insecure country boy is offered comradeship and a good time by two petty officers assigned to escort him to prison.
The Last Detail. 1973. Quaid, Randy

Meadows, Harold.
A tailor's apprentice who aspires to be an author stammers and stutters when he is nervous, and turns his many embarrassing moments into hilarious situations, especially when girls are involved.
Girl Shy. 1924. Lloyd, Harold

Meechum, Ben.
Eighteen-year-old Ben regards his authoritarian father with a mixture of fear, awe, love and hate, and struggles with his own sense of manhood by first resisting and then absorbing some of his dad's ideas.
The Great Santini. 1980. O'Keefe, Michael

Meechum, Bull.
Overpoweringly dedicated macho U.S. Marine Corps colonel, out of a sense of love, insists that his eldest son follow the same kind of life he had. Although Bull is competent in many other ways, he is unsuccessful in articulating the feelings he has for his family.
The Great Santini. 1980. Duvall, Robert

Meg.
In the throes of mid-life crisis and unable to meet the right man, Meg has compromised the ideals she had in the 1960s by signing with a corporate law firm rather than defending the poor. She declares herself ready to have a baby, even if the father wants to take no responsibility.
The Big Chill. 1983. Place, Mary Kay

Megan.
Eager, insensitive Miami reporter is duped into writing a damaging story about the disappearance of a union leader. She not only breaks the basic rules of journalism, neglecting to check her information and getting involved with the suspect, but her further reportage leads to tragedy.
Absence of Malice. 1981. Field, Sally

Melandez, Mrs.
An evil, cunning Fascist in London during the Spanish Civil War tries to stop a Loyalist agent from thwarting a business deal whereby the Fascists will receive coal from England.
Confidential Agent. 1945. Paxinou, Katina

Melanie Wilkes, see Hamilton, Melanie

Melisande.
Three American soldiers, billeted in her father's Champillon farmhouse, become infatuated with this charming, good-natured, affectionate girl. She falls in love with the Southern boy, but his company moves out one morning and she does not have the chance to say good-bye to him.
The Big Parade. 1925. Adoree, Renee

Melvin, see Dummar, Melvin

Merrick, John.

Born in 1864, this hideously deformed Englishman, with twisted spine, useless right arm, and head swollen to twice normal size, spends years in the workhouse as a child and later is exhibited by showmen. He is befriended by a London physician and becomes a fashionable figure, visited by members of highest society.
The Elephant Man. 1980. Hurt, John

Merrick, John P.

A grumpy old millionaire poses as a clerk in his own department store in order to investigate workers' complaints, and becomes a more mellow, understanding person because of his experiences.
The Devil and Miss Jones. 1941. Coburn, Charles

Merton.

The town grocer dreams of success as a movie actor and finally gets a part. Full of pride, he goes to the theatre to watch his performance, but slips out in shame and dejection at the hateful slapstick comedy in which he has appeared.
Merton of the Movies. 1924. Hunter, Glenn

Messala.

Once a boyhood friend of the Judean, Ben-Hur, this tribune becomes his mortal enemy after the Roman conquest of Judea. They climax their animosity in a mammoth chariot race.
Ben-Hur. 1959. Boyd, Stephen

Micawber, Wilkins.

Micawber is ever optimistic, prone to flowery rhetoric, and always on the edge of debtors' prison.
David Copperfield. 1935. Fields, W. C.

Michael.

Grotesque village idiot is aware of the relationship between the wife of the schoolteacher and the commander of the local garrison, and publicly reveals their secret.
Ryan's Daughter. 1970. Mills, John

Michael.

Disciplined, sensitive, strong young steelworker, a deer hunter, does not succumb to the horrors of the Vietnamese War, but has the will to save himself and the courage to try to help his friends survive.
The Deer Hunter. 1978. De Niro, Robert

Michael.
Fifteen years after the excitement has faded, Michael, now an edgy, inquisitive reporter for *People Weekly,* is reunited with a group of one-time campus radicals at the funeral of an old friend.
The Big Chill. 1983. Goldblum, Jeff

Michaels, Dorothy, see Dorsey, Michael

Michel.
Convict at Devil's Island becomes houseboy to the warden and falls in love with the man's wife.
Condemned. 1929. Colman, Ronald

Mick.
Idealistic young girl befriends a deaf-mute who lives in her family's boarding house, but cannot entirely accept his friendship because of a bad first sexual experience.
The Heart is a Lonely Hunter. 1968. Locke, Sondra

Mickey.
A charming young tomboy is sent to an aunt in the city to be educated, captures the heart of a wealthy man, and comes to his aid by masquerading as a jockey in a horse race.
Mickey. 1918. Normand, Mabel

Mickey.
Venerable, gruff-talking manager comes to believe that his problem prizefighter can actually win the championship.
Rocky. 1976. Meredith, Burgess

Miller, Constance.
Tough, ambitious, practical English madam becomes a partner in the saloon and whorehouse business at the turn of the century in a small, isolated mining camp in the American Northwest.
McCabe & Mrs. Miller. 1971. Christie, Julie

Miller, Skipper.
Kindly, gentle old man, who crudely prints out dollar bills on an antiquated hand press only when he needs money for his modest life, is eventually caught by a young Secret Service agent.
Mister 880. 1950. Gwenn, Edmund

Milligan, Connie.
This pretty young working girl in Washington, D.C., during World War II rents half of her apartment to a comical old gent.
The More the Merrier. 1943. Arthur, Jean

Milly.
After this perky, comely lass marries a backwoodsman, she learns that she must keep house for his six untidy brothers as well.
Seven Brides for Seven Brothers. 1954. Powell, Jane

Mimi.
In the bohemian Latin Quarter of Paris, Mimi is a beautiful, delicate, constantly coughing seamstress, rejected by her writer sweetheart who wrongly suspects her of being unfaithful. They are eventually brought together again, but she is fatally ill and dies.
La Boheme. 1926. Gish, Lillian

Min, see Divot, Min

Minafer, Fanny.
A nervous and bitter middle-aged spinster suffers unrequited love for her sister-in-law's suitor.
The Magnificent Ambersons. 1942. Moorehead, Agnes

Minafer, George Amberson.
A vain, arrogant, and spoiled young man, who everyone in town hopes will one day get his "come-uppance," wrecks the romance between his widowed mother and an old suitor.
The Magnificent Ambersons. 1942. Holt, Tim

Miner, Bill.
Released in 1901 after spending over 30 years in San Quentin for robbing stagecoaches, this courteous crook accepts the challenge of robbing those newfangled trains. Working valiantly to adapt his skills to the new technology, he is rewarded by small takes, a hard life on the run, and the animosity of the lawmen of both the U.S. and Canada.
The Grey Fox. 1983. Farnsworth, Richard

Miniver, Clem.
An upper-middle-class husband and father in a small English town is determined to do his best as a civilian during the Battle of Britain, and helps save British soldiers stranded at Dunkirk.
Mrs. Miniver. 1942. Pidgeon, Walter

Miniver, Kay.
A gentle and lovely upper-middle-class English wife and mother proves to be courageous and strong during the Battle of Britain.
Mrs. Miniver. 1942. Garson, Greer

Minnesota Fats.
Confident, seasoned pool expert and acknowledged master cooly beats a young hustler in a marathon pool match.
The Hustler. 1961. Gleason, Jackie

Miracle Man.
This deaf-blind faith healer is able to cure the body and mind, and with this gift and his innate goodness, he reforms a gang of small-time racketeers.
The Miracle Man. 1919. Dowling, Joseph J.

Mirande, Pierre.
An impoverished Parisian aristocrat makes a fortune producing liquor-flavored chewing gum.
The Big Pond. 1930. Chevalier, Maurice

Mireau, General.
Mireau is a French general of the school which believes that a military order, regardless of its absurd difficulty, must be carried out successfully. When a regiment fails in its assignment, he vengefully demands that several of its soldiers, selected arbitrarily, be executed for cowardice.
Paths of Glory. 1957. Macready, George

Miss Em.
Imperious, acid-tongued dowager of an old Southern family falls dangerously ill, is nursed by a young black woman, and makes her the beneficiary of her estate.
Pinky. 1949. Barrymore, Ethel

Mitch.
This awkward, boorish man seeks romance in his coarse environment as he responds to a fading, neurotic Southern belle.
A Streetcar Named Desire. 1951. Malden, Karl

Mitty, Walter.
A timid, thoroughly domesticated suburbanite daydreams that he is a man capable of heroic deeds and exciting adventures.
The Secret Life of Walter Mitty. 1947. Kaye, Danny

Moe.
Tired but sharp-tongued old woman sells ties, but is also a professional stool-pigeon so that she can make enough money to have a decent burial.
Pickup on South Street. 1953. Ritter, Thelma

Moffat, Miss.
An unmarried, intellectual middle-aged schoolteacher suppresses her deeper emotions and enthusiastically educates a promising Welsh mining boy.
The Corn is Green. 1945. Davis, Bette

Molly.
This insatiable, incorrigible slut is the cause of a big brawling fight in a churchyard in 18th-century England.
Tom Jones. 1963. Cilento, Diane

Monetti, Gino.
Papa Monetti, a prosperous, despotic Italian-American banker on New York's Lower East Side, is overbearing and unyielding to his three older boys, but spoils the youngest. When he realizes that those three have turned against him, he seeks revenge through the fourth.
House of Strangers. 1949. Robinson, Edward G.

Monster.
Bizarre, frightening, misshapen, manmade monster, unwilling to be separated from his creator, terrorizes both the community and his master.
Frankenstein. 1931. Karloff, Boris

Montana, Tony.
Ruthless, fearless, amoral Cuban gangster rises and falls in Miami's billion-dollar drug trade.
Scarface. 1983. Pacino, Al

Monteverdi, Giulio.
A charming and temperamental vocal teacher, reputedly the most talented in Italy, is determined not to mix romance with his music.
One Night of Love. 1934. Carminati, Tullio

Montgomery.
A loud-mouthed, vicious, anti-Semitic ex-sergeant murders a Jewish man in a drunken rage. When he is about to be arrested, his soldier buddies try to protect him out of pure misguided loyalty.
Crossfire. 1947. Ryan, Robert

Montour, Catherine.
Shortly before the Revolutionary War, a half-Indian woman with influence over King George III schemes to become Queen of America.
The Spirit of '76. 1917. Gleason, Adda

Moorhead, Ginny.
Pathetic small-town dance hall girl attaches herself to a returning soldier with literary aspirations.
Some Came Running. 1958. MacLaine, Shirley

More, Alice.
Sir Thomas More's stubborn, brusque but devoted wife cannot understand why her husband refuses to swear to the Act of Succession in support of Henry VIII.
A Man For All Seasons. 1966. Hiller, Wendy

More, Sir Thomas.
Learned, worldly, witty but exceptionally devout, Sir Thomas refuses to
swerve from his spiritual and intellectual convictions to condone King
Henry VIII's marriage to Anne Boleyn.
A Man For All Seasons. 1966. Scofield, Paul

Morel.
Rebellious, frustrated miner, capable of great tenderness even though he
has frequent temper flare-ups, is in constant conflict with his wife about the
proper future for their young artistic son.
Sons and Lovers. 1960. Howard, Trevor

Morgan.
During World War II, an expatriate American living in Vichy-controlled
Martinique, struggling to retain his freedom and individuality, is coerced
into rescuing a French resistance fighter by the lure of a sultry, fascinating
young woman.
To Have and Have Not. 1944. Bogart, Humphrey

Morgan.
Immature, bizarre prankster whose hero is King Kong, determined to deter
his beautiful wife from divorcing him and remarrying, flits through a series
of escapades which result in his incarceration in an insane asylum.
Morgan. 1966. Warner, David

Morgan, Angharad.
This beautiful young woman, the only daughter in a large Welsh mining
family, falls in love with the minister, but unhappily marries another man
when the pastor insists he is too poor to marry her.
How Green Was My Valley. 1941. O'Hara, Maureen

Morgan, Gwilym.
Strong but gentle Welsh miner, "dada" to his large family, quarrels with his
sons over union organization at the colliery and later dies in a cave-in.
How Green Was My Valley. 1941. Crisp, Donald

Morgan, Huw.
Young man looks back to when he was a sensitive small boy, youngest child
in a large Welsh mining family, and remembers his childhood, his first love,
and his beloved father's death in a cave-in.
How Green Was My Valley. 1941. McDowall, Roddy

Morgan, Mrs.
The cheerful, fearless, tireless mother of a large Welsh mining family sees
her loved ones through good times and bad.
How Green Was My Valley. 1941. Allgood, Sara

Morgan, Nathan Lee.
Loving, vigorous and strong, this father of a family of sharecroppers in Louisiana during the Depression is caught stealing food for his hungry children and is sentenced to a year's hard labor at a distant work camp.
Sounder. 1972. Winfield, Paul

Morgan, Pete.
A dour, crippled farmer is haunted by the horrible secret of an abandoned house set deep in the nearby woods, and tries to keep his adopted daughter away from the place.
The Red House. 1947. Robinson, Edward G.

Morgan, Rebecca.
Mother of a black family struggling for survival during the Depression in the deep South desperately fights to keep her family together and to instill in them a feeling of their own worth.
Sounder. 1972. Tyson, Cicely

Morrow, Jan.
Lonely, fashionable interior decorator cannot tolerate the songwriter with whom she shares a telephone party line, but changes her tune when they finally meet at a party.
Pillow Talk. 1959. Day, Doris

Moss, C.W.
Oafish, baby-faced hillbilly, blindly devoted to Clyde Barrow, is transported from his hometown, given a gun, and enlisted as the gang's mechanic and driver.
Bonnie and Clyde. 1967. Pollard, Michael J.

Motel.
Poor timid tailor marries the dairyman's daughter but can only promise her a life of "blissful hardship."
Fiddler on the Roof. 1971. Frey, Leonard

Mother Abbess.
Mother Abbess is sympathetic to the young postulant who cannot seem to conform to the abbey's discipline and regulations.
The Sound of Music. 1965. Wood, Peggy

Mother Emmanuel.
Powerful Mother Superior teaches the philosophy of and objectives in the life of a nun, and describes the unavoidable stresses in their training.
The Nun's Story. 1959. Evans, Edith

Mott, Ernie.
Although his wanderlust has kept him from being involved in the harsh realities of the world, this cocky, independent but lonely young man learns, through his love for his mother and his hopeless relationship with a young girl, that life is not easy, happiness is elusive, and detachment from other people is impossible.
None But the Lonely Heart. 1944. Grant, Cary

Mott, Ma.
Proprietor of a pawnshop, haggling daily with customers who are giving up their prized possessions, this sad and wonderful mother, dying of cancer, compromises her lifelong honesty for the love of her son, becomes part of a stolen goods ring and is arrested for possession of stolen property.
None But the Lonely Heart. 1944. Barrymore, Ethel

Mr. Chips, see Chipping, Arthur

Mr. Dussell, see Dussell

Mr. Hyde, see Hyde, Edward.

Mr. Roberts, see Roberts

Mr. Smith, see Smith, Jefferson

Mrs. Enders, see Enders, Mrs.

Muffley, President.
Simple, well-intentioned United States president tries his best to stop the war but is unable to lead the nation in its life-or-death crisis.
Dr. Strangelove: or, How I Learned to Stop Worrying and Love the Bomb. 1964. Sellers, Peter

Muldoon, Oscar.
Because of his whimsical interest in movies, this brassy, loud-mouthed press agent for an American multimillionaire discovers and supports a dancer in a nightclub in Madrid.
The Barefoot Contessa. 1954. O'Brien, Edmond

Muldoon, Roberta.
Former football player, a social and sexual misfit, now a transsexual, enjoys the unique position of viewing the battle of the sexes from both perspectives.
The World According to Garp. 1982. Lithgow, John

Muller, Kurt.
A quietly courageous anti-Nazi German, a leader of the underground who is worn out with fighting and suffering, comes to America with his family, but eventually returns to Europe to finish his work there.
Watch on the Rhine. 1943. Lukas, Paul

Muller, Max.
Humane sheriff wants to capture two escaped prisoners without harming them, but has to deal with racial conflict and resentment from his posse in doing so.
The Defiant Ones. 1958. Bikel, Theodore

Mulligan, Jerry.
An ex-GI-turned painter meets and woos a young French woman while studying in Paris.
An American in Paris. 1951. Kelly, Gene

Mullin, Tim.
Hard-fisted chaplain of a Barbary Coast mission makes a gambler friend see the error of his ways.
San Francisco. 1936. Tracy, Spencer

Mulwray, Evelyn.
Attractive big-time client uses a small-time detective while trying to escape her incestuous father in order to spirit her (and her father's) daughter to Mexico.
Chinatown. 1974. Dunaway, Faye

Munson, Vi.
Youthful, uninhibited, wise nurse at a VA hospital provides moral support for her patients and their loved ones as they experience the changes wrought upon them by the Vietnamese War.
Coming Home. 1978. Milford, Penelope

Murdstone.
David Copperfield's nefarious stepfather has become associated with sadistic behavior because of his cruel treatment of the sensitive boy.
David Copperfield. 1935. Rathbone, Basil

Mussabini, Sam.
This professional Turkish-Italian track coach provides the guidance and motivation that affords a Cambridge student the winning margin in the 1924 Olympics.
Chariots of Fire. 1981. Holm, Ian

Myra.
A graceful, fragile young ballet dancer falls madly in love with a British Army officer; when she thinks he has been killed in the war, she is forced by despair into a life of prostitution.
Waterloo Bridge. 1940. Leigh, Vivien

Myra.
Coercing her timid husband into helping her kidnap a child seems to be the way for this slightly seedy, middle-aged medium to gain recognition in her field, as she supplies the police and agitated parents with clues at the proper times.
Seance on a Wet Afternoon. 1964. Stanley, Kim

Nancy.
Saucy, impudent young maid, employed by a sadistic husband trying to drive his spouse insane, has a crush on her employer, and makes no effort to disguise her contempt for his wife.
Gaslight. 1944. Lansbury, Angela

Nanette.
Deeply troubled by the suffering of children during World War I, a young rural woman leaves her own child with a relative and follows her soldier husband to France as a nurse.
The Heart of Humanity. 1919. Phillips, Dorothy

Nanook.
Playing himself, this real-life Eskimo is a man of courage, strength and good humor in the face of ice and blizzards, and a master hunter whose life depends on killing walruses and seals.
Nanook of the North. 1922. Nanook

Napaloni, Benzini.
The amiable and extroverted dictator of Bacteria is a hilarious parody of Mussolini.
The Great Dictator. 1940. Oakie, Jack

Natalia.
Prim Jewish Berlin department store heiress wins the love of a young man who decides to re-embrace his deliberately concealed Jewish ancestry.
Cabaret. 1972. Berenson, Marisa

Nazerman, Sol.
Beyond pain, past caring, alienated from humanity after the loss of his family and friends in the Nazi death camps, this elderly Jewish survivor runs a pawnshop in Harlem. When his young Puerto Rican assistant sacrifices his life for him, he finally realizes that through his rejection of mankind, he has unnecessarily brought his concentration camp world with him to his new life.
The Pawnbroker. 1965. Steiger, Rod

Neary, Roy.

Power company workman in Indiana becomes alienated from his family and friends because of his obsessive preoccupation with a vision of the monolithic Devil's Tower. He finally leads the nonbelievers to the concealed landing site of the extraterrestrial.
Close Encounters of the Third Kind. 1977. Dreyfuss, Richard

Nero.

An egomaniac and a fool, the demented Nero rules the Roman Empire with wickedness and decadence mixed with cowardice.
Quo Vadis. 1951. Ustinov, Peter

Nesbit, Evelyn.

Pretty but brainless pre-World War I showgirl on the make is slipping into obscurity. She regains a degree of notoriety when her jealous husband kills her former lover, a world-renowned architect.
Ragtime. 1981. McGovern, Elizabeth

Nevins, Larry.

War-blinded veteran, frustrated by and despairing of his affliction, rather mechanically goes through the various stages of rehabilitation at the Valley Forge General Hospital in Pennsylvania. He begins to adjust only when he meets and falls in love with a young hospital volunteer.
Bright Victory. 1951. Kennedy, Arthur

Nicholson.

Seen first as a man of great dignity and resolve, this British colonel battles the Japanese over treatment of POW officers during the forced building of a bridge. He eventually becomes so obsessed with discipline that he loses all perspective and sacrifices many of his men.
The Bridge on the River Kwai. 1957. Guinness, Alec

Nick.

Physically attractive, young, innocent professor stops for drinks with his wife at an older faculty couple's home, is seduced by his hostess, exposed by his host, and enlightened as to the more complex aspects of love and marriage.
Who's Afraid of Virginia Woolf? 1966. Segal, George

Nick.

An American POW, previously a bright, sensitive young steelworker from a small Pennsylvania town, is forced to play Russian roulette by his Vietnamese captors. He is so horrified by his experience that his brain snaps and, after he escapes, he ends up in a gambling hideout, drugged and playing roulette for high stakes.
The Deer Hunter. 1978. Walken, Christopher

Nick.
Veteran, emasculated by wounds received in the Viet Nam Conflict, joins
with six of his friends at the funeral of a seventh. They commiserate about
their guilt over the loss of the ideals they espoused in the 1960s.
The Big Chill. 1983. Hurt, William

Ninotchka.
Impassive, no-nonsense Russian comrade is sent to frivolous pre-war Paris
to supervise three wayward trade emissaries who have been seduced by the
glamour of capitalist luxuries and customs. Hilariously, she herself
succumbs to these temptations via a love affair.
Ninotchka. 1939. Garbo, Greta

Nolan, Gypo.
In Dublin, a huge, brooding, slow-witted brute betrays his best friend to the
Black and Tans for 20 pounds sterling, then embarks on a drunken binge
to soothe his remorse.
The Informer. 1935. McLaglen, Victor

Nolan, Johnny.
This good-natured ne'er-do-well father of a slum family in Brooklyn's
Williamsburg district is unable to give material things to his poor household,
but bestows upon his little girl a wondrous love and affection.
A Tree Grows in Brooklyn. 1945. Dunn, James

Nordley, Linda.
Stuffy, respectably married English lady is smitten by the big-game hunter
on an African safari and is ready to walk out on her unexciting anthro-
pologist husband.
Mogambo. 1953. Kelly, Grace

Norma.
When her Chicago gangster boyfriend sends her home so that he can
pursue his sexual fantasies unhampered, this dizzy, peroxide sexpot returns
to Paris with a new hoodlum companion in tow.
Victor/Victoria. 1982. Warren, Lesley Ann

Norma Rae.
Aggressive, courageous young factory worker becomes the chief ally of an
organizer from New York as they fight for the better conditions in and the
unionization of a Southern textile mill.
Norma Rae. 1979. Field, Sally

Norris, Jody.
Impregnated by a World War I flying ace, Jody relinquishes her baby,
unselfishly worshiping him from afar until she meets him in London during
World War II, when he arrives there as a military pilot.
To Each His Own. 1946. De Havilland, Olivia

Norton, Blackie.
An arrogant nightclub proprietor and gambler has a tempestuous, doomed love affair with an opera singer. It takes an earthquake to make Blackie change his ways.
San Francisco. 1936. Gable, Clark

Nosferatu.
Living in a castle deep in the German woods, this horribly ghoulish vampire, a Dracula-like creature with a face like an emaciated rat, spends his days in a coffin and his nights sucking blood.
Nosferatu. 1922. Von Schreck, Max

Nowat, Farley.
Stubborn, plucky biologist is commissioned to collect data about wolves and their inpact on caribou herds. To the chagrin of his sponsors, Nowat reports that man is in fact the predator, and that the wolf plays the important function of selecting out the unfit caribou.
Never Cry Wolf. 1983. Smith, Charles Martin

Nubuo.
A small houseboat docks near a restaurant on the riverbank of Osaka where this active, though somewhat solitary, ten-year-old lives with his parents. Nubuo plays with the children on board, but when his friend shows him a secret game and, coincidentally, he sees their mother with a client, he is filled with inexplicable distress.
Muddy River. 1982. Asahara, Nobutaka

Nurse Alma.
In an isolated seaside house, a pretty, lonely, capable nurse cares for a famous actress who canot speak. She attempts to penetrate the silence by freely talking about herself, and as their friendship develops, there is an almost complete merging of the personalities of these two women.
Persona. 1967. Andersson, Bibi

Nurse Ratched, see Ratched, Nurse

Obi-Wan, see Kenobi, Ben

O'Day, Patricia.
A spunky, adventurous Irish lass comes to New York impersonating her dead brother so that she and her father can receive a relative's huge inheritance.
Little Old New York. 1923. Davies, Marion

O'Doul, Joan.
A confident, wisecracking Army nurse who has served in the battle for Bataan returns to the United States a weary and haunted veteran.
So Proudly We Hail. 1943. Goddard, Paulette

O'Hara.
In charge of shaping up rookies, this immaculately dressed sergeant maintains rigorous discipline by browbeating, cracking pitiless jokes and especially embarrassing shirkers, but he is always successful in turning out hardened, well-trained Marines.
Tell It to the Marines. 1926. Chaney, Lon

O'Hara, Scarlett.
This beautiful, but once-spoiled Georgia belle, mistress of Tara plantation after the Civil War, is passionately determined to survive and to keep Tara, whatever the cost.
Gone With the Wind. 1939. Leigh, Vivien

Ohlsson, Greta.
Conscientious, annoyingly good Swedish missionary-nurse is one of a dozen passengers under suspicion for murder on the Orient Express, a luxury train bound for Calais.
Murder on the Orient Express. 1974. Bergman, Ingrid

O'Houlihan, Margaret.
Pompous, inhibited but competent major in Korea is the butt of some dreadfully humiliating jokes. She is nicknamed "Hot Lips" after her seduction by a Bible-quoting fundamentalist is broadcast over the public address system.
M*A*S*H. 1970. Kellerman, Sally

O-Lan.
Once a kitchen slave, this selfless and faithful girl works with her husband in the fields, and even resorts to stealing when the ownership of their land is threatened during the Civil War in China.
The Good Earth. 1937. Rainer, Luise

Old Kate.
An old but still vital French Gypsy woman believes that her granddaughter will one day marry the King of the Gypsies.
Gypsy Passion. 1920. Rejane, Gabrielle

Old Lodge Skins.
Ancient Cheyenne chief teaches an adopted young white orphan Indian philosophy and ways of life even as he watches the virtual extinction of his tribe.
Little Big Man. 1970. George, Chief Dan

Old Man.
Weary, aging Cuban fisherman braves the rough seas alone as he fights to find, catch and bring home a big marlin.
The Old Man and the Sea. 1958. Tracy, Spencer

O'Leary, Molly.
In 1854, Molly, widow of Patrick and owner of the infamous cow that eventually kicks over the lantern which starts the Chicago fire, establishes a laundry and becomes both mother and father to her three boys, who ultimately become the political backbone of the town of Chicago.
In Old Chicago. 1938. Brady, Alice

Oliver, Mitzi.
Beautiful, flirtatious Mitzi tries to tempt a handsome Parisian doctor into an affair, even though his wife is her childhood friend.
One Hour With You. 1932. Tobin, Genevieve

Ollie, see Barrett, Oliver, IV

Oma.
Because of their common loneliness and despair, Oma, a flamboyant, drunken barfly whose black lover is currently in jail, takes up with Tully, a Skid Row bum hoping to stage a comeback in the boxing world.
Fat City. 1972. Tyrrell, Susan

O'Malley, Chuck.
A young, progressive priest is sent to the improverished parish of an elderly pastor, and in a humorous but dignified way meshes his new ideas with the older man's traditionalism.
Going My Way. 1944. Crosby, Bing

O'Malley, Father.
An easygoing, confident priest assumes a vacant pastorate, humorously spats with the beautiful nun who runs a failing parochial school, and helps her get a new school building.
The Bells of St. Mary's. 1945. Crosby, Bing

O'Neill, Eugene.
A young playwright forming the Provincetown Players has an affair with Louise Bryant, even though she is living with John Reed.
Reds. 1981. Nicholson, Jack

O'Neill, Patty.
Attractive, candid young lady, with a healthy but cautious interest in sex, stirs the passions of several gentlemen, but ultimately gets her man on her own terms.
The Moon is Blue. 1953. McNamara, Maggie

Ophelia.
This gentle, fair, and meek young girl, misguided in her relationship with Hamlet and shattered by the death of her father, becomes distracted and eventually totally mad.
Hamlet. 1948. Simmons, Jean

O'Queen, Johnny.
After committing murder for a political cause, this wounded Irish rebel, delirious and bleeding to death, desperately struggles to escape the police in the night-shrouded slums of Belfast.
Odd Man Out. 1946. Mason, James

O'Shea, Sugarpuss.
Flashy, seductive showgirl on the run from mobsters finds refuge with eight professors who are compiling a slang dictionary.
Ball of Fire. 1941. Stanwyck, Barbara

Oskar, Karl.
Tough, hard-working Swedish farmer whose land will no longer support his family, journeys to the United States and stakes his claim in Minnesota, never losing his dignity despite the hardships he and his loved ones are forced to endure.
The Emigrants. 1972. Von Sydow, Max

Othello.
Arrogant, violently jealous Moorish commander of Venetian forces, who "has lov'd not wisely but too well," is destroyed by his involvement with a society from which he stands apart.
Othello. 1965. Olivier, Laurence

Otterbourne, Salome.
Anyone on board a ship floating down the Nile could have murdered an arrogant millionairess, even this overdone, alcoholic vamp, a trashy novelist by trade.
Death on the Nile. 1978. Lansbury, Angela

Pablo.
A murderous, drunken, cruel and treacherous peasant guerrilla fights the Fascists from the hills of Spain during the Civil War.
For Whom the Bell Tolls. 1943. Tamiroff, Akim

Packard, Sarah.
Both a physical and a psychic cripple, this confused, hard-drinking woman has a relationship with a pool hustler which ends in tragedy.
The Hustler. 1961. Laurie, Piper

Page, Norman.
This shy young man is completely dominated by his possessive mother.
Peyton Place. 1957. Tamblyn, Russ

Paine, Joseph.
The senior senator from Wisconsin has a bill in the hopper to give the state a new dam, which will pay him rich real-estate profits.
Mr. Smith Goes to Washington. 1939. Rains, Claude

Paleologus, Faith.
In 1775, this shrewd and jealous woman is the housekeeper of a local leghorn merchant and the mistress of a middle-aged nobleman.
Anthony Adverse. 1936. Sondergaard, Gale

Pancho.
A happy-go-lucky carousel proprietor in a busy New Mexico resort town becomes involved with a bungling amateur blackmailer.
Ride the Pink Horse. 1947. Gomez, Thomas

Paoli, Marianna.
This Corsican girl seeks revenge on the unknown Englishman who killed her brother, but later discovers that the man she loves is the very one she has vowed to kill.
Vendetta. 1921. Negri, Pola

Papa Monetti, see Monetti, Gino

Paradine, Maddelena.
A heartless, contemptuous woman murders her blind husband and is brought to court, where her mystery and passion have a fascinating hold over both the judge and the young lawyer who represents her.
The Paradine Case. 1948. Valli, Alida

Parke, Godfrey.
Unflappable, downtrodden ex-Harvard man is picked up in a shack colony for the unemployed near the East River by two bored millionaires on a scavenger hunt. He becomes their butler and ultimately straightens out the lives of their entire family.
My Man Godfrey. 1936. Powell, William

Parker, Bonnie.
Thrill-seeking, sex-starved moll joins Clyde Barrow, and, although she finds him impotent, sticks with him as they pillage and terrorize small-town banks in Texas and Oklahoma in the early 1930s.
Bonnie and Clyde. 1967. Dunaway, Faye

Parkington, Susie.
Poor girl from a wretched frontier silver town marries a mining millionaire and has her ups and downs with him when they come to New York and become part of the social set.
Mrs. Parkington. 1944. Garson, Greer

Parmalee, Hannah.
A mother discovers her son after years of separation, helps him to establish proper values and become a useful member of society, and then leaves without revealing their relationship.
White Banners. 1938. Bainter, Fay

Paroo, Marian.
Man-shy "Marian the Librarian" comes to love and eventually to reform the silver-tongued con man in town to peddle musical instruments.
The Music Man. 1962. Jones, Shirley

Parrish, Homer.
A sailor who has lost both hands in World War II, returning home tense and anxious, must adjust not only to his mechanical "hands" but to his well-intentioned loved ones.
The Best Years of Our Lives. 1946. Russell, Harold

Pascal.
A French peasant, father of six motherless daughters, is outraged when one girl becomes pregnant; but after he visits the boy's parents and a marriage is planned, he feels that the dignity and honor of the family are restored.
The Well-Digger's Daughter. 1946. Raimu

Passepartout.
Absurd, ingenious servant accompanies his employer in an around-the-world jaunt.
Around the World in Eighty Days. 1956. Cantinflas

Pasteur, Louis.
Eminent French scientist, discoverer of anthrax vaccine and a cure for rabies, is a model of scientific detachment, a modest, sensitive and courageous man.
The Story of Louis Pasteur. 1936. Muni, Paul

Pastor.
A Swiss pastor takes a poor blind girl under his wing, but his attachment to her grows into an unconsciously selfish passion which destroys his household.
Symphonie Pastorale. 1947. Blanchar, Pierre

Patent Leather Kid.

Known as the Patent Leather Kid because of his smooth black hair, this cocky young boxer from New York's Lower East Side can stand up to anyone in the ring, but learns true courage as a doughboy in World War I.
The Patent Leather Kid. 1927. Barthelmess, Richard

Patton, George S., Jr.

Flamboyant, brilliant, self-confident general loves combat, writes poetry, quotes the Bible, and believes in reincarnation and predestination. A commander of the American forces in Europe and North Africa during World War II, he suffers great mental anguish upon being nationally disgraced for slapping a battle-fatigued GI.
Patton: A Salute to a Rebel. 1970. Scott, George C.

Patucci, Tony.

A good-natured and generous Italian-American grape grower finds a fiancee by correspondence, suffers quietly when he learns she has become pregnant by his foreman, but wants to marry her anyway.
They Knew What They Wanted. 1940. Laughton, Charles

Paul.

After his wife commits suicide, a middle-aged man living in Paris encounters a French girl who agrees to meet him at an apartment and have sex without knowing anything about each other. After three days of a purely physical affair, he demands a fuller relationship, only to be rebuffed.
Last Tango in Paris. 1973. Brando, Marlon

Paul I.

Sadistic, cowardly, lecherous and mad czar, ruler of Russia in 1801, is surrounded by murderous plots and is in constant fear of death. The only man he trusts is Count Phalen, the man who becomes his assassin.
The Patriot. 1928. Jannings, Emil

Paul, Maggie.

Wayward Seattle pool hustler meets and marries a sailor on liberty and is delivered from some of her more sordid habits by her new husband, who even plays surrogate father to her 11-year-old son.
Cinderella Liberty. 1973. Mason, Marsha

Paula.

Patient and loyal chorus girl marries a war victim, an amnesiac. He forgets her when his memory returns, and she becomes a secretary in his family's household so that she can help him remember their life together.
Random Harvest. 1942. Garson, Greer

Paulie.
A beer-guzzling meat packer becomes more interested in a young boxer's future when his sister and the prizefighter become emotionally involved.
Rocky. 1976. Young, Burt

Pearl.
With her decent, uncomplicated ideas of right and wrong and her dedicated belief in security and happiness, this plump, healthy, extroverted widow is completely different from the family of the man she is about to marry.
Interiors. 1978. Stapleton, Maureen

Pearson, Bruce.
Amiable but dumb, bumbling catcher for the New York Mammoths is the butt of the baseball players' jokes. When his teammates discover that he is dying from Hodgkins disease, he suddenly becomes accepted and an object of sympathy.
Bang the Drum Slowly. 1973. De Niro, Robert

Peggotty, Dan.
A kind-hearted Yarmouth fisherman makes himself the protector of his niece and nephew and of the widow of his former partner.
David Copperfield. 1935. Barrymore, Lionel

Pelliker, Dolly.
This willowy rustic lesbian, without imagination or many deep convictions, shares a run-down farmhouse with a cowgirl beautician and Karen Silkwood and her boyfriend. She has an intense argument with Karen, which ultimately leads to a touching reconciliation.
Silkwood. 1983. Cher

Pendlebury.
Genteel sculptor and paperweight manufacturer becomes a principal accomplice in a bank robbery in England, but loses his confidence when events don't go quite as planned.
Lavender Hill Mob. 1951. Holloway, Stanley

Pendleton, Joe.
Prizefighter dies by mistake before his time; when his body is cremated, he enlists the aid of an archangel to find another body for him so he can fight for the championship.
Here Comes Mr. Jordan. 1941. Montgomery, Robert

Pendleton, Joe.
Football quarterback involved in an automobile accident is declared dead, contrary to heaven's master plan. He is required to return to earth first in the body of a powerful industrialist, and subsequently as a football player, in which guise he helps his old coach to win a championship.
Heaven Can Wait. 1978. Beatty, Warren

Pennington, Doris.
When this very sane young woman is sent to a sanitarium by her greedy aunt, she comically turns the tables on everyone by convincing them that her nurse is the patient and that she is the nurse.
Turning the Tables. 1919. Gish, Dorothy

Penny.
Penny is the youngest of three teen-agers who rescue their father from the clutches of a gold digger and return him to the arms of his wife, whom he left ten years before.
Three Smart Girls. 1937. Durbin, Deanna

Pentangeli, Frankie.
This old-timer in the rackets, resistant to change because he has had an enjoyable life, informs on the family when he sees that things will not be the same as they were in Don Vito's heyday.
The Godfather, Part II. 1974. Gazzo, Michael V.

Pepe Le Moko, see Le Moko, Pepe

Peppina.
Kidnapped when she was a baby and reared by a poor Italian family, this lovely and sensitive teen-ager escapes an arranged marriage by masquerading as a boy and stowing away to America, where she is reunited with her real parents.
Poor Little Peppina. 1916. Pickford, Mary

Pete.
While trying to mask his sexual preference and his reluctance to associate with girls, Pete retreats into loneliness when his motorcycle buddy finds out he's a homosexual, and breaks up their friendship.
The Leather Boys. 1964. Sutton, Dudley

Peter.
The moody Russian Czar, known as Peter the Great, becomes aware of a plot to oust him and to put his dimwitted son Alexis on the throne. Feigning death, the furiously angry Peter later appears at Alexis' "coronation," reveals the conspiracy, and kills his son.
Peter the Great. 1922. Jannings, Emil

Peter Pan.
A delightful and agile fantasy boy, accompanied by his tiny fairy Tinker Bell, teaches the Darling children how to fly and takes them to his home in Never Never Land where no one has to grow up.
Peter Pan. 1924. Bronson, Betty

Petersen, Rudolf.
Unbalanced German witness testifies concerning his sterilization, done on the order of one of the Nazi judges now on trial.
Judgment at Nuremburg. 1961. Clift, Montgomery

Peterson, Constance.
A woman psychiatrist falls in love with one of her patients, an amnesiac, and proves him to be innocent of a suspected homicide.
Spellbound. 1945. Bergman, Ingrid

Petronius.
A member of Nero's court, suave, cynical Petronius constantly derides the stupid Emperor, and has a tragic romance with a slave girl.
Quo Vadis. 1951. Genn, Leo

Peyramale.
The reserved and practical dean of the Catholic Church at Lourdes first rejects but then becomes the most passionate defender of a young peasant girl who says she has seen a vision of the Virgin Mary.
The Song of Bernadette. 1943. Bickford, Charles

Phalen.
Because of his unswerving love and loyalty for Russia, Count Phalen, chief adviser and trusted friend of Paul I, betrays the mad czar by heading a conspiracy to kill him.
The Patriot. 1928. Stone, Lewis

Phantom of the Opera.
Feared by all but actually seen by only a few who have fled in terror, this masked creature who haunts the Paris Opera kidnaps one of the young singers and brings her to his subterranean abode.
The Phantom of the Opera. 1925. Chaney, Lon
The Phantom of the Opera. 1943. Rains, Claude

Phelps, Margaret.
A divorced parent herself, this warm, friendly, concerned friend of a separated pair has long talks about life and love with the husband, and suggests the possibility of a reconciliation at the custody hearing.
Kramer vs. Kramer. 1979. Alexander, Jane

Phillips, Helen.
Young, virtuous widow falls in love with the millionaire rake who was indirectly responsible for both her blindness and the loss of her husband.
Magnificent Obsession. 1954. Wyman, Jane

Pied Piper, see Howard

Pierce, Mildred.
During her rise from poverty to affluence, this suffering wife and mother, courageous though frequently mistaken, makes enormous, unrewarded sacrifices for her spoiled, greedy daughter.
Mildred Pierce. 1945. Crawford, Joan

Pierce, Veda.
Selfish, grasping daughter breaks her mother's heart as she makes love to her second husband, and eventually goes to prison for murder.
Mildred Pierce. 1945. Blyth, Ann

Pilar.
Forceful, strong-willed peasant woman leads a band of guerrilla fighters in the hills of Spain during the Civil War.
For Whom the Bell Tolls. 1943. Paxinou, Katina

Pina.
A strong and sincere woman working for the underground resistance in German-occupied Rome is killed during a raid on her apartment.
Open City. 1944. Magnani, Anna

Pine, Hugo.
Handsome, self-assured doctor of psychology helps a city editor win a journalism teacher's affections.
Teacher's Pet. 1958. Young, Gig

Pinky.
After returning to her childhood home in Mississippi, this light-complexioned black nurse feels the bitter sting of segregation and prejudice, but finds purpose in her life when she opens a school and nursing home on an estate which she inherits.
Pinky. 1949. Crain, Jeanne

Pinky Rose.
New staffer at the Palm Springs Spa idolizes another therapist, comes to be her roommate and finally takes over her life.
Three Women. 1977. Spacek, Sissy

Pirate.
A crazy, canine-loving tramp saves enough "two-bitses" to buy a gold candlestick for St. Francis, whom he credits with having saved the life of one of his dogs.
Tortilla Flat. 1942. Morgan, Frank

Place, Etta.
Understanding schoolteacher, a friend of Butch Cassidy and mistress of the Sundance Kid, is a complete woman who can cook, clean house, and shoot a gun when necessary. Together with her friends, she leaves the American West to start a new life in Bolivia, but tiring of the bandit life, she abandons them.
Butch Cassidy and the Sundance Kid. 1969. Ross, Katherine

Plato.
Shy, thoroughly lost teen-ager, unable to relate to his mother and dad, substitutes friendships with unhappy peers and comes to a tragic end.
Rebel Without a Cause. 1955. Mineo, Sal

Plimsoll, Miss.
Irritating, henpecking but loyal nurse tries to keep her patient, a British attorney recovering from a coronary, away from brandy, cigars, and participation in murder trials.
Witness for the Prosecution. 1957. Lanchester, Elsa

Po-Han.
On a gunboat patrolling the Yangtze River in 1926, this coolie member of the "black gang," the engine room crew, is cruelly sacrificed and suffers a brutal beating before the entire ship's company during one of the many local riots.
The Sand Pebbles. 1966. Mako

Poiccard, Michel.
Self-centered, sharp-witted, amoral young French hoodlum steals a car and quite casually kills a highway patrolman. He wants his girl friend to continue their one-sided love affair, but she betrays him and he is shot down, still not caring for anything or anybody.
Breathless. 1961. Belmondo, Jean-Paul

Poirot, Hercule.
The renowned, unflappable Belgian sleuth solves the murder of a passenger in the next compartment on a luxury express train traveling from Istanbul to Calais.
Murder on the Orient Express. 1974. Finney, Albert

Pokrifki, Paula.
Concerned that her job at the local paper mill is all that life will offer, this spunky, seductive, strong-willed girl hopes that a naval officer from the nearby flight officers' school will rescue her from a future of drudgery.
An Officer and a Gentleman. 1982. Winger, Debra

Pollock.

At a British seaside boarding house, this pitiable, blustering retired major brags about his Sandhurst background and World War II conquests, but ultimately turns out to be a fraud.
Separate Tables. 1958. Niven, David

Pollyanna.

This poor little orphan girl comes to live with her cross, domineering aunt, bringing with her the "glad" game, the object of which is to "find the silver lining in every dark cloud." Her cheerfulness and unshakeable optimism soon rub off on all those around her, including Aunt Polly.
Pollyanna. 1920. Pickford, Mary
Pollyanna. 1960. Mills, Hayley

Pookie.

Outrageous, love-starved, sad young woman relentlessly pursues an undergraduate entomologist, eventually wins his affection, but scares him away after they have a brief affair.
The Sterile Cuckoo. 1969. Minnelli, Liza

Pope, Johnny.

Young married man becomes addicted to drugs when he is hospitalized after fighting in Korea. His loved ones, ignorant of the problem, are bewildered and hurt by his eccentricities.
Hatful of Rain. 1957. Murray, Don

Popeye, see Doyle, Jimmy

Popper, Ruth.

In a small Texas town in the early 1950s, an unhappy middle-aged high-school football coach's wife has a short affair with the co-captain of the football team.
The Last Picture Show. 1971. Leachman, Cloris

Poppins, Mary.

In Edwardian England, a strict but wonderful English nanny with magical powers arrives on the East Wind to care for two London children and to take them on exciting adventures.
Mary Poppins. 1964. Andrews, Julie

Porter, Connie.

One of nine people in a lifeboat adrift from a torpedoed ship, this shrewd, cynical, materialistic journalist is stripped of her material possessions. With the boat under the forced command of a Nazi submariner, she proves to be a woman of substance and strength.
Lifeboat. 1944. Bankhead, Tallulah

Potter, Jessica.
Rich, chic young wife sends her husband away so that she can become
independent and make a career of singing and songwriting. She realizes
later that she may have acted too quickly.
Starting Over. 1979. Bergen, Candice

Potts, Miss.
Miss Potts, a scatterbrained painter of religious pictures, opens her home to
two French nuns who are trying to establish a children's hospital.
Come to the Stable. 1949. Lanchester, Elsa

Powell, John.
Thinking that his buddy has been killed in their fighter plane, this brave
World War I flier soars through the air seeking revenge on the Germans,
killing them in the sky and on the road, setting fires, and scattering troops.
Wings. 1927. Rogers, Charles

Prager, George.
Arrogant writer, fearful of serious relationships, aggressively propositions a
bored housewife. He so reminds her of her own insensitive and abusive
husband that their affair is short-lived.
Diary of a Mad Housewife. 1970. Langella, Frank

Prentice, John.
Charming, distinguished black scientist falls in love with a wealthy white
girl, but their plans to marry are not graciously received by either set of
parents.
Guess Who's Coming to Dinner. 1967. Poitier, Sidney

Prentice, Mrs.
Dignified black mother is faced with the true test of her beliefs when her
son decides to marry a white girl.
Guess Who's Coming to Dinner. 1967. Richards, Beah

Prewitt, Robert E. Lee.
Prew, a hardheaded youthful Kentucky soldier assigned to Schofield
Barracks in pre-World War II Hawaii, has such strong convictions that he
refuses to box as ordered, despite the knowledge that he will be persecuted
and probably "busted" by his captain.
From Here to Eternity. 1953. Clift, Montgomery

Price, Russel.
This stocky, thick-voiced, wary photographer, on assignment in Nicaragua,
views a succession of mean little moneymakers through his lens. Although
attempting to remain objective, he eventually loses patience with the
stupidity and decadence of the government officials, and joins the
Sandinista rebels.
Under Fire. 1983. Nolte, Nick

Prissy.
Called on to help deliver Melanie's child, this frightened young maid confesses that she knows "nothin' about birthin' no babies."
Gone With the Wind. 1939. McQueen, Butterfly

Prospector, see Lone Prospector

Prunella.
A young girl, sheltered by three maiden aunts, is charmed by a traveling mummer and becomes a member of his troupe.
Prunella. 1918. Clark, Marguerite

Prynne, Hester.
A delicate and passionate young woman in Puritan New England bears an illegitimate child and must struggle against the hateful bigotry of the townspeople, who label her an adulteress and force her to wear the letter "A."
The Scarlet Letter. 1926. Gish, Lillian

Pullman, Bea.
A young resourceful widow becomes a successful businesswoman only to find disappointment in her personal relationships.
Imitation of Life. 1934. Colbert, Claudette

Pulver.
Bumbling, amorous ensign, the "laundry and morale" officer on board a Navy cargo ship during World War II, rebelliously destroys the ship's laundry with a homemade giant firecracker.
Mister Roberts. 1955. Lemmon, Jack

Pupkin, Rupert.
Neat, agreeable young man, obsessed with fame, builds a fantasy in which he is as big a star as his idol, a popular TV host. When this star refuses to let Rupert perform on his show, Rupert kidnaps him and holds him for a ransom: a guest appearance on the program.
The King of Comedy. 1983. De Niro, Robert

Puzzlehead, see Sabre, Mark

Pyle, Ernie.
This journalist and unobtrusive observer records the hardships of the ordinary infantry soldier in World War II and is beloved by many GIs for his humility, and the respect he showed for them.
Story of G.I. Joe. 1945. Meredith, Burgess

Quartermain, Allan.
Capable guide and hunter leads a safari into the African veld to rescue a missing explorer lost while searching for the fabulous legendary diamond mines of King Solomon.
King Solomon's Mines. 1950. Granger, Stewart

Quasimodo.
Repellent, imbecilic Quasimodo, with a grotesque humpback, is the bellringer for Notre Dame cathedral. When he saves a Gypsy girl from the hangman and defends the church against an attacking mob, he shows that his exterior ugliness has been masking a warm and gentle soul.
The Hunchback of Notre Dame. 1923. Chaney, Lon
Hunchback of Notre Dame. 1939. Laughton, Charles

Queeg.
Neurotic, disciplinarian captain in the Pacific during World War II, cowering under a hard-boiled veneer, antagonizes all his officers, appears to crack under strain of command, and is finally destroyed while acting as a witness during a court martial.
The Caine Mutiny. 1954. Bogart, Humphrey

Queen Dowager.
Hard-of-hearing, this fuzzy Queen Dowager from a Balkan country comes to London to attend the coronation ceremony of King George V.
The Prince and the Showgirl. 1957. Thorndike, Sybil

Queen, Ellery.
Ellery Queen, author and sleuth, assistant-without-portfolio to his inspector father, manages, as always, to analyze the many motives and clues and to solve the mystery.
Ellery Queen, Master Detective. 1940. Bellamy, Ralph

Quint.
Crusty, cross, malevolent old shark hunter is hired to locate a killer shark lurking near a seaside resort. When he turns the pursuit into a personal vendetta and compounds the danger, he himself becomes the next victim.
Jaws. 1975. Shaw, Robert

Quirt.
This fearless Marine sergeant who has a way with women tangles with his hard-living captain over the affections of a French barkeeper's daughter, but on the battlefield is his loyal buddy and comrade-in-arms.
What Price Glory? 1926. Lowe, Edmund

Quonsett, Ada.
In the worst blizzard of the year, on a plane bound for Rome, this charming, perky, little old lady stowaway, who likes to visit her daughter without having to pay, helps to disarm a psychotic man with a homemade bomb in his briefcase.
Airport. 1970. Hayes, Helen

Rachel, see Cameron, Rachel

Radovich, Irving.
Bewildered, breezy photographer, sidekick of an American reporter in Rome, surreptitiously snaps an unsuspecting princess on holiday away from her dull court routine.
Roman Holiday. 1953. Albert, Eddie

Rafferty, Mary.
In 1873, this pretty young girl becomes the maid in the home of a Pittsburgh steel magnate, serves the household devotedly, marries one of the sons, and nobly brings her influence to bear on the next generation.
The Valley of Decision. 1945. Garson, Greer

Railton-Bell, Sibyl.
This sad, shy young woman, cursed with a cruel and possessive mother, becomes attracted to an ex-major while visiting a British seaside resort.
Separate Tables. 1958. Kerr, Deborah

Rainier, Charles.
A British war victim, an amnesiac known as "Smithy," marries and has an idyllic life, until an accident restores his memory. He leaves his wife and returns to his aristocratic family.
Random Harvest. 1942. Colman, Ronald

Rajah of Rukh.
A Hindu potentate schooled at Oxford, refined, monocled and satin-robed, holds a grudge against the British, and detains three of them as prisoners when their plane crashes in his kingdom.
The Green Goddess. (Silent version). 1923. Arliss, George
The Green Goddess. 1930. Arliss, George

Ralfe, Gordon.
A black man befriends a white girl whom he accidently meets in the park, gives her some assurance and self-respect, and arranges to send her away to school. However, his plans are thwarted by her slatternly mother.
A Patch of Blue. 1965. Poitier, Sidney

Ramirez, Helen.
Ex-girl friend of the sheriff in a small Western town urges him to leave with his new bride before a revengeful killer arrives.
High Noon. 1952. Jurado, Katy

Rand, Benjamin.
Rugged though dying financier and important politician, impressed by an innocent gardener's simplicity and seemingly wise aphorisms, makes him a trusted confidante.
Being There. 1979. Douglas, Melvyn

Randall, Aloysius.
Known as "Smacksie," this hard-bitten, defiant, and gallant Marine dies with his comrades in a desperate attempt to defend Wake Island from the Japanese.
Wake Island. 1942. Bendix, William

Randall, Terry.
Wealthy, arrogant Terry becomes a good performer by discovering her own deep feelings after she hears of the suicide of another hopeful young actress.
Stage Door. 1937. Hepburn, Katharine

Ratched, Nurse.
Vicious, oppressive nurse in a mental hospital, particularly hostile to men, resorts to psychological coercion, shock treatment, and even lobotomy to extend her power and to reinforce her authority.
One Flew Over the Cuckoo's Nest. 1975. Fletcher, Louise

Ratso, see Rizzo, Ratso

Raymond's Mother.
Ruthless, possessive, scheming, mother of a prisoner of war in Korea who has returned to the U.S. conditioned to carry out a series of assassinations, she manipulates him for her own purposes while also managing her rabid, red-baiting Senator husband.
Manchurian Candidate. 1962. Lansbury, Angela

Redmond, Barry, see Lyndon, Barry

Reed, John.
Flamboyant, radical American journalist takes part in the Russian Revolution and writes *Ten Days That Shook the World.* His dedication to social change leads him to commit himself totally to the new worldwide Communist movement.
Reds. 1981. Beatty, Warren

Reenie.
In a small Oklahoma town in the 1920s, a young girl, surrounded by a family beset by internal conflicts, begins to grow, develop, and find love.
The Dark at the Top of the Stairs. 1960. Knight, Shirley

Reese, Linnea.
Discontented gospel-singing wife and mother of two deaf children, fully aware of what she is doing, has a one-night affair with a singing star.
Nashville. 1975. Tomlin, Lily

Regan.
Once a sparkling, bright attractive youngster, this 12-year-old girl, possessed by the devil, becomes foul-mouthed, sex-obsessed and more physically repulsive each day.
The Exorcist. 1973. Blair, Linda

Regis.
Fat Regis, trying to avoid being killed by the police, tells them where the famous criminal, Pepe Le Moko, is hiding.
Algiers. 1938. Lockhart, Gene

Reisman, Major.
Tough Army major whips 12 convicted GIs, each a murderer, rapist or a thief, into an efficient fighting team assigned to wage guerrilla warfare behind enemy lines.
The Dirty Dozen. 1967. Marvin, Lee

Reles, Abe.
Brutal, professional hit man uses terrorist tactics and performs assassinations for Louie (Lepke) Buchalter's Brooklyn mob.
Murder, Inc. 1960. Falk, Peter

Renault, Louis.
An amoral and opportunistic French police captain in Casablanca during World War II is coerced into aiding the Nazis. He appears to cooperate until an opportunity arises to leave Casablanca.
Casablanca. 1942. Rains, Claude

Reynolds, Lillian.
Flinty, dedicated, chain-smoking career scientist dons a multisensory headset while in the throes of a heart attack and tape records all the sensations, so that others may profit from her experiences.
Brainstorm. 1983. Fletcher, Louise

Rhoda.
Innocent-looking but psychopathic eight-year-old maliciously kills three people, including one of her classmates.
The Bad Seed. 1956. McCormack, Patty

Rhoda.
Lonely, plain and plump teen-ager, anxious to make friends, is drawn to three pretty, more emancipated adolescents who alternately tease, taunt, and befriend, and ultimately destroy her.
Last Summer. 1969. Burns, Cathy

Rice, Archie.
Hollow, egotistical third-rate comedian at a small seaside resort in England has major expectations for his career but minor talent to achieve them.
The Entertainer. 1960. Olivier, Laurence

Richard III.
Dark, misshapen monster, twisted in mind and body, responsible for devious dealings and murders at court, seizes the throne and pursues bloody conquests on the battlefield.
Richard III. 1956. Olivier, Laurence

Richards, Julie Cullen.
Anguished, helpless, white divorcee, because of her marriage to a black man, loses custody of her daughter to her former errant, unstable husband, who objects to the child being brought up in a predominantly black household.
One Potato, Two Potato. 1964. Barrie, Barbara

Richardson, Robert.
With patience and understanding this modest young doctor in a Nova Scotia village helps an abused deaf-mute girl with an illegitimate child.
Johnny Belinda. 1948. Ayres, Lew

Ridgefield, John.
Sober, businesslike famous designer of planes keeps his inner tensions under control as he appears totally absorbed in and devoted to his experimentation with aircraft and the challenges of space.
Breaking Through the Sound Barrier. 1952. Richardson, Ralph

Riedenschneider, Erwin.
Doc is an evil, criminal mastermind with a lecherous eye for young ladies. With a motley group of crooks, he plots and nearly executes a brilliant multimillion-dollar jewel caper.
Asphalt Jungle. 1950. Jaffe, Sam

Rinaldi, Allesandro.
This major on the Italian Front in World War I helps to reunite his two wartime friends, a nurse and an ambulance driver.
A Farewell to Arms. 1932. Menjou, Adolphe
A Farewell to Arms. 1957. De Sica, Vittorio

Ringo, Jimmy.
A famous but broody and lonely gunman wants to hang up his sixguns and return to his wife and child. He is, however, constantly beset by vengeful kin of past victims and young punks eager to make their reputations on his dead body.
The Gunfighter. 1950. Peck, Gregory

Ringo Kid.
This outlaw intends to avenge the murder of his father and brother when the stagecoach on which he is traveling arrives at Lordsburg. But first he, a sympathetic marshall and seven others must make it through Indian country.
Stagecoach. 1939. Wayne, John

Rink, Jett.
Poor but arrogant Texas ranch hand, disliked and mistrusted by most who know him, strikes oil on a small piece of inherited land, becomes one of the richest and most powerful men in the state, but never gets over his unrequited love for his exemployer's wife.
Giant. 1956. Dean, James

Ripper, General Jack D.
Paranoid, cigar-chomping American Air Force general goes berserk and declares his own war against the strength-sapping menaces of sex, fluoridation and communism when he launches a nuclear attack on Russia.
Dr. Strangelove: or, How I Learned to Stop Worrying and Love the Bomb. 1964. Hayden, Sterling

Rita.
Uninhibited, lower-class, 26-year-old hairdresser, dissatisfied with her lot in life, craves formal education and enrolls in a tutorial program in literature at a British university. She tones down her clothes, hairdo and slang vocabulary as her studies progress, but never loses her infectious spirit and enthusiasm.
Educating Rita. 1983. Walters, Julie

Rita's Mother.
Querulous, impatient, argumentative mother, who passed on her quality of lovelessness to her well-off Manhattan daughter, offers these last words on her deathbed: "cancel my appointments."
Summer Wishes, Winter Dreams. 1973. Sidney, Sylvia

Rizzo, Ratso.
Ratso, a tubercular, crippled, unshaven, dirty, conniving con man, a loser in New York City, befriends a lonely Texas cowboy, and almost realizes his dream of living the posh life in Miami.
Midnight Cowboy. 1969. Hoffman, Dustin

Robarts, Sir Wilfrid.
Defense attorney for an Englishman accused of murdering a widow bullies, cajoles, and uses all his courtroom tricks to destroy the testimony of the opposition.
Witness for the Prosecution. 1957. Laughton, Charles

Roberts.
Although this modest, quietly strong Navy lieutenant is the chief support of the crew against the stupidity and tyranny of the captain, he is frustrated by the petty boredom of life on a cargo ship. He desperately wants to be transferred to a fighting vessel in order to contribute to victory.
Mister Roberts. 1955. Fonda, Henry

Robin Hood.
The dashing, gallant swashbuckler of Sherwood Forest, as quick to frolic as he is to fight, exploits his enemies and graciously pays court to Maid Marian.
The Adventures of Robin Hood. 1938. Flynn, Errol

Robin, Jack.
The former Jakie Rabinowitz, a cantor's son, breaks with family tradition and becomes a jazz singer.
The Jazz Singer. 1927. Jolson, Al

Robinson, Elaine.
Beautiful college senior, home on vacation from Berkeley, must adjust to the shocking fact that the young graduate she has just started to date has had an affair with her mother.
The Graduate. 1967. Ross, Katherine

Robinson, Mrs.
This sophisticated older woman, selfish and unhappy in her marriage, deliberately seduces the son of close friends. When he later falls in love with her daughter, she does everything she can to prevent him from seeing her.
The Graduate. 1967. Bancroft, Anne

Rocco, Johnny.
Run out of the country but now living on a Florida key, this vulgar and egotistical gangster waits for the day when he will make a vicious comeback.
Key Largo. 1948. Robinson, Edward G.

Rochester, Edward.
This moody, arrogant man is tormented by the secret of his insane wife whom he has locked away in his gloomy Victorian mansion.
Jane Eyre. 1944. Welles, Orson

Rocky.
Seedy, crude, cynical, overage promoter and master of ceremonies urges his contestants on to further acts of self-destruction in one of the infamous dance marathons of the Depression years.
They Shoot Horses, Don't They? 1969. Young, Gig

Rocky.
Lonely, simple, second-rate professional boxer renews his own self-respect and the support of his girl when he is given the chance to fight the heavyweight champion of the world.
Rocky. 1976. Stallone, Sylvester

Rodolphe.
This poor young writer living in the bohemian Latin Quarter of Paris is madly in love with a tragically ill young seamstress who becomes his inspiration; but he is a jealous man who wrongly suspects her of infidelity.
La Boheme. 1926. Gilbert, John

Roeder, Paul.
A comfortable, middle-class German helps out his old friend, an anti-Nazi who is on the run, despite the peril to himself and his family.
The Seventh Cross. 1944. Cronyn, Hume

Rolfe, Hans.
Masterful, proud German defense attorney provides an eloquent defense during the 1948 trial of Nazi leaders accused by the Allies of terrible crimes against humanity.
Judgment at Nuremburg. 1961. Schell, Maximilian

Rolls Royce.
An alcoholic ex-lawyer is grateful to a fearless burglar who once gave him some money. When this burglar commits murder and is wanted by the police, he remains loyal to him and tries to help him escape.
Underworld. 1927. Brook, Clive

Roman, Dan.
Still haunted by the death of his wife and young son in a plane crash, this veteran copilot nevertheless keeps his cool and courage on a crippled airliner, and makes the right decision when the pilot loses control.
The High and the Mighty. 1954. Wayne, John

Romeo.
Heir of the Montagues attends a ball given by Lord Capulet, a bitter enemy
of his family, and falls in love with Juliet.
Romeo and Juliet. 1936. Howard, Leslie
Romeo and Juliet. 1954. Harvey, Laurence
Romeo and Juliet. 1968. Whiting, Leonard

Romoff, Panthea.
A young Russian musician, married to a despairing English composer,
agrees to become the mistress of an unscrupulous baron who is in a position
to help her husband.
Panthea. 1917. Talmadge, Norma

Romola.
This pretty maiden of Florence, a faithful and loving daughter of a blind
scholar, is betrayed by her scoundrel husband.
Romola. 1924. Gish, Lillian

Roosevelt, Eleanor.
While tenderly nursing her polio-stricken husband and giving love and
understanding to her five growing children, this once-shy and introspective
wife and mother emerges as a distinctive, humane, and politically conscious
woman.
Sunrise at Campobello. 1960. Garson, Greer

Roosevelt, Franklin D.
Warm, vibrant, energetic man, stricken with polio as he enters politics in the
prime of his life, is determined to triumph over his problems.
Sunrise at Campobello. 1960. Bellamy, Ralph

Rose.
In a role based on the late Janis Joplin, this spoiled, willful, rock'n'roll
singer tries to reach her emotional limits through song and burns herself
out on alcohol, drugs, and the stresses of stardom.
The Rose. 1979. Midler, Bette

Rosemary, see Woodhouse, Rosemary

Rosen, Lillian.
Before World War II, on a ship carrying Jews from Hamburg, Germany, to
Havana, Cuba, this worried wife tries to control her melancholic husband
who "is retreating into himself."
Voyage of the Damned. 1976. Grant, Lee

Rosenberg, Eva.
This concert violinist not only has her desire to have a child destroyed, but also finds her entire life shattered, when the civil war that is ravaging the mainland engulfs the remote island where she and her husband live.
Shame. 1968. Ullman, Liv

Rosita.
This lively and beautiful girl sings to the accompaniment of her guitar and completely enthralls King Carlos of Spain. He brings her to his palace to live, though she is really in love with a young man in prison.
Rosita. 1923. Pickford, Mary

Ross, Mattie.
Shrewd and plucky 14-year-old vows to avenge her father's murder and hires a gruff one-eyed Federal marshall to help her.
True Grit. 1969. Darby, Kim

Ross, Mrs.
Lonely, frightened 72-year-old woman, living alone in a tumble-down tenement, communicates with imaginary voices, complains to the police about conspiracies that never materialize, and assures the welfare people that she will soon become wealthy and no longer need them.
The Whisperers. 1967. Evans, Edith

Rosy.
Appealing Irish girl, daughter of Kirrary's publican, marries a widowed schoolteacher twice her age, has a rapturous affair with the lame commander of the British occupation forces in her town, and is punished by the villagers.
Ryan's Daughter. 1970. Miles, Sarah

Roth, Hyman.
Powerful, aging, businessman-gangster, said to be modeled on Meyer Lansky, is a partner of the Mafia as they try, with Battista's cooperation, to open Havana for gambling.
The Godfather, Part II. 1974. Strasberg, Lee

Roth, Lillian.
Lillian rises to fame as a singer-actress, becomes an alcoholic, and through the help of an Alcoholics Anonymous group, wins a tough, courageous victory over her drinking problem.
I'll Cry Tomorrow. 1955. Hayward, Susan

Rozanov.
Courtly Russian naval officer, barely able to speak English, hilariously leads a party of Russians ashore to an island off Cape Cod to beg, borrow or steal a power boat so that they can pull their grounded submarine free.
The Russians Are Coming, The Russians Are Coming. 1966. Arkin, Alan

Rubino, Marcello.
Young newspaperman, with hopes of becoming a serious writer, searches for material for his paper while on an endless round of parties and orgies. His life proves rich with excitement, but totally empty of serious relationships and personal satisfaction.
La Dolce Vita. 1961. Mastroianni, Marcello

Ruggles, Marmaduke.
As a result of a poker game in Paris, this very proper British manservant is transported to America where he experiences life in the raw in the bustling frontier community of Red Gap.
Ruggles of Red Gap. 1935. Laughton, Charles

Rummy, The, see Eddie

Russo, Buddy.
Together with his partner, Popeye, a New York City narcotics detective helps crack a lucrative heroin smuggling operation.
The French Connection. 1971. Scheider, Roy

Ryan, Monsignor.
Jovial priest, the friend of a family whose daughter is contemplating a racially mixed marriage, gives his blessings with a lighthearted casualness.
Guess Who's Coming to Dinner. 1967. Kellaway, Cecil

Sabre, Mark.
Known as "Puzzlehead," this young English husband personifies the "little man" who tries to do the right thing but is beset by constant troubles.
If Winter Comes. 1923. Marmont, Percy

Sabrina, see Fairchild, Sabrina

Saito.
Stubborn Japanese commandant of a prisoner-of-war camp in the Burmese jungle insists that the British officers contribute manual labor to the building of a bridge. This forces a battle of wills with a fanatical British officer.
The Bridge on the River Kwai. 1957. Hayakawa, Sessue

Sally.
This poor follies girl is courted by a prince, but the king and queen prevent the marriage. She spitefully marries the richest man in the kingdom, becomes a widow on her wedding night, and is eventually reunited with her true love.
The Merry Widow. 1925. Murray, Mae

Sally.

Trying to escape her past, this eager, tough young woman works in a hotel oyster bar, and in her spare time studies to be a croupier so that she can become a part of the glamorous life on the Riviera. Her career is threatened when her former husband and her sister return to town with hijacked cocaine.
Atlantic City. 1981. Sarandon, Susan

Sam.

Loyal and sympathetic pianist in Rick's Cafe Americaine in Casablanca during World War II is remembered for his rendition of "As Time Goes By," which Rick asks him to play again and again.
Casablanca. 1942. Wilson, Dooley

Sam.

Sam has gained nationwide fame on television, but is morose because of his recent divorce. He is one of a group of college friends from the 1960s grieving together over the loss of an old pal and of their old ideals.
The Big Chill. 1983. Berenger, Tom

Sam the Lion.

Because he owns three businesses, a movie house, a pool hall, and an all-night cafe, Sam has become the romantic father figure for two lonely, confused adolescents.
The Last Picture Show. 1971. Johnson, Ben

Sandy.

Giggling schoolgirl becomes a subtle, sensuous adolescent, spitefully betrays and finally destroys a teacher because she is jealous of the teacher's attention to another student.
The Prime of Miss Jean Brodie. 1969. Franklin, Pamela

Sandy.

This actress is deeply hurt and frustrated when she is turned down for a role for which she feels ideally suited. Her complaints to her boyfriend, an unemployed actor, goad him into trying out for the very same role.
Tootsie. 1982. Garr, Teri

Sanger, Tessa.

A happy, free-spirited schoolgirl falls in love with a composer and becomes his inspiration.
The Constant Nymph. 1943. Fontaine, Joan

Sarah.

Anna, a cool, detached actress, plays the part of a mysterious, tragic Victorian governess, Sarah, who is dishonored by her affair with a French officer. She becomes involved with a wealthy Englishman attracted to her beauty and sadness.
The French Lieutenant's Woman. 1981. Streep, Meryl

Sarah.
Physician, who seems to feel the loss of her ideals more deeply than do the old friends gathered in her home to attend a funeral, selflessly condones a night of love between her husband and a close chum.
The Big Chill. 1983. Close, Glenn

Sarah Jane.
Light-skinned daughter of a black servant successfully passes for white, rejects her mother, and finally runs away.
Imitation of Life. 1959. Kohner, Susan

Savage, General.
World War II commander of a bomber unit based in England goes about rebuilding his group's shattered morale with a fierce passion, which finally pays off in the revitalization of aggressiveness and pride among his men.
Twelve O'Clock High. 1949. Peck, Gregory

Saxel, Walter.
Selfish man, climbing steadily to fame, values his position over the promise of happiness through divorce and remarriage. He makes great demands on his mistress, leaning heavily on her for spiritual and emotional sustenance.
Back Street. 1932. Boles, John
Back Street. 1941. Boyer, Charles

Sayer, Rose.
Prissy, forbidding lady missionary finds her prudishness turning into warmth and tolerance as she discovers love on a riverboat adventure with an uncouth skipper, Charlie Allnutt, on an African river during World War I.
The African Queen. 1952. Hepburn, Katharine

Scarecrow, see Hunk

Schaefer, Betty.
This studio reader tries to persuade her script-writer boyfriend to leave the silent movie queen with whom he is living and to start to write again.
Sunset Boulevard. 1950. Olson, Nancy

Schiller, August.
A respectable bank cashier, who is also a devoted husband and father, has a wild night on the town and is too ashamed to return to his family.
The Way of All Flesh. 1927. Jannings, Emil

Schmid, Al.
After killing 200 Japanese at Guadalcanal, this real-life Marine is blinded by a bursting grenade. He struggles to adjust to his handicap and to recover his self-reliance and pride.
Pride of the Marines. 1945. Garfield, John

Schmidt, Ray.
Beautiful, sweet woman loves a married man and spends over 25 years in his shadow, sacrificing everything for him and complying with his every demand.
Back Street. 1932. Dunne, Irene
Back Street. 1941. Sullavan, Margaret

Schnell, Dutch.
Casey Stengel-like manager of the New York Mammoths baseball team appears to be concerned strictly with winning the pennant, until he learns that his second-string catcher is dying of Hodgkins disease. His compassionate reaction to this news reveals the humane side of his nature.
Bang the Drum Slowly. 1973. Gardenia, Vincent

Schumacher, Louise.
Even after her TV news department head husband forsakes her for an affair with a high-powered TV executive, the suffering Louise still has the capacity to be a loving woman.
Network. 1976. Straight, Beatrice

Schumacher, Max.
Scrupulous news division chief at UBS television network refuses to participate in some of his colleagues' ruthless programming schemes and is rendered impotent in the corporation.
Network. 1976. Holden, William

Schumann, Dr.
Sad, tired, dedicated ship's physician falls in love with a woman he knows is a drug addict on her way to prison, and literally dies of a broken heart aboard ship.
Ship of Fools. 1965. Werner, Oskar

Scolastica, Sister.
This sweet, starry-eyed nun has many trials and tribulations when she leaves her abbey in France to come to America to find land and resources for a new children's hospital.
Come to the Stable. 1949. Holm, Celeste

Scott, Diana.
Beautiful, ambitious but immoral London photographer's model succeeds socially by having a series of affairs, but winds up unhappily married to an Italian prince.
Darling. 1965. Christie, Julie

Scratch, Mr.
A clever, affable, and thoroughly charming devil with battered hat and thick stubble convinces a poor farmer to sell him his soul.
All That Money Can Buy. 1941. Huston, Walter

Scrooge, Ebenezer.
This is an offbeat but remarkable portrayal of literature's most easily salvaged, miserly, Christmas-hating misanthrope.
Scrooge. 1970. Finney, Albert

Sea Hawk, see Tressilian, Oliver

Sebastian, Alexander.
The shrewd and hateful leader of a gang of Nazis exiled in South America marries an American girl and later learns she has been sent there to spy on him.
Notorious. 1946. Rains, Claude

Sefton.
In a German prisoner-of-war camp during World War II this cynical, clever, calculating GI spends his prison time haggling to earn special privileges, and, until he redeems himself, is suspected of being a traitor by his fellow soldiers.
Stalag 17. 1953. Holden, William

Selky, Susan.
Susan's six-year-old son is missing. She waits alone, berating her estranged husband, turning on her best friend, suppressing her anger, choking on her agony, not daring to despair or to give up hope.
Without a Trace. 1983. Nelligan, Kate

Senate President.
The President of the Senate believes the young senator from Wisconsin to be honest and assists him in his dealings with other congressional members.
Mr. Smith Goes to Washington. 1939. Carey, Harry

Serpico.
Dogged, dedicated New York policeman, appalled by police corruption and graft, decides to expose brutality and bribe-taking but is frustrated at every turn, finding only contempt and hostility for his honesty.
Serpico. 1973. Pacino, Al

Seton, Linda.
Born into a socially prominent family, Linda is intelligent, critical and highly sensitive. She becomes attracted to a young nonconformist because he, too, is trying to discover his role in society.
Holiday. 1938. Hepburn, Katharine

Seven Beauties, see Frafuso, Pasqualino

Severi, Giovanni.
A young Italian soldier captured in the African desert, but reported slain, returns home. He finds his fiancee has become a nun, and when he begs her to have the Pope release her from her vows to marry him, she remains committed to the Church.
The White Sister. 1923. Colman, Ronald

Severine.
Once popular Hollywood actress returns to Europe to live and to play the part of a middle-aged mother in "Meet Pamela," a film in which the male lead is her former lover.
Day for Night. 1974. Cortese, Valentina

Shane.
In Wyoming, a strong, silent ex-gunfighter arrives out of nowhere in time to help a family of homesteaders fight a decisive battle against the cattlemen and their gunman, Wilson. He departs to nowhere to the echoes of the plaintive calls of the homesteader's son, Joey Starrett.
Shane. 1953. Ladd, Alan

Shanghai Lily.
When a train bound for Shanghai is waylaid by Chinese revolutionaries, this fearless high-class prostitute, although repentant of her past life, offers herself to a sinister Chinese warlord in an effort to save the other passengers.
Shanghai Express. 1932. Dietrich, Marlene

Shawnessy, John Wickliff.
Idealistic Indiana man, hoping to find the mythical rain tree which holds the secret of life, falls in love with a beautiful, disturbed Southern belle and throws his life into disarray.
Raintree County. 1957. Clift, Montgomery

She.
In modern Hiroshima to make a film, this French actress meets a Japanese architect, and is constantly reminded of the devastation caused by the atomic bomb and of her tragic love affair with a young German soldier during the French occupation.
Hiroshima Mon Amour. 1959. Riva, Emmanuelle

Sheik.
A handsome and exotic desert sheik, the orphaned son of a Spanish father and an English mother who has been raised by an older sheik, kidnaps and gently romances a well-bred English girl.
The Sheik. 1921. Valentino, Rudolph

Shelleen, Kid.
Once a dreaded gunslinger, but now over the hill and whiskey-soaked, the Kid is hired to eliminate a vicious killer. The challenge breaks through his alcoholic haze and rekindles some of his combative spark.
Cat Ballou. 1965. Marvin, Lee

Sherif Ali.
During World War I, this handsome, fierce Arab fighter is rescued by T.E. Lawrence and becomes his best friend and supporter.
Lawrence of Arabia. 1962. Sharif, Omar

Sheriff, see Muller, Max

Sherwood, Eileen.
A pretty and innocent girl from Ohio arrives in Greenwich Village with her sister and hopes to become an actress.
My Sister Eileen. 1942. Blair, Janet

Sherwood, Ruth.
This aspiring writer comes with her sister from Ohio to Greenwich Village where they share an apartment and try to get started on their careers.
My Sister Eileen. 1942. Russell, Rosalind

Shields, Jonathan.
Talented but arrogant and ruthless Hollywood producer builds his reputation by bringing professional success to others, but in doing so ruins their personal lives.
Bad and the Beautiful. 1952. Douglas, Kirk

Shirley.
Chic swinger socialite meets a male prostitute in cowboy clothes at a psychedelic party and gives him $20 to spend one wild night with her.
Midnight Cowboy. 1969. Vaccaro, Brenda

Shoplifter.
A wisecracking but frightened Brooklynesque shoplifter is booked at the ramshackle 21st Precinct in New York City.
Detective Story. 1951. Grant, Lee

Silkwood, Karen.
Betrayed by almost everyone in her life, this promiscuous, stubborn, sometimes unpleasant nuclear materials factory worker is motivated partly by fear, but also by an element of selfless heroism. She is obsessed with the idea of exposing her employer for operating a criminally unsafe plant.
Silkwood. 1983. Streep, Meryl

Silvernose.
Darkly menacing killer, meanest gun in the West, Silvernose is hired to kill a rancher with valuable property coveted by a greedy land baron. He meets his match in the reinvigorated Kid Shelleen, hired by the rancher's daughter.
Cat Ballou. 1965. Marvin, Lee

Simmons, Toni.
Young Greenwich village hippie, a dentist's mistress, is forsaken when the dentist and his nurse admit their love for each other.
Cactus Flower. 1969. Hawn, Goldie

Simmons, Veta Louise.
Despairing, much-abused sister is constantly apologizing for her brother's erratic behavior. She attempts to have him treated at a rest home but is herself mistakenly committed.
Harvey. 1950. Hull, Josephine

Simpson, Arthur.
Tourist guide in a Greek seaport town makes a travesty of the fine art of burglary when he is duped into driving the car for a group of thieves intent on stealing jewels from the Topkapi Palace Museum in Istanbul.
Topkapi. 1964. Ustinov, Peter

Singer.
Attractive, bright, kindhearted deaf-mute positively influences the lives of others, but nonetheless feels so abandoned and friendless that he is led to commit suicide.
The Heart is a Lonely Hunter. 1968. Arkin, Alan

Singer, Alvy.
Pessimistic, gloomy New York comedy writer and nightclub performer, hypersensitive about being Jewish, tries unsuccessfully to rekindle his romance with a budding young singer.
Annie Hall. 1977. Allen, Woody

Sister Luke.
Sensitive young Belgian nun is denied the right to serve as a nurse in the Belgian underground following her father's murder by the Nazis. After years of self-discipline, she decides she cannot endure the restraints of her order and asks to be released.
The Nun's Story. 1959. Hepburn, Audrey

Skeffington, Job.
A dignified Jewish bank broker, wishing to possess a beautiful wife, marries an exquisite but vain woman. When he loses his sight in a concentration camp and can no longer see her, she remains beautiful to him despite her advancing age.
Mr. Skeffington. 1944. Rains, Claude

Skid.
Success causes this funny and charming male half of a husband-wife song and dance team to separate from his wife, but love brings them together again.
When My Baby Smiles At Me. 1948. Dailey, Dan

Skinner, Skippy.
Both devious and charming, disobedient and lovable, this impersonation of a comic-strip character has many amusing adventures as he tries to raise $3.00 to free his friend Sooky's pet mongrel from the dogcatcher.
Skippy. 1931. Cooper, Jackie

Skinner, Tessibel.
When a wealthy man buys a stretch of waterfront that has always "belonged" to poor fishermen and squatters, this determined fisherman's daughter enlists the aid of the man's son in getting the property back.
Tess of the Storm Country. 1922. Pickford, Mary

Skippy, see Skinner, Skippy

Slade, Larry.
Embittered old anarchist, awaiting imminent death, views the foibles of the human debris in Harry Hope's Bar with a stern pity tempered by an occasional smile.
The Iceman Cometh. 1973. Ryan, Robert

Sledge, Mac.
Lonely, alcoholic former country singer gives up his career to marry a poor Texas widow. Mac struggles to build a new life and to come to terms with his songwriting, his country star ex-wife, and the 18-year-old daughter he left behind.
Tender Mercies. 1983. Duvall, Robert

Slim, see Marie

Sloper, Austin.
Wealthy, charming doctor with a touch of cruelty successfully prevents his daughter's marriage to a mercenary suitor, and condemns her to a life of loneliness and revenge.
The Heiress. 1949. Richardson, Ralph

Sloper, Catherine.
Homely, timid young heiress falls in love with her first suitor, but her father prevents their marriage because he feels the young man is a fortune hunter.
The Heiress. 1949. De Havilland, Olivia

Smith, Cora.
A cheap and cold California blonde, beset with the idea that she can "be somebody" through crime, seduces a young bum and convinces him to kill her unwanted husband.
The Postman Always Rings Twice. 1946. Turner, Lana
The Postman Always Rings Twice. 1981. Lange, Jessica

Smith, Homer.
While teaching them to speak English and to sing Negro spirituals, this gentle, irreverent, independent jack-of-all-trades helps a group of German nuns build a chapel in the Arizona desert.
Lilies of the Field. 1963. Poitier, Sidney

Smith, Jefferson.
Naive but totally honest junior senator from Wisconsin encounters corruption in the nation's capital. He embarks on a one-man campaign to uproot the evil Senator Joseph Paine and to spoil his plans for making personal profit from an unnecessary dam.
Mr. Smith Goes to Washington. 1939. Stewart, James

Smithy, see Rainier, Charles

Smollett, Colonel.
An impertinent and selfish retired Army colonel comes to lodge with a brave and cheerful family whose men are off fighting the war, and through this experience he becomes a warmer and more mellow person.
Since You Went Away. 1944. Woolley, Monte

Snyder, Carrie.
Big-hearted, disreputable Carrie finds her first real loves, a little boy of 11 and his five-year-old pal, who staunchly refuse to believe that their adopted mother was ever bad.
Valiant is the Word for Carrie. 1936. George, Gladys

Snyder, Martin.
This uncouth, brutal racketeer, better known as the Gimp, propels Ruth Etting's career from dance hall to Ziegfeld Follies, but is also responsible for her unhappiness.
Love Me or Leave Me. 1955. Cagney, James

Sonny.
Childishly inept bisexual tries to satisfy everybody, his wife, children, a dim-witted accomplice and a homosexual lover. He is driven to his limits when he is trapped in the middle of a bank robbery in an attempt to raise money for a sex operation for his boyfriend, Leon.
Dog Day Afternoon. 1975. Pacino, Al

Sonny, see Crosby, Charles

Sophie.
Despite her tragic and secret past, this beautiful Roman Catholic Polish survivor of Auschwitz is still hopeful that life can hold some happiness for her with her lover and her friend in a Brooklyn rooming house after the war.
Sophie's Choice. 1982. Streep, Meryl

Soubirous, Bernadette.
A simple French peasant girl sees a vision of the Virgin Mary. She holds steadfast, against widespread disbelief, in her claim to have had this mystical experience.
The Song of Bernadette. 1943. Jones, Jennifer

Soubirous, Louise.
The mother of a young girl who has seen a holy vision is outwardly reserved but inwardly truly warm-hearted and sympathetic.
The Song of Bernadette. 1943. Revere, Anne

Souse, Egbert.
Indigent, child-hating, henpecked barfly, living in a town called Lompoc, accidently captures a holdup man and is rewarded with the job of bank guard.
The Bank Dick. 1940. Fields, W.C.

Spade, Sam.
This tough, shrewd, cynical detective becomes involved in finding a priceless jewel-studded statuette, first in cooperation, then in competition, with a motley gang of international thieves and thugs.
The Maltese Falcon. 1941. Bogart, Humphrey

St. James, Henry.
Since his childhood, Captain St. James has been searching for paradise, and he finally finds it. He becomes a two-timing ferryboat skipper, with a proper British wife in Gibraltar who satisfies his domestic yearnings; an Arab wife in North Africa caters to his more exotic desires.
The Captain's Paradise. 1953. Guinness, Alec

St. Maugham, Mrs.
Concerned primarily with her arid flower garden, this haughty, aging English matron does not discipline her granddaughter; rather, she selfishly spoils her, until a new governess with an undisclosed past appears.
The Chalk Garden. 1964. Evans, Edith

Standish, Peter.

Modern Peter Standish becomes absorbed in an ancestor's diary, is transformed into his own past, and falls in love with a girl from 150 years ago.
Berkeley Square. 1933. Howard, Leslie

Starbuck.

Phony con man is a poet and a dreamer who wants people to believe in themselves. He is more successful at seducing a confirmed spinster than in delivering the rain he promises.
The Rainmaker. 1956. Lancaster, Burt

Stark, Willie.

Honest small-town politician (resembling Huey Long) starts out trying to improve conditions for his Southern state. He is elected governor, becomes fatally corrupt in office, and ruthlessly crushes everybody who opposes him.
All the King's Men. 1949. Crawford, Broderick

Starrett, Joey.

Bright, inquisitive farmboy idolizes the mysterious stranger, Shane, who is helping his family on their homestead. His plaintive calls of "Shane, come back, Shane!" are unsuccessful in keeping his idol close by.
Shane. 1953. De Wilde, Brandon

Stella.

Employed in a diner, this sultry, money-loving waitress, with a roving eye and a desire to be married, is found murdered.
Fallen Angel. 1946. Darnell, Linda

Stephens, Drew.

Drew gives the appearance of protecting his girl friend, Karen Silkwood, but is quick to abandon her when he sees suspicious changes in her behavior.
Silkwood. 1983. Russell, Kurt

Stephenson, Al.

A middle-aged sergeant returns home from World War II with some anxiety, but with his old good humor and wit, and with the love of his wife and children, he makes a fairly smooth adjustment to civilian life.
The Best Years of Our Lives. 1946. March, Fredric

Steuben, Lieutenant von.

Haughty, flashy, pretentious Prussian officer pursues a neglected American wife with gifts and sweet talk.
Blind Husbands. 1919. Stroheim, Erich von

Stevenson, Leona.
A selfish and nervous hypochondriac, confined to her New York City penthouse, overhears on the telephone a plot to kill her, and works herself up into a frenzy of terror.
Sorry, Wrong Number. 1948. Stanwyck, Barbara

Stevenson, Ralph.
An American officer in Europe after World War II takes a grief-stricken, homeless Czech boy under his wing.
The Search. 1948. Clift, Montgomery

Stewart, Mrs.
This is the mother of a successful Broadway musical comedy star who attained fame the hard way and has become a lonely woman projecting a tough image.
Torch Song. 1953. Rambeau, Marjorie

Stock, Mizzie.
Bored with her professor husband, this selfish Viennese wife has several humorous and mildly diverting flirtations.
The Marriage Circle. 1924. Prevost, Marie

Stoller, Mr.
This used-car salesman and former stonecutter is torn between affection for and apoplexy over his son because he cannot understand the boy's newly acquired "Italian" ways.
Breaking Away. 1979. Dooley, Paul

Stoller, Mrs.
Baffled by her son's attraction to things Italian, this understanding mother is supportive of his desire for a life beyond Bloomington, Indiana. She is also sympathetic to her husband's confusion at and resentment of this strange creature their son has become, and tries to resolve the conflicts between them.
Breaking Away. 1979. Barrie, Barbara

Stoneman, Elsie.
Lovely young Northern girl, in love with a Southern colonel condemned to death on false charges, visits President Lincoln, who agrees to pardon the officer.
The Birth of a Nation. 1915. Gish, Lillian

Stoner, Harry.
This sweet-natured super salesman has become a troubled, middle-aged businessman. He is at the breaking point because he has juggled the books to keep his company alive and is again desperate for money to keep it solvent.
Save the Tiger. 1973. Lemmon, Jack

Storm, Sarah.
A young mother attempts to find her son who had been taken away by his father and reared by a wealthy couple.
Sarah and Son. 1930. Chatterton, Ruth

Stosh.
In a Nazi prisoner-of-war camp, this dumb, oafish GI, always referred to as Animal, is tortured by thoughts of women in general, but Betty Grable in particular.
Stalag 17. 1953. Strauss, Robert

Stovall, Major.
Loyal, perceptive, middle-aged major, a former attorney, helps the new general of the devastated 918th Bomb Squad enforce the discipline so important for the rebuilding of morale and leadership among the men.
Twelve O'Clock High. 1949. Jagger, Dean

Strang, Alan.
This teen-ager, a part-time stablehand who blinded six horses, is caught between an anti-religious father and a devout mother, and has transferred his mother's religious devotion into equine worship.
Equus. 1977. Firth, Peter

Strangelove, Dr.
Impotent in his wheelchair, this mad German scientist, called on to aid the United States, cannot prevent his artificial arm from jerking into a Nazi salute.
Dr. Strangelove: or, How I Learned to Stop Worrying and Love the Bomb. 1964. Sellers, Peter

Streinikoff, see Antipov, Pasha

Strickland, Charles.
After leaving his English family and struggling in Paris, this tortured artist finally escapes to the South Seas, where he paints prodigiously.
The Moon and Sixpence. 1942. Sanders, George

Stroud, Elizabeth.
Passionately devoted to her convicted killer son, Mrs. Stroud is instrumental in saving him from death through her pleas to Mrs. Woodrow Wilson.
Birdman of Alcatraz. 1962. Ritter, Thelma

Stroud, Robert E.
Convicted killer spends more than 40 years in solitary confinement with birds as his only companions, and becomes a world authority and author of a definitive book on the illnesses of birds.
Birdman of Alcatraz. 1962. Lancaster, Burt

Stryker.
Tough, unrelenting but softhearted Marine sergeant must convert young recruits into disciplined combat troops in the Pacific during World War II.
Sands of Iwo Jima. 1949. Wayne, John

Sullivan, Anne.
A poor, determined near-blind teacher comes to care for a blind and deaf girl, Helen Keller. In spite of showing patience and fortitude, she is nearly defeated by the child's stubbornness, but finally succeeds in teaching her to communicate.
The Miracle Worker. 1962. Bancroft, Anne

Sullivan, John L.
A comedy film director decides to make a serious picture, and to get experience with hardship, he disguises himself as a tramp and goes slumming. He learns that poverty and cruelty are not what the world wants, but laughter is.
Sullivan's Travels. 1942. McCrea, Joel

Sullivan, Rocky.
Brazen, tough East Side hood develops a conscience and feigns cowardice on his way to the electric chair, so that he will not become an object of hero worship for the slum kids who idolize him.
Angels with Dirty Faces. 1938. Cagney, James

Sundance Kid.
This amiable member of the Hole-in-the-Wall Gang is chased to Bolivia by a Union Pacific posse. His gun wizardry and bank robbing prove to be as profitless there as his train robbing had become in the States.
Butch Cassidy and the Sundance Kid. 1969. Redford, Robert

Suyin, Han.
Lovely, intense widowed Eurasian physician falls in love with an unhappily married American correspondent in Hong Kong during the Korean War.
Love is a Many-Splendored Thing. 1955. Jones, Jennifer

Swann, Alan.
Matinee idol whose career is declining, invited to make his TV debut, suffers a horrible case of stage fright when he learns that the show will be done live in front of millions of viewers. His search for courage from a bottle makes things difficult for the program host.
My Favorite Year. 1982. O'Toole, Peter

Swede.
A young boxer is ruined by a sexy woman and big-time mobsters. When he is too down-and-out and tired to make another move, he quietly waits in his rented room for the gunmen who have been hired to kill him.
The Killers. 1946. Lancaster, Burt

Sweetie.
Babied by his mother and his nurse, this young man declares his independence at age 21 and proceeds to seek a wild life with an amusement park showgirl.
The Cradle Buster. 1922. Hunter, Glenn

Sycamore, Penny.
An eccentric mother, married to a millionaire, keeps busy writing thrillers because someone left a typewriter on her doorstep.
You Can't Take It With You. 1938. Byington, Spring

Szell.
Sadistic, egotistical former Nazi dentist, in an attempt to save his hoard of stolen diamonds, pursues and torments a young innocent West Side New Yorker.
Marathon Man. 1976. Olivier, Laurence

Talbot, Larry.
Young Larry returns to his family's English home, is bitten by a werewolf, and assumes a dual personality. He changes both mentally and physically into the Wolf Man during nights of the full moon, and commits horrifying atrocities, until he is discovered and killed by his father.
The Wolf Man. 1941. Chaney, Lon, Jr.

Tarzan.
English boy, lost in the wilds of Africa, is adopted by a tribe of apes and grows up with simian strength and human intelligence. He becomes the magnificent lord of the jungle, achieving impossible feats of power and daring.
Tarzan of the Apes. 1918. Lincoln, Elmo
Tarzan, the Apeman. 1932. Weissmuller, Johnny

Ted.
Square, ultraconventional husband "gets with it" after his more swinging friends convince him that by sharing with everybody he will expand his capacity for love.
Bob & Carol & Ted & Alice. 1969. Gould, Elliott

Templeton, Elliott.
With his fancy Paris apartment and magnificent Riviera mansion, this boastful and witty social titan is the epitome of 1920s snobbery.
The Razor's Edge. 1946. Webb, Clifton

Templeton, Scottie.
Middle-aged Broadway press agent, a compulsive joker who has wasted his life, loused up his marriage, and alienated his son, is now dying of cancer and has one last chance for a reconciliation with his son.
Tribute. 1980. Lemmon, Jack

Teresa.
Only this emotionally disturbed, frightened Catholic girl knows that the prime suspect in a crime was with her in Atlanta, helping her to arrange an abortion. When she confesses, begs the reporter for anonymity and is ignored, she commits suicide.
Absence of Malice. 1981. Dillon, Melinda

Tess.
Beautiful young woman, forced to seek social status by her ambitious family, is raped at 16 by a wealthy scoundrel, and is then misunderstood by the weakling she loves and marries.
Tess. 1980. Kinski, Nastassia

Tevye.
Poor dairyman, struggling for a meagre existence in Czarist Russia in 1905, cannot reconcile himself with his daughters' defiance of tradition, or God's unwillingness to cast him in the role of a rich man.
Fiddler on the Roof. 1971. Topol

Tharon.
This close-cropped, mannishly dressed, two-gun heroine of the Old West knows how to take care of herself, and leads the cattlemen of Lost Valley in their victorious war against the rustlers.
The Crimson Challenge. 1922. Dalton, Dorothy

Thatcher, Emma.
Devoted and loving servant in a widower's family, Emma marries her wealthy employer when the children are grown, and must endure their hostility and resentment.
Emma. 1932. Dressler, Marie

Thayer, Ethel.
Nearing her 70th birthday, a wife of 50 years and now the sole source of strength and stability in her failing husband's narrowing world, Ethel comes with him to Golden Pond to enjoy perhaps their last summer together.
On Golden Pond. 1981. Hepburn, Katharine

Thayer, Norman, Jr.
Cranky, intentionally rude, retired professor, celebrating his 80th birthday, is very aware of his physical deterioration and is constantly preoccupied with death. In perhaps his last summer at Golden Pond, he makes peace with his daughter and finds a new pal in her fiance's young son.
On Golden Pond. 1981. Fonda, Henry

Theodora, see Lynn, Theodora

Thief of Bagdad, see Abu

Thompson, Sadie.
This prostitute, trying to hide her identity in the South Seas, is about to marry a Marine when a heartless reformer, obsessed with her immorality, threatens to turn her in to the police.
Sadie Thompson. 1928. Swanson, Gloria

Thornton, Sean.
Ex-steelworker and prizefighter from Pittsburgh quits the ring after he accidently kills a fighter. He settles down to a quiet life in his native Ireland, and tempestuously woos a willful Irish lass, Mary Kate Danaher.
The Quiet Man. 1952. Wayne, John

Thunderbolt.
Gangster on death row repents at the eleventh hour and exonerates another prisoner who has been framed.
Thunderbolt. 1929. Bancroft, George

Thursday, Colonel.
A stubborn and sullen Army colonel takes over the command of an Arizona frontier post, during the Indian wars. He proves to be ignorant of the ways of the Apaches, unresponsive to the advice of those who are not, and, consequently leads his men to massacre.
Fort Apache. 1948. Fonda, Henry

Tibbs, Virgil.
Cool, arrogant black Philadelphia detective wins a modicum of respect in Sparta, Mississippi, when he joins forces with the bigoted redneck police chief to solve a murder.
In the Heat of the Night. 1967. Poitier, Sidney

Tigna, Uncle.
Despite the danger, this good-humored but determined Italian peasant hides in his barn two Americans who are being pursued by the Nazis.
To Live in Peace. 1947. Fabrizi, Aldo

Tilford, Amelia.
Impressionable grandmother is convinced by her evil granddaughter who is attending a private girls' school that two young teachers at the school have a lesbian relationship.
The Children's Hour. 1962. Bainter, Fay

Tilford, Mary.
Evil, venomous little girl, enrolled at a school for young girls, tells a lie about a teacher whom she hates, and causes three lives to be irrevocably changed.
These Three. 1936. Granville, Bonita
The Children's Hour. 1962. Balkin, Karen

Tin Woodman, see Hickory

Tindle, Milo.
Lower-class Italian hairdresser, and current lover of his host's wife, is invited by that eccentric author for a night of sport and humiliation. However, he becomes surprisingly adept as the games become increasingly intricate and deadly.
Sleuth. 1972. Caine, Michael

Toby.
Vain, shallow beauty, who can only boast about the many rich men who have fallen in love with her, remains the best girl friend of a rehabilitated alcoholic actress now trying to get her life in order.
Only When I Laugh. 1981. Hackett, Joan

Toddy.
While suffering a temporary career setback, this gay, somewhat decadent nightclub master of ceremonies becomes the manager of an out-of-work actress made up as a man who impersonates females.
Victor/Victoria. 1982. Preston, Robert

Tom.
Arrogant, edgy and truculent, a bully with women as well as with men, Tom starts out as a small-time hood, graduates to the top rungs of crime, and meets a cruel death at the hands of rival mobsters.
The Public Enemy. 1931. Cagney, James

Tompkins, Jim.
In spite of being awarded a medal for an act of bravery, this young corporal considers himself a coward. He is coaxed into taking sodium pentathol to help relieve his guilt for deserting another soldier in a burning plane.
Captain Newman, M.D. 1963. Darin, Bobby

Tondelayo.
Voluptuous but scheming native girl, who utters the famous phrase, "I, Tondelayo," entices the British managers of a rubber plantation in the hot, sticky tropics.
White Cargo. 1942. Lamarr, Hedy

Topouzoglou, Stavros.
This poor Greek boy, struggling to escape the persecutions that his people suffered in Turkey, makes his way across the sea to America, fulfilling his obsessive dream of reaching the promised land.
America America. 1963. Giallelis, Stathis

Topper, Cosmo.
Timid, humorless banker is always accompanied by a husband-and-wife team of ghosts, who have pledged to liberate him from his nagging wife and to brighten his impeccable and humdrum life.
Topper. 1937. Young, Roland

Tori.
This wealthy and menacing man from the Orient lends a socialite a large sum of money. When she tries to return it, he calls her a cheat and brands her shoulder to prove that she is his property.
The Cheat. 1915. Hayakawa, Sessue

Toulouse-Lautrec.
In Paris in the Gay Nineties, this dignified, self-deprecating but talented painter has a sad outlook on life because the tragic deformity he suffered as a child repulses the women he loves.
Moulin Rouge. 1952. Ferrer, Jose

Tower, Alexander.
At the turn of the century in a small town, this mysterious local physician, haunted by the fear of insanity in his family, murders his daughter and then kills himself.
Kings Row. 1941. Rains, Claude

Tracey, Blaze.
This Western outlaw is feared by all, but is also respected for his unique code of honor, which moves him to fight and to kill for justice.
Hell's Hinges. 1916. Hart, William S.

Tracy.
Beautiful 17-year-old, able to hold her own with adults on all levels, has an affair with a much older television writer. She adapts well, but he cannot accept the difference in their ages.
Manhattan. 1979. Hemingway, Mariel

Traherne, Judith.
Gay, self-centered Long Island socialite, dying from a malignant brain tumor and with less than a year to live, falls in love with and marries her surgeon.
Dark Victory. 1939. Davis, Bette

Trainee, Milos.
Shy young man gets a job as an apprentice train dispatcher at a village railway station near Prague during World War II. He tries to emulate his superior's sexual prowess and nonchalance in his job, but fails in a moment of crisis and is thrown into despair.
Closely Watched Trains. 1966. Neckar, Vaclav

Tramp.
The comical mustachioed derelict, complete with derby and cane, finds an abandoned baby and decides to bring him up as his window fixing assistant.
The Kid. 1921. Chaplin, Charles

Tramp.
A hobo on the run from the police finds refuge in a circus where he becomes a clown and falls in love with an equestrienne, only to lose her to the tightrope walker.
The Circus. 1928. Chaplin, Charles

Tramp.
Penniless vagabond falls in love with a blind flower girl who mistakes him for a rich man. With the inadvertent aid of a drunken millionaire, he is able to provide the money for an operation. With her restored sight, she finds it difficult to believe that this comical little tramp could be her Prince Charming.
City Lights. 1931. Chaplin, Charles

Tramp.
The little vagabond, complete with dog-eared shoes, baggy pants, bamboo cane, and incongruous derby, is the embodiment of the awkward underdog out of place in the hectic modern world.
Modern Times. 1936. Chaplin, Charles

Tramp, in *The Gold Rush,* see Lone Prospector

Trask, Cal.
Confused, sensitive, rebellious adolescent is tormented by his sense of jealousy toward his brother and by his father's rejection.
East of Eden. 1955. Dean, James

Traynor, Karen.
Clever, irresistible Southern labor lawyer has an affair with a young, handsome senator who cannot solve the problem of having two desirable women in his life at the same time.
The Seduction of Joe Tynan. 1979. Streep, Meryl

Trelkovsky.
Filing clerk moves into an apartment made available because of the attempted suicide of the previous tenant. He becomes convinced that the other occupants of the building are responsible for that suicide attempt and are now forcing him, against his will, to assume the identity of the now dead tenant.
The Tenant. 1976. Polanski, Roman

Trellis, Fanny.
An extremely beautiful but vain woman tries to live on the admiration and attention she has always received from men, despite her advancing age and eventual loss of beauty.
Mr. Skeffington. 1944. Davis, Bette

Trent, Hilary.
Reported as missing in action, this blinded war hero does not want to burden his sweetheart with his handicap. When they are finally reunited in her home, he pretends that he can see since he knows every inch of the house.
The Dark Angel. 1925. Colman, Ronald

Tressilian, Oliver.
An aristocrat is kidnapped and carried away on a ship by a henchman of his half brother, who wants to frame him for murder. The ship is captured by a Moorish fighting vessel and Sir Oliver becomes the first lieutenant, adopts the name Sea Hawk, and sails to England for his revenge.
The Sea Hawk. 1924. Sills, Milton

Trilby.
A charming young French girl, full of life and adventure, loathes the gruesome Svengali, but comes under his hypnotic spell and is ruined.
Trilby. 1923. Lafayette, Andree

Trina.
Cold and nagging wife wins a large sum of money, and becomes so obsessed with a greed for more that she lies and cheats, and eventually drives her husband to such desperation that he kills her.
Greed. 1923. Pitts, Zasu

Trina.
One of a large Norwegian family who settled in San Francisco in the early 1900s, this twittering, painfully timid old maid needs moral support from the boss of the family, Mama, to marry an equally timid undertaker.
I Remember Mama. 1948. Corby, Ellen

Tripp, Alice.
Poor, lonely, frumpy working girl wants to marry her socially ambitious boyfriend so that their child will not be illegitimate.
A Place in the Sun. 1951. Winters, Shelley

Trotwood, Betsey.
Eccentric, sharp-tongued but kindly great-aunt helps educate her nephew, establishes him in his literary career, and lives to see him happily married to his childhood sweetheart.
David Copperfield. 1935. Oliver, Edna May

Truesmith, Woodrow.
Urged on by six buddies, this ingenuous and charming Marine returns to his small town wearing their medals as a conquering hero, although he was actually medically discharged for hay fever.
Hail the Conquering Hero. 1944. Bracken, Eddie

Truman, Harry S
Feisty, plain-speaking president recalls meetings with Douglas MacArthur, Joseph McCarthy, and the Ku Klux Klan as he reminisces about his colorful years in American politics.
Give 'Em Hell, Harry. 1975. Whitmore, James

Tucker, Sam.
A young and hopeful poor white sharecropper is determined to make a better life for his family despite hunger, disease, and flood.
The Southerner. 1945. Scott, Zachary

Tully.
A young yet over-the-hill boxer returns to the ring, wins his first bout, but does not have the endurance to follow through. He returns to picking onions by day and sleeping in Skid Row flop houses at night.
Fat City. 1972. Keach, Stacy

Turgidson, General Buck.
Hawkish general, always stuffing his mouth with wads of chewing gum, wants the total annihilation of Russia as a follow-up to an accidental American nuclear attack.
Dr. Strangelove: or, How I Learned to Stop Worrying and Love the Bomb. 1964. Scott, George C.

Tweedledee.
A greedy, ill-tempered midget leaves the circus sideshow where he and two cronies have been picking pockets. The three embark on a new robbery scheme in which Tweedledee's size enables him to masquerade as a baby in a carriage, so that no one suspects him of being a thief.
The Unholy Three. 1925. Earles, Harry

Twillie, Cuthbert J.
This comically pretentious, lewd, and scowling misanthrope weds the town's buxom bawdy lady, and then discovers she has married him for legal reasons only.
My Little Chickadee. 1940. Fields, W. C.

Twist, Oliver.
Angelic, appealing, much abused orphan is taught the skills of the pickpocket trade on the streets of London. He is involved in many calamitous episodes before he is finally given a home by one of his early pickpocket victims.
Oliver Twist. 1922. Coogan, Jackie

Tybalt.
Fiery cousin of Juliet Capulet challenges Romeo on his attendance at the Capulet ball and finally meets his end at sword's point.
Romeo and Juliet. 1936. Rathbone, Basil

Tyree.
A former Rebel cavalryman, who still harbors a dislike of Yankees, becomes a highly efficient advance scout for Company C of the Seventh Cavalry at Fort Starke.
She Wore a Yellow Ribbon. 1949. Johnson, Ben

Tyrone, James.
An aging, vain, autocratic father and husband of 35 years, formerly a wealthy and successful matinee idol, cannot shake the miserly habits brought on by his insecurity.
Long Day's Journey into Night. 1962. Richardson, Ralph

Tyrone, Jamie.
Drunken older son, a misfit, continually quarrels with his father and devastates his younger brother in an argument during a summer vacation in their Connecticut home.
Long Day's Journey into Night. 1962. Robards, Jason

Tyrone, Mary.
Married to an overbearing actor, her eldest son an alcoholic, this middle-aged woman turns to drugs to relieve her tension and to lessen her disappointment at not becoming a concert pianist.
Long Day's Journey into Night. 1962. Hepburn, Katharine

Udo, Tommy.
This sadistic, giggling, psychopathic killer seeks revenge after a convict rats on his pals to gain his own release from prison.
Kiss of Death. 1947. Widmark, Richard

Ugarte.
Despicable, sleezy black marketeer kills some Germans to acquire signed exit visas permitting departure from wartime Casablanca. He is unable to benefit from these valuable papers before the Nazis track him down.
Casablanca. 1942. Lorre, Peter

Urban, Sylvester.
In gay and reckless prewar Vienna, a kindly old man, saddened by the loss of his wife, gets great pleasure and satisfaction from making children laugh at the amusement park where he is a clown and a puppeteer.
Merry Go Round. 1923. Cravina, Cesare

Vale, Charlotte.
An ugly duckling, made neurotic by her mother, becomes a confident and self-assured woman through the help of a psychiatrist and the love of a married man.
Now, Voyager. 1942. Davis, Bette

Vale, Mrs.
This wealthy Boston Back Bay mother totally dominates her unattractive daughter and drives her to a nervous breakdown.
Now, Voyager. 1942. Cooper, Gladys

Valjean, Jean.
Nineteenth-century French convict, sentenced to imprisonment for stealing a loaf of bread, is granted his freedom. He becomes an almost saintly, generous factory owner, but is never allowed to forget his past.
Les Miserables. 1935. March, Fredric

Vampire.
An evil temptress ensnares a diplomat, causes him to desert his wife and child, and coldly gloats as he becomes powerless in her grasp.
A Fool There Was. 1915. Bara, Theda

Van der Besh, Philip.
Wealthy, charming, whimsical young American meets an older, sedate Parisian woman, falls in love, and begins a passionate affair. He is devastated when she rejects him to accept a marriage proposal from her former lover.
Goodbye Again. 1961. Perkins, Anthony

Van Gogh, Vincent.
Lonely, tormented genius, a man of tempestuous moods, encounters great anguish in pursuing his great artistic talent.
Lust for Life. 1956. Douglas, Kirk

Van Hossmere, Muzzy.

In the jazzy 1920s, this darling of the sophisticated Long Island social set and widow of an enormously wealthy gentleman, herself a fun-loving playgirl, makes sure she lives life to the fullest.
Thoroughly Modern Millie. 1967. Channing, Carol

Van Meer.

In Europe of 1939, this honest Dutch diplomat memorizes a secret clause in an Allied treaty for his country. A spy ring, needing this information, kidnaps him and assassinates an impostor to give the impression that Van Meer is dead.
Foreign Correspondent. 1940. Basserman, Albert

Van Pelham, Harold.

This wealthy hypochondriac seeks rest in a sleepy Mexican town but is mistaken for a spy. Thrown into prison and totally dismayed, he meets a giant with a toothache, who helps him escape. In gratitude Harold extracts the painful molar.
Why Worry? 1923. Lloyd, Harold

Vane, Kitty.

When her boyfriend is reported missing in action, this beautiful girl clings to the hope that he may be found. Years later, on her wedding day, she learns that he is alive, cancels the ceremony and is tearfully reunited with her sweetheart, who has been blinded in battle.
The Dark Angel. 1925. Banky, Vilma
The Dark Angel. 1935. Oberon, Merle

Vane, Sibyl.

A luckless and virginal music hall singer is seduced by an enigmatic debaucher.
The Picture of Dorian Gray. 1945. Lansbury, Angela

Vauzos, Marie Theresa.

When a young girl claims she has seen a holy vision, this harsh and tormented nun becomes resentful of the girl and contemptuously treats her as a fraud.
The Song of Bernadette. 1943. Cooper, Gladys

Velma.

Weird, witch-like housekeeper, slovenly but faithful to the old demented woman whom she serves, is murdered when she returns to the old mansion after being discharged.
Hush ... Hush, Sweet Charlotte. 1964. Moorehead, Agnes

Venable, Mrs.
Domineering, aging Southern belle insists that her niece is insane, and requests a lobotomy be performed to insure that this young woman will never reveal the circumstances of Mrs. Venable's son's death.
Suddenly Last Summer. 1959. Hepburn, Katharine

Vergerus, Edvard.
In provincial Sweden this fanatically pious, handsome bishop preaches "love of truth." Many of his women parishioners find his severity erotic. Soon after a church member's husband dies, the bishop marries her and brings her family to his castle to live.
Fanny and Alexander. 1983. Malmsjo, Jan

Veronica.
During World War II, a sensitive young Russian girl, under the strain of wartime, the loss of her family, and the loneliness of waiting, is unfaithful to her sweetheart while he is at the front, thus destroying their love affair.
The Cranes Are Flying. 1958. Samoilova, Tatiana

Vickers, Angela.
Vibrant, voluptuous society debutante wants to marry a blue-collar factory worker.
A Place in the Sun. 1951. Taylor, Elizabeth

Victor.
In Paris of 1934, a hungry, unemployed English actress allows herself to be made up as Victor, a Polish-born count and female impersonator known professionally as Victoria.
Victor/Victoria. 1982. Andrews, Julie

Victoria, see Victor

Villa, Pancho.
Gruff Mexican peasant turned bandit and patriot tries to control Mexico after the fall of President Porfirio Diaz in 1910.
Viva Villa. 1934. Beery, Wallace

Von Geigern, Baron Felix.
Although this handsome aristocrat-turned-petty-larcenist is very eager for wealth, he is still a sympathetic and caring man who wins the love of Grusinskaya and returns the wallet he has stolen.
Grand Hotel. 1932. Barrymore, John

Von Mayerling, Max.
In his prime days as a director, Max was the discoverer and ex-husband of the fading movie queen he now serves as devoted butler.
Sunset Boulevard. 1950. Von Stroheim, Erich

Von Obersdorf, Baroness.
Mother of a young German nobleman tells his current amorata, the roving wife of an American manufacturer, why older wives of younger husbands are invariably miserable.
Dodsworth. 1936. Ouspenskaya, Maria

Von Shtupp, Lili.
Seductive dance hall queen, to please her paramour, seduces the black sheriff in the town of Ridge Rock. However, instead of breaking his heart as planned, she falls in love with him.
Blazing Saddles. 1974. Kahn, Madeline

Walden, Rita.
Well-tailored Manhattan housewife married for 24 years to a devoted oculist, has nothing to do but fight with her canary and redecorate her apartment. Upon the death of her mother, she feels guilty and regretful, and agonizes over those dreams of fulfillment that may never come true.
Summer Wishes, Winter Dreams. 1973. Woodward, Joanne

Walker.
This taciturn infantry captain in the North African and Italian campaigns of World War II has a deep understanding of his soldiers, and a belief in the innate dignity of man.
Story of G.I. Joe. 1945. Mitchum, Robert

Walker, Coalhouse, Jr.
Well-mannered, soft-spoken black jazz pianist demands justice when his new Model T Ford is defaced by members of the New Rochelle volunteer fire company. When he cannot gain legal redress, he forms a band of black militants who resort to extreme measures as they wage guerrilla war on all fire stations.
Ragtime. 1981. Rollins, Howard E.

Walker, Nora.
Tough and witty, a singer and dancer, Nora is the mother of Tommy, a boy who becomes deaf, dumb and blind after he sees his stepfather murder his real father.
Tommy. 1975. Ann-Margret

Wandrous, Gloria.
Beautiful, tempestuous, high-priced call girl, whose wealthy clientele allows her to live an elegant life, is willing to settle down when she meets a charming millionaire, a married man.
Butterfield 8. 1960. Taylor, Elizabeth

Wang.
Poor Chinese farmer becomes Lord of the Great House, but this rise to success and wealth ends in disaster when he neglects the land that he was taught to worship and discovers that O-Lan, his first wife, is dying.
The Good Earth. 1937. Muni, Paul

Warden, Milton.
First sergeant and solid career soldier, a man's man who is also a ladies' man, Warden is respected by both the GIs and officers in his company. He can easily achieve promotion to a higher rank, but refuses to manipulate the system.
From Here to Eternity. 1953. Lancaster, Burt

Warne, Peter.
Wandering newspaperman, tough and cynical on the surface but tender and romantic underneath, meets a helpless young rich girl on the bus from Florida, and falls in love against his will.
It Happened One Night. 1934. Gable, Clark

Warren, Mrs.
In a New England town terrorized by a psychopathic killer, this cranky invalid is the matriarch of a sinister household in which family hatreds run deep.
The Spiral Staircase. 1946. Barrymore, Ethel

Warriner, Jerry.
Estranged husband flaunts his paramours right in front of his wife, but ultimately wishes for a reconciliation.
The Awful Truth. 1937. Grant, Cary

Warriner, Lucy.
Lucy, suspicious and jealous of her husband, tries to have romances with other men, but changes her mind about a divorce at the last minute.
The Awful Truth. 1937. Dunne, Irene

Warwick.
Sloppy, bearded Warwick is the picture of a Tennessee mountain man at his worst: lazy, brutal, and virtually uncaring about the unfortunate and ignorant women who slave for their menfolk.
Stark Love. 1927. Miracle, Silas

Warwick, Rob.
Unlike the other lazy and brutish Tennessee mountaineers, young Rob thinks that women should not be slaves to their men. He is mocked by all when he falls for a girl who should be "protected, respected and pleasured."
Stark Love. 1927. James, Forrest

Waters, Mrs.
Brazen and bold Mrs. Waters helps Tom Jones devour a sumptuous meal, waits until he's finished slobbering, and seduces him with her eyes.
Tom Jones. 1963. Redman, Joyce

Watson, Dr.
Blustering, rotund physician, with a good-natured yet pompous personality, is a friend and assistant to the brilliant and somewhat brusque detective, Sherlock Holmes.
Sherlock Holmes. 1922. Young, Roland
The Hound of the Baskervilles. 1939. Bruce, Nigel

Watty, Bessie.
Her sly tricks obstructed in every instance by a very proper English schoolteacher in a small Welsh mining village, this pretty, cheap little temptress is paid to leave when she is impregnated by the star pupil in the school. On her return, the teacher adopts her unwanted child.
The Corn is Green. 1945. Lorring, Joan

Wayne, Chelsea Thayer.
Fortyish, divorced woman, suffering from feelings of inferiority and neglect, is still intimidated by her father, who appears to show resentment because she was not the boy he so desired.
On Golden Pond. 1981. Fonda, Jane

Webb, Emily.
Sweet, intelligent young girl grows up in a small New Hampshire town, dates the school's star baseball player, marries him, and starts a family.
Our Town. 1940. Scott, Martha

Weed, Bull.
With his roaring voice and raging temper, this burglar is feared by all, but when he commits murder he is helped by a derelict to whom he once gave a lot of money.
Underworld. 1927. Bancroft, George

Wells, Ira.
Trying to eke out a living and maintain his self-respect in the sleazy underworld of Los Angeles, this scrupulously honest, paunchy, over-the-hill private eye pursues the killer of an old pal.
The Late Show. 1977. Carney, Art

Wells, Kimberly.
When a nuclear accident occurs at a nuclear power plant while she is there on a routine assignment, this ambitious TV newscaster tries to persuade the nuclear control room manager to help expose what really happened.
The China Syndrome. 1979. Fonda, Jane

Western, Miss.
The goodhearted but wrong-minded visiting sister of Squire Western agrees with him when he insists that his daughter marry a man whom she absolutely detests.
Tom Jones. 1963. Evans, Edith

Western, Squire.
Rabelaisian Squire Western, snorting and cursing, bolts his food and guzzles his drinks, and interrupts the search for his daughter to join in a hunt he sees along the way.
Tom Jones. 1963. Griffith, Hugh

Westrum, Gil.
Aging, down-and-out ex-lawman joins an old pal in the job of protecting a gold shipment. In a moment of bitterness, he plans to make off with the gold; but, disarmed by his friend's quiet honesty and dignity, he returns to fight by his friend's side.
Ride the High Country. 1962. Scott, Randolph

Whitaker, Angela.
In this witty look at Hollywood, a stagestruck young woman goes to the film capital to act, but never gets a part. After several relatives, including her own children, and even the family parrot, find acting work, poor Angela realizes she is only a pretty face.
Hollywood. 1923. Brown, Hope

Whitaker, Joel.
A poor old man accompanies his stagestruck granddaughter to Hollywood and is given a part by a director who sees him by chance. He becomes a star and, dizzy with success, decides to take up golf and to have his name printed on his cigarettes.
Hollywood. 1923. Cosgrave, Luke

Whitcomb, Josiah.
An unpretentious Yankee farmer from New England leaves home to search for his son, who has gone to New York to seek his fortune.
The Old Homestead. 1915. Lossee, Frank

White, Margaret.
Filling her house with candles and chanting hysterical prayers, this neurotically religious mother tries to keep her teen-aged daughter, who has telekinetic powers, from going to the senior prom.
Carrie. 1976. Laurie, Piper

Wilkes, Ashley.
Aristocratic, idealistic and sensitive scion of Twelve Oaks plantation marries Melanie and resists Scarlett's jealous love and ardent devotion.
Gone With the Wind. 1939. Howard, Leslie

Wilkes, Melanie see Hamilton, Melanie

Wilkins, Mary.
Pioneer mother sacrifices to send her son through medical college. He becomes a successful surgeon in the Union Army, but neglects his mother who is now widowed.
Of Human Hearts. 1938. Bondi, Beulah

Willard.
In Vietnam this laconic, low-keyed intelligence captain is given a top-secret hazardous mission to proceed upriver into Cambodia and to assassinate a renegade colonel.
Apocalypse Now. 1974. Sheen, Martin

Williams, Chick.
A ruthless ex-convict plans a perfect murder.
Alibi. 1929. Morris, Chester

Wilson.
Mean, ugly, icy-nerved professional killer, hired by ranchers to see that the range remains unfenced by homesteaders, is eventually killed in a shoot-out with Shane.
Shane. 1953. Palance, Jack

Wilson, Joe.
Young Midwestern gasoline station owner, falsely accused of kidnapping, is thought to be destroyed by a lynch mob. However, he miraculously escapes death in a jailhouse fire, then vengefully conspires to see members of the mob punished for the crime they almost committed.
Fury. 1936. Tracy, Spencer

Wilson, Mary.
Married to a Denver lawyer for 16 years, this bored, still-beautiful matron, approaching middle age, is addicted to drugs and drink because her life is empty.
The Happy Ending. 1969. Simmons, Jean

Wilson, Woodrow.
This president tries with strength and dignity to keep the country out of World War I, struggles for peace during the war, and intelligently and forcefully battles for the League of Nations after the armistice.
Wilson. 1944. Knox, Alexander

Winemiller, Alma.
Lonely, inhibited preacher's daughter, confused by a combination of sexual, moral, and social taboos, nevertheless offers herself to the town's handsome, rakish heel.
Summer and Smoke. 1961. Page, Geraldine

Winemiller, Mrs.
Wife of a dominating, dictatorial husband, Mrs. Winemiller is a demented kleptomaniac who broke down under the strain of excessive poverty and repression, and who now jeers at and makes mocking revelations about her daughter, and treats her like a nursemaid.
Summer and Smoke. 1961. Merkel, Una

Winslow, Frank.
A sensitive Rebel soldier, who flees in terror from his first night on duty and hides in his family's attic, redeems himself when he bravely warns the Confederates of a Union attack.
The Coward. 1915. Ray, Charles

Winters, Eloise.
When her young lover is killed in a plane crash before they can be married, Eloise, finding herself pregnant, weds an old flame. Years later, when the unhappy marriage is over, her husband allows her custody of the child.
My Foolish Heart. 1949. Hayward, Susan

Wizard of Oz, see Marvel, Professor

Wolf Man, see Talbot, Larry

Wolsey.
Firm, single-minded but amoral Cardinal degenerates into a pathetic, powerless old man.
Anne of the Thousand Days. 1969. Quayle, Anthony

Woman.
Lonely, pathetic young widow almost convinces an escaped convict to stay with her.
The Defiant Ones. 1958. Williams, Cara

Woodhouse, Rosemary.
Young pregnant woman believes that her husband, in return for his success as an actor, has arranged a diabolical bargain with the people next door concerning the future of her unborn child.
Rosemary's Baby. 1968. Farrow, Mia

Woodward, Bob.
Young, dogged Washington Post reporter coaxes out information and plays his hunches as he untiringly tries to break the Watergate scandal.
All the President's Men. 1976. Redford, Robert

Wriford, Philip.
An amiable young writer and newspaper editor grows increasingly nervous and irritable due to overwork. When his mind finally snaps, he disappears from home and becomes a vagabond.
The Clean Heart. 1924. Marmont, Percy

Writer.
In late 19th-century Kristiania, this ragged, starving young writer, proud but secretly desperate, is unable to find a publisher. He takes refuge in his daydreams, wanders around the busy wintry streets, meets a young woman who later shuns him, and leaves the city to work as a deck hand.
Hunger. 1968. Oscarsson, Per

Wyke, Andrew.
Aristocratic, cruel English mystery writer with a penchant for gamesmanship invites his wife's lover for a social evening. His efforts to trick the young man backfire, and result in his own humiliation.
Sleuth. 1972. Olivier, Laurence

Wyverne, Kathryn.
The beautiful and bored wife of an English sportsman hunting in Algeria hopes to find an extramarital romance in an exotic setting.
Barbary Sheep. 1917. Ferguson, Elsie

Yang, General.
Insanely cruel and sinister Chinese warlord conquers a province in Shanghai, but must battle against idealistic Americans who hate oppression and believe in democracy.
The General Died at Dawn. 1936. Tamiroff, Akim

Yeager, Chuck.
Cool, taciturn test pilot, the first man to exceed the speed of sound, is passed over for astronaut training because he does not have a college degree. Because he is a prime example of someone with "the right stuff," he continues to test the limits of new aircraft, while the astronauts receive all the publicity.
The Right Stuff. 1983. Shepard, Sam

Yegor.
A singing bandit dresses up as a Cossack and woos a Russian princess.
The Rogue Song. 1930. Tibbett, Lawrence

Yente.
This outrageous matchmaker does business in the tiny Russian village of Anatevka.
Fiddler on the Roof. 1971. Picon, Molly

Yentl.
Yentl, a strong-willed woman living in Eastern Europe at the turn of the century, is determined to study the Torah, the Jewish Bible, although such study was forbidden to women. Disguised as a boy, she attends a Yeshiva in another village, but complications arise when she falls in love.
Yentl. 1983. Streisand, Barbra

York, Alvin C.
This real-life Tennessee mountain farmer is first a conscientious objector during World War I, but later joins the Army and becomes a hero by single-handedly capturing 132 German soldiers.
Sergeant York. 1941. Cooper, Gary

Younger, Ruth.
Attempting to leave the black ghetto to live in a white neighborhood this sweet, hard-working wife in a family of Chicago blacks realistically pursues happiness only in terms of peace and contentment within her own home.
A Raisin in the Sun. 1961. Dee, Ruby

Yuri.
Sexy, magnetic Russian-born ballet star has a fling with an aspiring young dancer, but does not allow her or any other woman to distract him from his art.
The Turning Point. 1977. Baryshnikov, Mikhail

Zampano.
Brutish, animalistic, itinerant carnival performer buys a simple, childlike farm girl, Gelsomina, to help in his act. He kills a circus performer because he is jealous of his friendship with the girl, and abandons Gelsomina. Only after finding that she has died does Zampano realize his love for her and his terrifying loneliness without her.
La Strada. 1954. Quinn, Anthony

Zapata, Emiliano.
During the Mexican Civil War, this selfless Mexican rebel leader, with a hatred for injustice and a passionate devotion to the poor and oppressed, is betrayed by the political leaders who fear him.
Viva Zapata. 1952. Brando, Marlon

Zeb.
Veteran trapper and trader, a typical mountain man, leaves civilization for life "in a big and wide country."
The Big Sky. 1952. Hunnicutt, Arthur

Zeke.
The comical Cowardly Lion is so timid that he is afraid of even a mouse. He wants to find the Wizard so that he will regain his courage and become king of the forest.
The Wizard of Oz. 1939. Lahr, Bert

Zelig, Leonard.
Possessed of a weak personality combined with a neurotic need to be liked, this human chameleon is capable of assuming the appearance and personality of anyone he is with. Zelig's progress from medical marvel to a celebrity in his own right in the '20s and '30s is traced by interviews, newsreels and recordings.
Zelig. 1983. Allen, Woody

Zhivago, Yuri.
Orphaned son of an impoverished Russian nobleman, raised by a wealthy aristocratic family, Yuri matures into a sensitive, passionate, idealistic poet and physician, and marries the family's daughter. However, the horrors of the Russian Revolution, World War I, and the Bolshevik Revolution throw the Zhivagos' lives into disruption and tragedy.
Doctor Zhivago. 1965. Sharif, Omar

Ziegfeld, Florenz, Jr.
Great Broadway showman becomes a legend because of his creative imagination, infallible eye for talent, and the courage to follow his own beliefs.
The Great Ziegfeld. 1936. Powell, William

Zola, Emile.
Young compassionate writer becomes successful as the author of *Nana* and a number of other novels, all protesting oppression and social injustice in France. In later years, Zola becomes complacent but is forced to renew his struggle for freedom and truth as he defends Captain Dreyfus.
The Life of Emile Zola. 1937. Muni, Paul

Zorba, Alexis.
Earthy, exuberant Greek, of uncertain age and origin, tries to share his joy in life with a timid Englishman by teaching him to accept both happiness and pain.
Zorba the Greek. 1964. Quinn, Anthony

Zorro.

In California in the 1820s, a pampered nobleman named Don Diego Vega disguises himself as a dashing and daring masked bandit, Zorro, who fights oppression and injustice.

The Mark of Zorro. 1920. Fairbanks, Douglas

The Mark of Zorro. 1940. Power, Tyrone

BIBLIOGRAPHY

Baer, D. Richard, ed. *Film Buff's Checklist of Motion Pictures, 1912-1979*. Hollywood, Calif.: Hollywood Film Archive, 1979.

Bawden, Liz-Anne, ed. *Oxford Companion to Film*. New York: Oxford University Press, 1976.

Boyum, Jay Gould and Scott, Adrienne. *Film as Film*. Boston: Allyn and Bacon, 1971.

Corliss, Richard. *Talking Pictures: Screenwriters in the American Cinema, 1927-1973*. Woodstock, N.Y.: The Overlook Press, 1974.

Crist, Judith. *The Private Eye, the Cowboy and the Very Naked Girl: Movies from Cleo to Clyde*. Chicago: Holt, Rinehart and Winston, 1968.

Crowther, Bosley. *Reruns: Fifty Memorable Films*. New York: Putnam, 1978.

Everson, William K. *American Silent Film*. New York: Oxford University Press, 1978.

Garbicz, Adam and Klinowski, Jacek. *Cinema, the Magic Vehicle: A Guide to its Achievement*. Vol. 1: *Journey One: The Cinema Through 1949*. Metuchen, N.J.: Scarecrow Press, 1975.

Garbicz, Adam and Klinowski, Jacek. *Cinema, the Magic Vehicle: A Guide to its Achievement*. Vol. 2: *Journey Two: The Cinema in the Fifties*. Metuchen, N.J.: Scarecrow Press, 1979.

Gianetti, Louis. *Master of the American Cinema*. Englewood Cliffs, N.J.: Prentice-Hall, 1981.

Griffith, Richard. *The Movie Stars*. Garden City, N.Y.: Doubleday, 1972.

Halliwell, Leslie. *The Filmgoer's Companion*. 6th ed. New York: Hill and Wang, 1977.

Halliwell, Leslie. *Halliwell's Film Guide*. 4th ed. New York: Charles Scribner's Sons, 1983.

Higham, Charles and Greenberg, Joel. *Hollywood in the Forties*. New York: Paperback Library, 1970.

Hyams, Jay. *The Life and Times of the Western Movie*. New York: W.H. Smith, 1983.

Kael, Pauline. *Deeper Into Movies*. New York: Warner Books, 1969.

Kael, Pauline. *5001 Nights at the Movies: A Guide From A to Z*. New York: Holt, Rinehart and Winston, 1982.

Kael, Pauline. *Going Steady*. Boston: Little, Brown, 1970.

Kael, Pauline. *Reeling*. Boston: Little, Brown, 1976.

Kael, Pauline. *When the Lights Go Down*. New York: Holt, Rinehart and Winston, 1979.

Kauffmann, Stanley. *Before My Eyes*. New York: Harper & Row, 1980.

Kauffmann, Stanley. *Figures of Light: Film Criticism and Comment*. New York: Harper & Row, 1970.

Kauffmann, Stanley. *Living Images*. New York: Harper & Row, 1974.

Magill's Survey of Cinema: English Language Films: First Series. 4 vols. Englewood Cliffs, N.J.: Salem Press, 1980.

Magill's Survey of Cinema: English Language Films: Second Series. 6 vols. Englewood Cliffs, N.J.: Salem Press, 1981.

Magill's Survey of Cinema: Silent Films. 3 vols. Englewood Cliffs, N.J.: Salem Press, 1982.

Maltin, Leonard, ed. *TV Movies*. New York: New American Library, 1978.

Michael, Paul. *The American Movies Reference Book: The Sound Era*. Englewood Cliffs, N.J.: Prentice-Hall, 1969.

New York Times Film Reviews, 1913-1968. 6 vols. New York: New York Times, 1970. Supplements: 1969-70, 1971-72, 1973-74, 1975-76.

Osborne, Robert A. *50 Golden Years of Oscar: The Official History of the Academy of Motion Picture Arts and Sciences*. La Habra, Calif.: ESE California, 1979.

Pechter, William S. *Movies Plus One*. New York: Horizon Press, 1982.

Pickard, Roy. *The Award Movies: A Complete Guide From A to Z*. New York: Schocken Books, 1980.

Sarris, Andrew. *Confessions of a Cultist: On the Cinema, 1955-1969*. New York: Simon and Schuster, 1971.

Schickel, Richard. *Second Sight: Notes on Some Movies, 1965-1970.* New York: Simon and Schuster, 1972.

Seidman, Steve. *Comedian Comedy: A Tradition in Hollywood Film.* Ann Arbor, Mich.: UMI Research Press, 1981.

Shipman, David. *The Great Movie Stars: The Golden Years.* New York: Bonanza Books, 1975.

Simon, John. *Movies Into Film: Film Criticism 1967-1970.* New York: Simon and Schuster, 1971.

Slide, Anthony. *Fifty American Silent Films, 1912-1920: A Pictorial Survey.* New York: Dover Publications, 1980.

Slide, Anthony. *Selected Film Criticism.* Metuchen, N.J.: Scarecrow Press, 1982-1983. Vol. 1: 1896-1911. Vol. 2: 1912-1920. Vol. 3: 1921-1930. Vol. 4: 1931-1940. Vol. 5: 1941-1950.

Steinberg, Cobbett S. *Film Facts.* New York: Facts on File, 1980.

Variety Film Reviews, 1907-1980. New York: Garland, 1983.

Von Gunden, Kenneth and Stock, Stuart H. *Twenty All-Time Great Science Fiction Films.* New York: Arlington House, 1982.

Walker, Alexander. *Double Takes: Notes and Afterthoughts on the Movies, 1955-76.* London: Elm Tree Books, 1977.

Zinman, David. *50 Classic Motion Pictures: The Stuff That Dreams Are Made Of.* New York: Crown, 1972.

Zinman, David. *50 From the 50's: Vintage Films From America's Mid-Century.* New Rochelle, N.Y.: Arlington House, 1979.

Periodical Indexes

In addition to the books listed, important sources for descriptions of film characters included individual film reviews from magazines, journals, and newspapers too numerous to list.

Alternative Press Index: An Index to Alternative and Radical Publications. 1969- . Baltimore, Md.: Alternative Press Centre.

Art Index. 1929- . New York: H.W. Wilson.

Arts and Humanities Citation Index. 1977- . Philadelphia, Pa.: Institute for Scientific Information.

Film Literature Index. 1973- . Albany, N.Y.: Filmdex.

Humanities Index. 1974- . New York: H.W. Wilson.

Index to the Christian Science Monitor. 1960- . Wooster, Ohio: Bell and Howell.

New York Times Index. 1861- . New York: New York Times.

Popular Periodical Index. 1973- . Collingswood, N.J.: Robert M. Bottorff.

Readers' Guide to Periodical Literature. 1900- . New York: H.W. Wilson.

FILM INDEX

Abe Lincoln in Illinois
Lincoln, Abraham

Absence of Malice
Gallagher
Megan
Teresa

Across the Pacific
Lorenz, Dr.

Actress, The
Jones, Clinton
Jones, Ruth Gordon

Adventures of Robin Hood, The
Robin Hood

Adventures of Robinson Crusoe, The
Crusoe, Robinson

Affairs of Cellini, The
Duke of Florence

African Queen, The
Allnutt, Charlie
Sayer, Rose

Airport
Guerrero, Inez
Quonsett, Ada

Alfie
Alfie
Lily

Algiers
Gaby
Le Moko, Pepe
Regis

Alibi
Williams, Chick

Alice Adams
Adams, Alice
Malena

Alice Doesn't Live Here Anymore
Flo
Hyatt, Alice

All About Eve
Birdie
DeWitt, Addison
Eve
Karen
Margo

All My Sons
Keller, Joe

All Quiet on the Western Front
Baumer, Paul

All That Jazz
Gideon, Joe

All That Money Can Buy
Scratch, Mr.

All the King's Men
Burden, Jack
Burke, Sadie
Stark, Willie

All the President's Men
Bernstein, Carl
Bookkeeper
Bradlee, Ben
Deep Throat
Woodward, Bob

All This and Heaven Too
De Praslin, Duc
De Praslin, Duchesse
Deluzy-Desportes, Henriette

Along Came Jones
Jones, Melody

America America
Topouzoglou, Stavros

American Graffiti
Debbie

An American in Paris
Bourvier, Lise
Mulligan, Jerry

Anastasia
Anastasia
Empress

Anatomy of a Murder
Biegler, Paul
Dancer, Claude
McCarthy, Parnell

Anchors Aweigh
Brady, Joseph

And Justice For All
Kirkland, Arthur

Angels With Dirty Faces
Connolly, Jerry
Sullivan, Rocky

Anna and the King of Siam
Anna
King

Anna Christie
Christie, Anna
Marthe

Anna Karenina
Karenina, Anna

Anne of the Thousand Days
Boleyn, Anne
Henry VIII
Wolsey

Annie Hall
Hall, Annie
Singer, Alvy

Anthony Adverse
Paleologus, Faith

Apartment, The
Baxter, C.C
Dreyfuss, Dr.
Kubelik, Fran

Apocalypse Now
Kilgore
Kurtz
Willard

Apprenticeship of Duddy Kravitz
Duddy

Around the World in Eighty Days
Fogg, Phileas
Passepartout

Arrowsmith
Arrowsmith, Leora
Arrowsmith, Martin

Arthur
Bach, Arthur
Hobson

Ashes of Vengeance
De Breux, Yoeland
Duc de Tours

Asphalt Jungle
Emmerich, Alonzo D
Handley, Dix
Riedenschneider, Erwin

Atlantic City
Lou
Sally

Ben-Hur
   Ben-Hur, Judah
   Ilderim, Sheik
   Messala

Berkeley Square
   Standish, Peter

Best Little Whorehouse in Texas, The
   Governor

Best Man, The
   Hockstader, Arthur

Best Years of Our Lives, The
   Parrish, Homer
   Stephenson, Al

Bicycle Thief, The
   Antonio
   Bruno

Big Chill, The
   Meg
   Michael
   Nick
   Sam
   Sarah

Big Country, The
   Hannassey, Rufus

Big House, The
   Butch

Big Parade, The
   Apperson, James
   Melisande

Big Pond, The
   Mirande, Pierre

Big Sky, The
   Deakins, Jim
   Zeb

Big Sleep, The
   Marlowe

Billy Budd
   Budd, Billy

Birdman of Alcatraz
   Gomez, Feto
   Stroud, Elizabeth
   Stroud, Robert E.

Birth of a Nation, The
   Cameron, Ben
   Cameron, Flora
   Stoneman, Elsie

Black Narcissus
   Clodagh, Sister

Black Pirate, The
   Black Pirate

Black Stallion, The
   Dailey, Henry

Blazing Saddles
   Von Shtupp, Lili

Blind Husbands
   Armstrong, Margaret
   Armstrong, Robert
   Steuben, Lieutenant von

Blood and Sand
   Gallardo, Juan

Blossoms in the Dust
   Gladney, Edna

Blue Veil, The
   Mason, Louise

Bob & Carol & Ted & Alice
   Alice
   Bob
   Carol
   Ted

Body and Soul
   Davis, Charlie

Boheme, La
Mimi
Rodolphe

Bold and the Brave, The
Dooley

Bonnie and Clyde
Barrow, Buck
Barrow, Clyde
Blanche
Moss, C.W
Parker, Bonnie

Born Yesterday
Dawn, Billie

Bound for Glory
Guthrie, Woody

Boys From Brazil, The
Lieberman, Ezra

Boys' Town
Flanagan, Father
Marsh, Whitey

Brainstorm
Reynolds, Lillian

Brat, The
Brat

Breakfast at Tiffany's
Golightly, Holly

Breaking Away
Dave
Stoller, Mr.
Stoller, Mrs.

Breaking Through the Sound Barrier
Ridgefield, John

Breathless
Poiccard, Michel

Bridge on the River Kwai, The
Nicholson
Saito

Brief Encounter
Jesson, Laura

Bright Victory
Nevins, Larry

Broadway Melody
Hank

Broken Arrow
Cochise

Broken Blossoms
Burrows, Lucy
Cheng, Huan

Broken Lance
Devereaux, Matt
Devereaux, Senora

Bronco Billy
Bronco Billy

Brothers Karamazov, The
Karamazov, Fyodor

Browning Version, The
Crocker-Harris, Andrew

Buddy Holly Story, The
Holly, Buddy

Bulldog Drummond
Drummond, Hugh

Bus Stop
Bo
Cherie

Butch Cassidy and the Sundance Kid
Cassidy, Butch
Place, Etta
Sundance Kid

Butterfield 8
Wandrous, Gloria

Butterflies are Free
Baker, Mrs.
Jill

Cabaret
Bowles, Sally
Master of Ceremonies
Natalia

Cabinet of Dr. Caligari, The
Caligari, Dr.
Cesare

Cabiria or the Nights of Cabiria
Cabiria

Cactus Flower
Simmons, Toni

Caged
Allen, Marie
Harper, Evelyn

Caine Mutiny, The
DeVriess
Queeg

California Suite
Barrie, Diana

Camille
Gautier, Marguerite

Captain Blood
Blood, Peter

Captain Newman, M.D
Tompkins, Jim

Captains Courageous
Cheyne, Harvey
Manuel

Captain's Paradise, The
St. James, Henry

Cardinal, The
Glennon, Cardinal

Carmen Jones
Carmen

Carnal Knowledge
Bobbie

Carrie
Carrie
White, Margaret

Casablanca
Blaine, Rick
Ferrari, Senor
Lund, Ilsa
Renault, Louis
Sam
Ugarte

Cat Ballou
Shelleen, Kid
Silvernose

Cat on a Hot Tin Roof
Big Daddy
Brick
Maggie

Cat People
Dubrovna, Irena

Cavalcade
Marryot, Jane

Chalk Garden, The
St. Maugham, Mrs.

Champ, The
Champ
Dink

Champion
Kelly, Connie
Kelly, Midge

Chapter Two
MacLaine, Jennie

Come and Get It
Bostrom, Swan

Come Back, Little Sheba
Delaney, Doc
Delaney, Lola
Loring, Marie

Come Fill the Cup
Copeland, Boyd
Marsh, Lew

Come to the Stable
Margaret, Sister
Potts, Miss
Scolastica, Sister

Comes a Horseman
Dodger

Coming Home
Hyde, Robert
Hyde, Sally
Martin, Luke
Munson, Vi

Condemned
Michel

Confidential Agent
Denard
Melandez, Mrs.

Constant Nymph, The
Sanger, Tessa

Conversation, The
Caul, Harry

Cool Hand Luke
Dragline
Luke

Coquette
Beasant, Norma

Corn is Green, The
Evans, Morgan
Moffat, Miss
Watty, Bessie

Count of Monte Cristo, The
Dantes, Edmond

Country Girl, The
Elgin, Frank
Elgin, Georgie

Cousin, Cousine
Marthe

Coward, The
Winslow, Frank

Cradle Buster, The
Sweetie

Crainquebille
Crainquebille

Cranes Are Flying, The
Veronica

Cries and Whispers
Agnes
Anna
Maria

Crimson Challenge, The
Tharon

Crossfire
Ginny
Montgomery

Cyrano de Bergerac
De Bergerac, Cyrano

Dangerous
Heath, Joyce

Dark Angel, The
Trent, Hilary
Vane, Kitty

Dark at the Top of the Stairs, The
Reenie

Dark Victory
Traherne, Judith

Dodsworth
Dodsworth, Samuel
Von Obersdorf, Baroness

Dog Day Afternoon
Leon
Sonny

Dolce Vita, La
Rubino, Marcello

Double Indemnity
Dietrichson, Phyllis

Double Life, A
John, Anthony

Dr. Dolittle
Dolittle, Dr. John

Dr. Jekyll and Mr. Hyde
Hyde, Edward
Jekyll, Henry

Dr. No
Bond, James

Dr. Strangelove: or, How I Learned to Stop Worrying and Love the Bomb
Mandrake, Group Captain
Muffley, President
Ripper, General Jack D
Strangelove, Dr.
Turgidson, General Buck

Dracula
Dracula

Dramatic Life of Abraham Lincoln, The
Lincoln, Abraham

Drums Along the Mohawk
McKlennar, Mrs.

Duel in the Sun
Chavez, Pearl
McCanles, Laurabelle

E.T. the Extra-Terrestrial
Elliott

East of Eden
Kate
Trask, Cal

Easy Rider
Hanson, George

Ebb Tide
Davis

Educating Rita
Bryant, Frank
Rita

Edward, My Son
Boult, Evelyn

Effect of Gamma Rays on Man-in-the-Moon Marigolds
Beatrice

Egg and I, The
Kettle, Ma

Elephant Man, The
Merrick, John

Ellery Queen, Master Detective
Queen, Ellery

Elmer Gantry
Bains, Lulu
Gantry, Elmer

Elvira Madigan
Elvira

Emigrants, The
Kristine
Oskar, Karl

Emma
Thatcher, Emma

Entertainer, The
Rice, Archie

Fortune Cookie, The
Gingrich, Willie

42nd Street
Dillon, Abner
Marsh, Julian

Four Daughters
Borden, Mickey

Fourteen Hours
Cosick, Robert

Frances
Farmer, Frances
Farmer, Lillian

Frankenstein
Frankenstein
Monster

Frankenstein Meets the Wolfman
Frankenstein

Free Soul, A
Ashe, Jan
Ashe, Stephen

French Connection, The
Doyle, Jimmy
Russo, Buddy

French Lieutenant's Woman, The
Sarah

Freshman, The
Lamb, Harold

Friendly Persuasion
Birdwell, Josh

From Here to Eternity
Alma
Holmes, Karen
Maggio, Angelo
Prewitt, Robert E. Lee
Warden, Milton

Front Page, The
Burns, Walter
Johnson, Hildy

Funny Girl
Brice, Fanny

Fury
Wilson, Joe

Gallipoli
Dunne, Frank

Gandhi
Gandhi, Mahatma

Gaslight
Alquist, Paula
Anton, Gregory
Nancy

Gay Divorcee, The
Glossop, Mimi
Holden, Guy

General, The
Gray, Johnnie

General Died at Dawn, The
Yang, General

Generale della Rovere
Della Rovere

Gentleman Jim
Corbett, Jim

Gentleman's Agreement
Anne
Green, Phil
Kathy

Georgy Girl
Georgy
James

Giant
Benedict, Bick
Benedict, Luz
Rink, Jett

Great White Hope
Eleanor
Jefferson, Jack

Great Ziegfeld, The
Held, Anna
Ziegfeld, Florenz, Jr.

Greed
McTeague
Trina

Green Goddess, The
Rajah of Rukh

Green Years, The
Gow, Alexander

Grey Fox, The
Miner, Bill

Guardsman, The
Actor
Actress

Guess Who's Coming to Dinner
Drayton, Christina
Drayton, Matt
Prentice, John
Prentice, Mrs.
Ryan, Monsignor

Gunfighter, The
Ringo, Jimmy

Gypsy Passion
Old Kate

Hail the Conquering Hero
Truesmith, Woodrow

Hamlet
Hamlet
Ophelia

Happy Ending, The
Wilson, Mary

Hard Way, The
Chernen, Helen

Harry and Tonto
Harry

Harvey
Dowd, Elwood P
Simmons, Veta Louise

Hasty Heart, The
Lachie

Hatful of Rain
Pope, Johnny

Hawaii
Malama

He Who Gets Slapped
Beaumont

Heart is a Lonely Hunter, The
Mick
Singer

Heart of Humanity, The
Nanette

Heartbreak Kid, The
Corcoran, Mr.
Lenny
Lila

Hearts of the West
Kessler

Heaven Can Wait
Corkle, Max
Farnsworth, Julia
Pendleton, Joe

Heaven Knows, Mr. Allison
Angela, Sister

Hedda
Hedda

Hustler, The
Felson, Eddie
Gordon, Bert
Minnesota Fats
Packard, Sarah

I am a Fugitive from a Chain Gang
Allen, James

I Never Sang for My Father
Garrison, Gene
Garrison, Tom

I Remember Mama
Chris
Katrin
Mama
Trina

I Want to Live
Graham, Barbara

Iceman Cometh, The
Slade, Larry

If I Were King
Louis XI

If Winter Comes
Sabre, Mark

I'll Cry Tomorrow
Roth, Lillian

Imitation of Life
Delilah
Johnson, Annie
Pullman, Bea
Sarah Jane

In Old Arizona
Cisco Kid

In Old Chicago
O'Leary, Molly

In the Heat of the Night
Gillespie, Bill
Tibbs, Virgil

In Which We Serve
Kinross, Captain

Incredible Shrinking Man
Carey, Scott

Informer, The
Nolan, Gypo

Inherit the Wind
Brady, Matthew Harrison
Drummond, Henry

Inside Daisy Clover
Dealer

Inside Moves
Louise

Interiors
Eve
Pearl

Interlude
Antonia

Interrupted Melody
Lawrence, Marjorie

Invaders, The
Hirth

Irma La Douce
La Douce, Irma

Isadora
Duncan, Isadora

Isn't Life Wonderful?
Inga

It Happened One Night
Andrews, Ellie
Warne, Peter

Italian, The
Donnetti, Beppo

Kramer vs. Kramer
Kramer, Billy
Kramer, Joanna
Kramer, Ted
Phelps, Margaret

L-Shaped Room, The
Jane

Lacombe, Lucien
Horn, Albert

Ladies in Retirement
Ellen

Lady for a Day
Apple Annie
Dave, the Dude

Lady Sings the Blues
Holiday, Billie

Landlord, The
Enders, Mrs.
Fanny

Last Angry Man, The
Abelman, Sam

Last Command, The
Dolgorucki

Last Detail, The
Buddusky
Meadows

Last Laugh, The
Doorman

Last Picture Show, The
Farrow, Lois
Jackson, Duane
Popper, Ruth
Sam the Lion

Last Summer
Rhoda

Last Tango in Paris
Paul

Late Show, The
Wells, Ira

Laura
Lydecker, Waldo

Lavender Hill Mob
Holland
Pendlebury

Lawrence of Arabia
Lawrence
Sherif Ali

Leather Boys, The
Pete

Leave Her to Heaven
Ellen

Lenny
Bruce, Honey
Bruce, Lenny

Letter, The
Crosbie, Leslie
Joyce, Howard

Letter From an Unknown Woman
Berndle, Lisa

Life and Times of Judge Roy Bean, The
Bean, Roy

Life of Emile Zola, The
Dreyfus, Alfred
Zola, Emile

Life With Father
Father

Lifeboat
Porter, Connie

Lili
Berthalet, Paul
Daurier, Lili

Lilies of the Field
Maria, Mother
Smith, Homer

Lion in Winter, The
Eleanor of Aquitaine
Henry II

Little Big Man
Crabb, Jack
Old Lodge Skins

Little Caesar
Little Caesar

Little Foxes, The
Giddens, Regina

Little Old New York
O'Day, Patricia

Little Women
Jo
March, Aunt

Live and Let Die
Bond, James

Lolita
Haze, Charlotte

Lonelyhearts
Doyle, Fay

Long Day's Journey into Night
Tyrone, James
Tyrone, Jamie
Tyrone, Mary

Looking for Mr. Goodbar
Dunn, Katherine
Dunn, Theresa

Lost Horizon
Chang
Conway, Robert
High Lama

Lost Weekend, The
Birnam, Don

Lost World, The
Challenger, Professor

Love Affair
MacKay, Terry
Marnay, Mme

Love is a Many-Splendored Thing
Suyin, Han

Love Light, The
Angela

Love Me or Leave Me
Snyder, Martin

Love Parade, The
Alfred, Count

Love Story
Barrett, Oliver, IV
Cavilleri, Jenny
Cavilleri, Phil

Love With the Proper Stranger
Angie

Lovers and Other Strangers
Frank

Luck of the Irish, The
Horace

Lust for Life
Gauguin, Paul
Van Gogh, Vincent

M
M

Macomber Affair, The
Macomber, Margaret

Madame Curie
Curie, Marie
Curie, Pierre

Madame Rosa
Madame Rosa

Madame X
Floriot, Jacqueline

Magnificent Ambersons, The
Minafer, Fanny
Minafer, George Amberson

Magnificent Obsession
Phillips, Helen

Magnificent Yankee, The
Holmes, Oliver Wendell

Major and the Minor, The
Applegate, Sue

Majority of One, A
Jacoby, Bertha

Maltese Falcon, The
Cairo, Joel
Gutman, Casper
Spade, Sam

Man and a Woman, A
Gauthier, Anne

Man for All Seasons, A
Henry VIII
More, Alice
More, Sir Thomas

Man in the Glass Booth, The
Goldman, Arthur

Man Who Played God, The
Arden, John

Man Who Would Be King, The
Carnehan, Peachy
Dravot, Daniel

Man With the Golden Arm, The
Frankie

Manchurian Candidate
Raymond's Mother

Manhandled
McGuire, Tessie

Manhattan
Tracy

Marathon Man
Babe
Szell

Marie Antoinette
Antoinette, Marie
Louis XVI

Mark, The
Fuller, Jim

Mark of Zorro, The
Zorro

Marriage Circle, The
Stock, Mizzie

Marriage Italian Style
Marturano, Filomena

Marty
Angie
Clara
Marty

Mary Poppins
Poppins, Mary

Mary, Queen of Scots
Mary, Queen of Scots

M*A*S*H
O'Houlihan, Margaret

Monte Cristo
  Dantes, Edmond

Moon and Sixpence, The
  Strickland, Charles

Moon is Blue, The
  O'Neill, Patty

Moon is Down, The
  Lanser, Colonel

Moontide
  Bobo

More the Merrier, The
  Dingle, Benjamin
  Milligan, Connie

Morgan
  Leonie
  Morgan

Morning Glory
  Lovelace, Eva

Morocco
  Jolly, Amy

Moulin Rouge
  Charlet, Marie
  Toulouse-Lautrec

Mourning Becomes Electra
  Mannon, Lavinia
  Mannon, Orin

**Mr. Blandings Builds His Dream
  House**
  Blandings, Jim

Mr. Deeds Goes to Town
  Deeds, Longfellow

Mr. Skeffington
  Skeffington, Job
  Trellis, Fanny

Mr. Smith Goes to Washington
  Paine, Joseph
  Senate President
  Smith, Jefferson

Mrs. Miniver
  Ballard
  Beldon, Carol
  Beldon, Lady
  Miniver, Clem
  Miniver, Kay

Mrs. Parkington
  Parkington, Susie

Muddy River
  Nubuo

Murder, Inc.
  Reles, Abe

Murder on the Orient Express
  Ohlsson, Greta
  Poirot, Hercule

Music Man, The
  Hill, Harold
  Paroo, Marian

Mutiny on the Bounty
  Bligh, William
  Byam
  Christian, Fletcher

My Cousin Rachel
  Ashley, Philip

My Fair Lady
  Doolittle, Alfred
  Doolittle, Eliza
  Higgins, Henry
  Higgins, Mrs.

My Favorite Year
  Swann, Alan

My Foolish Heart
  Winters, Eloise

Old Homestead, The
Whitcomb, Josiah

Old Man and the Sea, The
Old Man

Oliver
Artful Dodger
Fagin

Oliver Twist
Fagin
Twist, Oliver

On Golden Pond
Thayer, Ethel
Thayer, Norman, Jr.
Wayne, Chelsea Thayer

On the Waterfront
Barry, Father
Doyle, Edie
Friendly, Johnny
Malloy, Charley
Malloy, Terry

Once is Not Enough
Linda

One Flew Over the Cuckoo's Nest
Bibbitt, Billy
Bromden, Chief
McMurphy, R.P
Ratched, Nurse

One Glorious Day
Botts, Ezra

One Hour With You
Bertier, Andre
Bertier, Colette
Oliver, Mitzi

One Night of Love
Barrett, Mary
Monteverdi, Giulio

One of Our Aircraft is Missing
De Vries, Jo

One Potato, Two Potato
Richards, Julie Cullen

Only When I Laugh
Georgia
Jimmy
Toby

Open City
Pina

Ordinary People
Berger
Beth
Calvin
Conrad

Orphans of the Storm
Henriette
Louise

Othello
Desdemona
Emilia
Iago
Othello

Our Town
Webb, Emily

Ox-Bow Incident, The
Carter, Gil

Panic
Hire, Monsieur

Panic in Needle Park
Helen

Panthea
Romoff, Panthea

Paper Chase, The
Kingsfield

Paper Moon
Delight, Trixie
Loggins, Addie

Pocketful of Miracles
Joy Boy

Pollyanna
Pollyanna

Poor Little Peppina
Peppina

Poor Little Rich Girl, A
Gwendolyn

Poseidon Adventure, The
Belle

Possessed
Howell, Louise

Postman Always Rings Twice, The
Chambers, Frank
Smith, Cora

Pride and Prejudice
Bennet, Elizabeth

Pride of the Marines
Schmid, Al

Pride of the Yankees, The
Gehrig, Lou

Prime of Miss Jean Brodie, The
Brodie, Jean
MacKay, Miss
Sandy

Primrose Path
Adams, Mamie

Prince and the Showgirl, The
Queen Dowager

Private Benjamin
Benjamin, Judy
Lewis, Doreen

Private Life of Henry VIII, The
Anne of Cleves
Henry VIII

Producers, The
Bloom, Leo

Providence
Langham, Clive

Prunella
Prunella

Psycho
Bates, Norman
Crane, Marion

Public Enemy, The
Tom

Pumpkin Eater, The
Jo

Pygmalion
Doolittle, Eliza
Higgins, Henry

Quiet Man, The
Danaher, Mary Kate
Danaher, "Red" Will
Flynn, Michaleen
Thornton, Sean

Quo Vadis
Nero
Petronius

Rachel, Rachel
Cameron, Rachel
Mackie, Calla

Raging Bull
La Motta, Jake
La Motta, Joey
La Motta, Vickie

Ragtime
Conklin, Willie
Nesbit, Evelyn
Walker, Coalhouse, Jr.

Raiders of the Lost Ark
Indy

Romeo and Juliet
Juliet
Romeo
Tybalt

Romola
Romola

Room at the Top
Aisgill, Alice
Elspeth
Lampton, Joe

Rose, The
Dyer
Rose

Rose Tattoo, The
Delle Rose, Rosa
Delle Rose, Serafina

Rosemary's Baby
Castevet, Minnie
Woodhouse, Rosemary

Rosita
Carlos
Rosita

Royal Family of Broadway, The
Cavendish, Tony

Ruggles of Red Gap
Ruggles, Marmaduke

Ruling Class, The
Jack, 14th Earl of Gurney

Russians Are Coming, The Russians Are Coming
Rozanov

Ryan's Daughter
Michael
Rosy

Sabrina
Fairchild, Sabrina
Larrabee, David
Larrabee, Linus

Sadie Thompson
Thompson, Sadie

Sahara
Giuseppe
Gunn, Joe

Same Time, Next Year
Doris
George

San Francisco
Mullin, Tim
Norton, Blackie

Sand Pebbles, The
Holman, Jake
Po-Han

Sands of Iwo Jima
Stryker

Sarah and Son
Storm, Sarah

Saratoga Trunk
Angelique
Dulaine, Clio

Saturday Night and Sunday Morning
Arthur

Saturday Night Fever
Manero, Tony

Save the Tiger
Greene, Phil
Stoner, Harry

Sayonara
Gruver
Katsumi
Kelly

Scarface
Camonte, Tony
Montana, Tony

Street Angel
Angela

Streetcar Named Desire, A
Blanche
Kowalski, Stanley
Kowalski, Stella
Mitch

Stunt Man, The
Cameron
Cross, El

Subject Was Roses, The
Cleary, John
Cleary, Nettie

Sudden Fear
Blaine, Lester
Hudson, Myra

Suddenly Last Summer
Holly, Catherine
Venable, Mrs.

Sullivan's Travels
Sullivan, John L

Summer and Smoke
Winemiller, Alma
Winemiller, Mrs.

Summer Wishes, Winter Dreams
Rita's Mother
Walden, Rita

Summertime
Hudson, Jane

Sunday Bloody Sunday
Greville, Alex
Hirsh, Daniel

Sundowners, The
Carmody, Ida
Firth, Mrs.

Sunrise at Campobello
Roosevelt, Eleanor
Roosevelt, Franklin D.

Sunset Boulevard
Desmond, Norma
Gillis, Joe
Schaefer, Betty
Von Mayerling, Max

Sunshine Boys, The
Clark, Willy
Lewis, Al

Suspicion
McLaidlaw, Lina

Sweet Bird of Youth
Del Lago, Alexandra
Finley, Boss
Finley, Heavenly

Symphonie Pastorale
Pastor

Tale of Two Cities, A
Carton, Sydney

Talk of the Town, The
Dilg, Leopold

Tarzan of the Apes
Tarzan

Tarzan, the Apeman
Jane
Tarzan

Taste of Honey, A
Geoffrey
Jo

Taxi Driver
Bickle, Travis
Iris

Teacher's Pet
Pine, Hugo

Tell It to the Marines
Burns, Skeet
O'Hara

To Kill a Mockingbird
Finch, Atticus
Finch, Scott

To Live in Peace
Tigna, Uncle

Tol'able David
David

Tom Jones
Jones, Tom
Molly
Waters, Mrs.
Western, Miss
Western, Squire

Tommy
Walker, Nora

Tootsie
Dorsey, Michael
Julie
Sandy

Topkapi
Simpson, Arthur

Topper
Topper, Cosmo

Torch Song
Stewart, Mrs.

Tortilla Flat
Pirate

Touch of Class, A
Allessio, Vicki
Blackburn, Steve

Towering Inferno, The
Claiborne, Harlee

Travels With My Aunt
Augusta

Treasure of Sierra Madre
Dobbs, Fred C.
Gold Hat
Howard

Tree Grows in Brooklyn, A
Nolan, Johnny

Trespasser, The
Donnell, Marion

Trial
Barney

Tribute
Templeton, Scottie

Trilby
Trilby

Trojan Women, The
Helen of Troy

True Grit
Cogburn, Rooster
Ross, Mattie

Tugboat Annie
Annie

Turning Point, The
Deedee
Emilia
Emma
Yuri

Turning the Tables
Pennington, Doris

Twelve Angry Men
Juror 3
Juror 8

Twelve O'Clock High
Savage, General
Stovall, Major

Twilight of Honor
Brown, Ben

ACTOR INDEX

Abel, Alfred
Masterman, John

Adams, Nick
Brown, Ben

Adjani, Isabelle
H., Adele

Adoree, Renee
Melisande

Aherne, Brian
Maximillian

Aimee, Anouk
Gauthier, Anne

Albert, Eddie
Corcoran, Mr.
Radovich, Irving

Albertson, Jack
Cleary, John

Alda, Alan
George

Alexander, Jane
Bookkeeper
Eleanor
Phelps, Margaret

Allen, Woody
Singer, Alvy
Zelig, Leonard

Allgood, Sara
Morgan, Mrs.

Anderson, Judith
Danvers, Mrs.

Andersson, Bibi
Nurse Alma

Andersson, Harriett
Agnes
Justina

Andrews, Julie
Maria
Poppins, Mary
Victor

Ann-Margret
Bobbie
Walker, Nora

Arkin, Alan
Kessler
Rozanov
Singer

Arliss, George
Arden, John
Disraeli, Benjamin
Rajah of Rukh

Armendariz, Pedro
Kino

Arthur, Jean
Milligan, Connie

Asahara, Nobutaka
Nubuo

Astaire, Fred
Claiborne, Harlee
Holden, Guy

Astor, Mary
Kovack, Sandra

Auer, Mischa
Carlo

Ayres, Lew
Baumer, Paul
Kildare, James
Richardson, Robert

Bacall, Lauren
Marie

Baddeley, Hermione
Elspeth

Badham, Mary
Finch, Scott

Bainter, Fay
Belle, Aunt
Parmalee, Hannah
Tilford, Amelia

Baker, Carroll
Baby Doll

Balkin, Karen
Tilford, Mary

Balsam, Martin
Arnold

Bancroft, Anne
Emma
Jo
Robinson, Mrs.
Sullivan, Anne

Bancroft, George
Thunderbolt
Weed, Bull

Bankhead, Tallulah
Porter, Connie

Banky, Vilma
Vane, Kitty

Bannen, Ian
Crow

Bara, Theda
Cleopatra
Lazar, Vania
Vampire

Barrault, Marie-Christine
Marthe

Barrie, Barbara
Richards, Julie Cullen
Stoller, Mrs.

Barrymore, Ethel
Miss Em
Mott, Ma
Warren, Mrs.

Barrymore, John
Brummel, George
Holmes, Sherlock
Hyde, Edward
Jekyll, Henry
Von Geigern, Baron Felix

Barrymore, Lionel
Ashe, Stephen
Gillespie, Leonard
Kringelein, Otto
Peggotty, Dan

Barthelmess, Richard
Bartlett, David
Cheng, Huan
Crosby, Charles
David
Marden, Joe
Patent Leather Kid

Bartholomew, Freddie
Cheyne, Harvey
Copperfield, David

Baryshnikov, Mikhail
Yuri

Basehart, Richard
Cosick, Robert
Matto

Bergner, Elisabeth
Gemma

Berlin, Jeannie
Lila

Bickford, Charles
Clancy
McDonald, Black
Peyramale

Bikel, Theodore
Muller, Max

Billings, George A
Lincoln, Abraham

Billington, Francelia
Armstrong, Margaret

Bisset, Jacqueline
Hamilton, Liz

Black, Karen
Dipesto, Rayette

Blair, Betsy
Clara

Blair, Janet
Sherwood, Eileen

Blair, Linda
Regan

Blakley, Ronee
Barbara Jean

Blanchar, Pierre
Pastor

Blinn, Holbrook
Carlos

Blondell, Joan
Lady Fingers

Blue, Monte
Girard, Dr.

Blyth, Ann
Pierce, Veda

Bogart, Humphrey
Allnutt, Charlie
Blaine, Rick
Dobbs, Fred C.
Earle, Roy
Gunn, Joe
Larrabee, Linus
Marlowe
Martin, Baby Face
Morgan
Queeg
Spade, Sam

Boles, John
Saxel, Walter

Bolger, Ray
Hunk

Bondi, Beulah
Jackson, Rachel
Wilkins, Mary

Booth, Shirley
Delaney, Lola

Borgnine, Ernest
Marty

Boyd, Stephen
Messala

Boyer, Charles
Anton, Gregory
Cesar
De Praslin, Duc
Denard
Iscovescu, Georges
Le Moko, Pepe
Saxel, Walter

Bracken, Eddie
Truesmith, Woodrow

Brady, Alice
O'Leary, Molly

Brando, Marlon
Antony, Marc
Christian, Fletcher
Corleone, Don Vito
Gruver
Kowalski, Stanley
Kurtz
Malloy, Terry
Paul
Zapata, Emiliano

Brennan, Eileen
Lewis, Doreen

Brennan, Walter
Bean, Roy
Bostrom, Swan
Eddie
Goodwin, Peter

Bridges, Jeff
Jackson, Duane
Lightfoot

Broderick, Matthew
David

Bronson, Betty
Peter Pan

Brook, Clive
Rolls Royce

Broune, Leslie
Emilia

Brown, Hope
Whitaker, Angela

Bruce, Nigel
Watson, Dr.

Brynner, Yul
King

Bujold, Genevieve
Boleyn, Anne

Buono, Victor
Flagg, Edwin

Burke, Billie
Cameron, Peggy
Kilbourne, Emily

Burns, Cathy
Rhoda

Burns, George
God
Lewis, Al

Burstyn, Ellen
Doris
Farrow, Lois
Hyatt, Alice
MacNeil, Chris
McCauly, Edna

Burton, Richard
Ashley, Philip
Becket, Thomas
Dysart, Dr.
Gallio, Marcellus
George
Henry VIII
Leamas, Alec

Busey, Gary
Holly, Buddy

Buttons, Red
Kelly

Byington, Spring
Sycamore, Penny

Caan, James
Corleone, Sonny

Cabot, Bruce
Hickock, Bill

Cagney, James
Captain
Cohan, George M.
Marsh, Lew
Snyder, Martin
Sullivan, Rocky
Tom

Caine, Michael
Alfie
Bryant, Frank
Carnehan, Peachy
Tindle, Milo

Calhern, Louis
Emmerich, Alonzo D.
Holmes, Oliver Wendell

Cannon, Dyan
Alice
Farnsworth, Julia

Cantinflas
Passepartout

Carey, Harry
Senate President

Carlin, Lynn
Forst, Maria

Carminati, Tullio
Monteverdi, Giulio

Carney, Art
Harry
Wells, Ira

Caron, Leslie
Bourvier, Lise
Daurier, Lili
Gigi
Jane

Carradine, David
Guthrie, Woody

Carroll, Diahann
Claudine

Carroll, Nancy
Hobart, Hallie

Carson, Jack
Libby, Matt

Cass, Peggy
Gooch, Agnes

Cassavetes, John
Franko, Victor

Cassel, Seymour
Chet

Castellano, Richard
Frank

Chakiris, George
Bernardo

Chandler, Jeff
Cochise

Chaney, Lon
Beaumont
Blizzard
Echo
Fagin
Frog
O'Hara
Phantom of the Opera
Quasimodo

Chaney, Lon, Jr.
Lennie
Talbot, Larry

Channing, Carol
Van Hossmere, Muzzy

Chaplin, Charles
Hynkel, Adenoid
Lone Prospector
Tramp, in *The Circus*
Tramp, in *City Lights*
Tramp, in *The Kid*
Tramp, in *Modern Times*

Cooper, Gary
Deeds, Longfellow
Gehrig, Lou
Geste, Michael
Henry, Frederic
Jones, Melody
Jordan, Robert
Kane, Will
York, Alvin C.

Cooper, Gladys
Higgins, Mrs.
Vale, Mrs.
Vauzos, Marie Theresa

Cooper, Jackie
Aldrich, Henry
Dink
Skinner, Skippy

Corby, Ellen
Trina

Cortese, Valentina
Severine

Cosgrave, Luke
Whitaker, Joel

Cotten, Joseph
Leland, Jedediah

Courtenay, Tom
Antipov, Pasha

Coward, Noel
Kinross, Captain

Crain, Jeanne
Pinky

Cravina, Cesare
Urban, Sylvester

Crawford, Broderick
Stark, Willie

Crawford, Joan
Flaemmchen
Howell, Louise
Hudson, Myra
Pierce, Mildred

Crisp, Donald
Morgan, Gwilym

Cronyn, Hume
Roeder, Paul

Crosby, Bing
Elgin, Frank
O'Malley, Chuck
O'Malley, Father

Cross, Ben
Abrahams, Harold

Crosse, Rupert
McCaslin, Ned

Culp, Robert
Bob

Cummings, Quinn
McFadden, Lucy

Curtis, Tony
Jackson, John

Dailey, Dan
Skid

Dall, John
Evans, Morgan

Dalton, Dorothy
Tharon

Dandridge, Dorothy
Carmen

Daniels, Hattie
Malena

Darby, Kim
Ross, Mattie

Dix, Richard
Cravat, Yancey

Donat, Robert
Chipping, Arthur
Dantes, Edmond
Manson, Andrew

Donlevy, Brian
Markoff

Dooley, Paul
Stoller, Mr.

Douglas, Kirk
Dax, Colonel
Deakins, Jim
Kelly, Midge
McLeod, James
Shields, Jonathan
Van Gogh, Vincent

Douglas, Melvyn
Bannon, Homer
Garrison, Tom
Rand, Benjamin

Dourif, Brad
Bibbitt, Billy

Dowling, Joseph J.
Miracle Man

Dressler, Marie
Annie
Divot, Min
Marthe
Thatcher, Emma

Dreyfuss, Richard
Duddy
Garfield, Elliot
Neary, Roy

Duke, Patty
Keller, Helen

Dunaway, Faye
Christensen, Diana
Crawford, Joan

Mulwray, Evelyn
Parker, Bonnie

Dunn, James
Nolan, Johnny

Dunn, Michael
Glocken

Dunne, Irene
Anna
Cravat, Sabra
Lynn, Theodora
MacKay, Terry
Mama
Schmidt, Ray
Warriner, Lucy

Dunnock, Mildred
Comfort, Rose
Loman, Linda

Durbin, Deanna
Penny

Durning, Charles
Erhardt
Governor

Duvall, Robert
Hagen, Tom
Kilgore
Meechum, Bull
Sledge, Mac

Duvall, Shelley
Lammoreaux, Millie

Eagels, Jeanne
Crosbie, Leslie

Earles, Harry
Tweedledee

Eastwood, Clint
Bronco Billy

Eddy, Nelson
Actor

Fonda, Henry
Carter, Gil
Joad, Tom
Juror 8
Roberts
Thayer, Norman, Jr.
Thursday, Colonel

Fonda, Jane
Daniel, Bree
Gloria
Hellman, Lillian
Hyde, Sally
Wayne, Chelsea Thayer
Wells, Kimberly

Fontaine, Joan
Berndle, Lisa
De Winter, Mrs.
Eyre, Jane
McLaidlaw, Lina
Sanger, Tessa

Fontanne, Lynn
Actress

Ford, Harrison
Indy

Forrest, Frederic
Dyer

Foster, Jodie
Iris

Francis, Alec
Gaunt, Dr.

Franklin, Pamela
Sandy

Fresnay, Pierre
De Paul, Vincent

Frey, Leonard
Motel

Frolong, Ewa
Ekdahl, Emilie

Gabin, Jean
Bobo
Le Moko, Pepe

Gable, Clark
Butler, Rhett
Christian, Fletcher
Norton, Blackie
Warne, Peter

Garbo, Greta
Cavallini
Christie, Anna
Gautier, Marguerite
Grusinskaya
Karenina, Anna
Ninotchka

Gardenia, Vincent
Schnell, Dutch

Gardner, Ava
Kelly, Eloise Y.

Garfield, John
Borden, Mickey
Chambers, Frank
Davis, Charlie
Schmid, Al

Gargan, William
Joe

Garland, Judy
Blodgett, Esther
Dorothy
Hoffman, Irene

Garr, Teri
Sandy

Gould, Elliott
Ted

Gowland, Gibson
McTeague

Grahame, Gloria
Bartlow, Rosemary
Ginny

Granger, Stewart
Quartermain, Allan

Grant, Cary
Adams, Roger
Blandings, Jim
Case, Johnny
Dilg, Leopold
Mott, Ernie
Warriner, Jerry

Grant, Lee
Enders, Mrs.
Felicia
Rosen, Lillian
Shoplifter

Granville, Bonita
Tilford, Mary

Greenstreet, Sydney
Ferrari, Senor
Gutman, Casper
Lorenz, Dr.

Grey, Joel
Master of Ceremonies

Griffith, Hugh
Ilderim, Sheik
Western, Squire

Grodin, Charles
Lenny

Guinness, Alec
Holland
Kenobi, Ben
Nicholson
St. James, Henry

Guve, Bertil
Ekdahl, Alexander

Gwenn, Edmund
Kringle, Kris
Miller, Skipper

Haas, Dolly
Burrows, Lucy

Hackett, Joan
Toby

Hackman, Gene
Barrow, Buck
Caul, Harry
Doyle, Jimmy
Garrison, Gene

Hagen, Jean
Lamont, Lina

Haines, William
Burns, Skeet

Haley, Jack
Hickory

Hall, Grayson
Fellowes, Judith

Hardwicke, Cedric
Lanser, Colonel

Harris, Barbara
Allison

Harris, Ed
Glenn, John

Harris, Julie
Addams, Frankie

Harris, Richard
Byam
Machin, Frank

Harrison, Rex
  Caesar, Julius
  De Carter, Alfred
  Dolittle, Dr. John
  Higgins, Henry
  King

Hart, William S.
  Tracey, Blaze

Hartman, Elizabeth
  D'Arcey, Selina

Harvey, Laurence
  Lampton, Joe
  Romeo

Hatfield, Hurd
  Gray, Dorian

Hawn, Goldie
  Benjamin, Judy
  Jill
  Simmons, Toni

Hayakawa, Sessue
  Saito
  Tori

Hayden, Sterling
  Handley, Dix
  Ripper, General Jack D.

Hayes, Helen
  Arrowsmith, Leora
  Barkley, Catherine
  Claudet, Madelon
  Empress
  Quonsett, Ada

Hayward, Susan
  Angie
  Froman, Jane
  Graham, Barbara
  Roth, Lillian
  Winters, Eloise

Heckart, Eileen
  Baker, Mrs.
  Daigle, Mrs.

Heflin, Van
  Hartnett, Jeff

Hemingway, Mariel
  Tracy

Henry, Justin
  Kramer, Billy

Hepburn, Audrey
  Anne
  Doolittle, Eliza
  Fairchild, Sabrina
  Golightly, Holly
  Hendrix, Susy
  Sister Luke

Hepburn, Katharine
  Adams, Alice
  Curry, Lizzie
  Drayton, Christina
  Eleanor of Aquitaine
  Harding, Tess
  Hudson, Jane
  Jo
  Lord, Tracy
  Lovelace, Eva
  Randall, Terry
  Sayer, Rose
  Seton, Linda
  Thayer, Ethel
  Tyrone, Mary
  Venable, Mrs.

Heston, Charlton
  Ben-Hur, Judah

Hiller, Wendy
  Cooper, Miss
  Doolittle, Eliza
  More, Alice

Hirsch, Judd
  Berger

Hoffman, Dustin
Babe
Bernstein, Carl
Braddock, Ben
Bruce, Lenny
Crabb, Jack
Dorsey, Michael
Kramer, Ted
Rizzo, Ratso

Holbrook, Hal
Deep Throat

Holden, William
Carter, Hal
Gillis, Joe
Larrabee, David
Schumacher, Max
Sefton

Holliday, Judy
Dawn, Billie

Holloway, Stanley
Doolittle, Alfred
Pendlebury

Holm, Celeste
Anne
Karen
Scolastica, Sister

Holm, Ian
Mussabini, Sam

Holt, Tim
Minafer, George Amberson

Homolka, Oskar
Chris

Houseman, John
Kingsfield

Howard, Leslie
Higgins, Henry
Romeo
Standish, Peter
Wilkes, Ashley

Howard, Trevor
Bligh, William
Morel

Hudson, Rock
Benedict, Bick

Hull, Josephine
Simmons, Veta Louise

Hunnicutt, Arthur
Zeb

Hunt, Linda
Kwan, Billy

Hunter, Glenn
Merton
Sweetie

Hunter, Kim
Kowalski, Stella

Hurt, John
Max
Merrick, John

Hurt, William
Nick

Hussey, Olivia
Juliet

Hussey, Ruth
Imbrie, Elizabeth

Huston, John
Cross, Noah
Glennon, Cardinal

Huston, Walter
Cohan, Jerry
Dodsworth, Samuel
Howard
Scratch, Mr.

Hutton, Timothy
Conrad

Kedrova, Lila
Hortense, Madame

Keel, Howard
Adam

Kellaway, Cecil
Horace
Ryan, Monsignor

Kellerman, Sally
O'Houlihan, Margaret

Kelly, Gene
Brady, Joseph
Mulligan, Jerry

Kelly, Grace
Elgin, Georgie
Nordley, Linda

Kelly, Nancy
Christine

Kennedy, Arthur
Barney
Cross, Lucas
Hirsh, Frank
Kelly, Connie
Nevins, Larry

Kennedy, George
Dragline

Kerr, Deborah
Angela, Sister
Anna
Boult, Evelyn
Carmody, Ida
Clodagh, Sister
Curtis, Elizabeth
Holmes, Karen
Railton-Bell, Sibyl

Kibbee, Guy
Dillon, Abner

Kingsley, Ben
Gandhi, Mahatma

Kinski, Nastassia
Tess

Knight, Shirley
Finley, Heavenly
Reenie

Knox, Alexander
Wilson, Woodrow

Kohner, Susan
Sarah Jane

Krauss, Werner
Caligari, Dr.

Kroner, Josef
Brtko, Tono

Kruschen, Jack
Dreyfuss, Dr.

La Garde, Jocelyne
Malama

Ladd, Alan
Shane

Ladd, Diane
Flo

Lafayette, Andree
Trilby

Lahr, Bert
Zeke

Lamarr, Hedy
Gaby
Tondelayo

Lancaster, Burt
Delaney, Doc
Gantry, Elmer
Lou
Starbuck
Stroud, Robert E.
Swede
Warden, Milton

Long, Walter
Dooley, Biff

Loren, Sophia
Antonietta
Cesira
Marturano, Filomena

Lorre, Peter
Cairo, Joel
M
Ugarte

Lorring, Joan
Watty, Bessie

Lossee, Frank
Whitcomb, Josiah

Love, Bessie
Hank

Lowe, Edmund
Quirt

Lowenadler, Holger
Horn, Albert

Loy, Myrna
Charles, Nora

Lugosi, Bela
Dracula
Frankenstein

Lukas, Paul
Muller, Kurt

Lunt, Alfred
Actor

Lupino, Ida
Chernen, Helen
Ellen

MacDonald, Jeanette
Bertier, Colette

MacGraw, Ali
Brenda
Cavilleri, Jenny

MacLaine, Shirley
Aurora
Deedee
Kubelik, Fran
La Douce, Irma
Moorhead, Ginny

Macready, George
Mireau, General

Maggiorani, Lamberto
Antonio

Magnani, Anna
Delle Rose, Serafina
Gioia
Pina

Main, Marjorie
Kettle, Ma

Mako
Po-Han

Malden, Karl
Barry, Father
Mitch

Malmsjo, Jan
Vergerus, Edvard

Malone, Dorothy
Hadley, Marylee

Mantell, Joe
Angie

McLaglen, Victor
Danaher, "Red" Will
Flagg
Hercules
Nolan, Gypo

McMillan, Kenneth
Conklin, Willie

McNamara, Maggie
O'Neill, Patty

McQueen, Butterfly
Prissy

McQueen, Steve
Holman, Jake

Melvin, Murray
Geoffrey

Menjou, Adolphe
Albert
Burns, Walter
Durant, Albert
Rinaldi, Allesandro

Merchant, Vivien
Lily

Mercouri, Melina
Ilya

Meredith, Burgess
George
Harry
Mickey
Pyle, Ernie

Merkel, Una
Winemiller, Mrs.

Midler, Bette
Rose

Mifune, Toshiro
Bandit

Miles, Sarah
Rosy

Miles, Sylvia
Cass
Florian, Mrs.

Milford, Penelope
Munson, Vi

Milland, Ray
Birnam, Don

Miller, Jason
Karras, Father

Miller, Patsy Ruth
Esmeralda

Mills, Hayley
Pollyanna

Mills, John
George
Michael

Mineo, Sal
Landau, Dov
Plato

Minnelli, Liza
Bowles, Sally
Pookie

Miracle, Silas
Warwick

Mitchell, Millard
Connie, James

Mitchell, Thomas
Boone, Josiah
Kersaint

Mitchum, Robert
Hunnicutt, Wade
Walker

Monroe, Marilyn
Cherie

Montgomery, Robert
Danny
Pendleton, Joe

Moody, Ron
Fagin

Moore, Dudley
Bach, Arthur

Moore, Grace
Barrett, Mary

Moore, Juanita
Johnson, Annie

Moore, Mary Tyler
Beth

Moore, Roger
Bond, James

Moore, Terry
Loring, Marie

Moore, Victor
Fadden, Chimmie

Moorehead, Agnes
Minafer, Fanny
Velma

Moran, Lois
Dallas, Laurel

Moreno, Rita
Anita

Morgan, Frank
Duke of Florence
Marvel, Professor
Pirate

Moriarty, Cathy
La Motta, Vickie

Morley, Robert
Louis XVI
Max

Morris, Chester
Williams, Chick

Movin, Lisbeth
Anne

Munday, Helen
Allen, Barbara

Muni, Paul
Abelman, Sam
Allen, James
Camonte, Tony
Dyke, James
Pasteur, Louis
Wang
Zola, Emile

Murray, Don
Bo
Pope, Johnny

Murray, Mae
Sally

Naish, J. Carrol
Giuseppe
Martini, Charley

Nanook
Nanook

Napierkowska, Stacia
Antinea

Natwick, Mildred
Banks, Ethel

Nazimova, Alla
Brat

Neal, Patricia
Alma
Cleary, Nettie

Neckar, Vaclav
Trainee, Milos

Negri, Pola
Catherine
Du Barry, Madame
Paoli, Marianna

Nelligan, Kate
Selky, Susan

Newman, Paul
Bannon, Hud
Bean, Roy
Ben Canaan, Ari
Brick
Cassidy, Butch
Felson, Eddie
Gallagher
Galvin, Frank
Gondorff, Henry
Luke

Nicholson, Jack
Buddusky
Chambers, Frank
Dupea, Robert Eronica
Garrett
Gittes, J.J.
Hanson, George
McMurphy, R.P.
O'Neill, Eugene

Niven, David
Fogg, Phileas
Pollock

Nolte, Nick
Price, Russel

Normand, Mabel
Mickey

Novarro, Ramon
Ben-Hur, Judah
Leonnec, Jean

Oakie, Jack
Napaloni, Benzini

Oberon, Merle
Cathy
Vane, Kitty

O'Brien, Edmond
Clark, Raymond
Muldoon, Oscar

O'Brien, Pat
Connolly, Jerry
Johnson, Hildy

O'Connell, Arthur
Bevans, Howard
McCarthy, Parnell

O'Hara, Maureen
Danaher, Mary Kate
Morgan, Angharad

O'Herlihy, Dan
Crusoe, Robinson

O'Keefe, Michael
Meechum, Ben

Oland, Warner
Chan, Charlie

Oliver, Edna May
March, Aunt
McKlennar, Mrs.
Trotwood, Betsey

Olivier, Laurence
De Winter, Maxim
Hamlet
Heathcliff
Henry V
Lieberman, Ezra
Othello
Rice, Archie
Richard III
Szell
Wyke, Andrew

Olson, Nancy
Schaefer, Betty

O'Neal, Ryan
Barrett, Oliver, IV
Lyndon, Barry

O'Neal, Tatum
Loggins, Addie

O'Neil, Barbara
De Praslin, Duchesse

Oscarsson, Per
Writer

O'Sullivan, Maureen
Jane

O'Toole, Peter
Chipping, Arthur
Cross, El
Henry II, in *Becket*
Henry II, in *The Lion in Winter*
Jack, 14th Earl of Gurney
Lawrence
Swann, Alan

Ouspenskaya, Maria
Marnay, Mme.
Von Obersdorf, Baroness

Pacino, Al
Corleone, Michael, in *The Godfather*
Corleone, Michael, in *The Godfather, Part II*
Kirkland, Arthur
Montana, Tony
Serpico
Sonny

Page, Geraldine
Angie
Chanticleer, Margery
Del Lago, Alexandra
Eve
Winemiller, Alma

Palance, Jack
Blaine, Lester
Wilson

Papas, Irene
Helen of Troy

Parker, Eleanor
Allen, Marie
Lawrence, Marjorie
McLeod, Mary

Parks, Larry
Jolson, Al

Parsons, Estelle
Blanche
Mackie, Calla

Patinkin, Mandy
Avigdor

Pavan, Marisa
Delle Rose, Rosa

Paxinou, Katina
Melandez, Mrs.
Pilar

Peck, Gregory
Baxter, Penny
Chisholm, Francis
Finch, Atticus
Green, Phil
Ringo, Jimmy
Savage, General

Peppard, George
Copley, Rafe

Perkins, Anthony
Bates, Norman
Birdwell, Josh
Van der Besh, Philip

Perkins, Millie
Frank, Anne

Perrine, Valerie
Bruce, Honey

Pesci, Joe
La Motta, Joey

Phillips, Dorothy
Nanette

Pickford, Mary
Angela
Beasant, Norma
Blake, Unity
Gwendolyn
Maris, Stella
Peppina
Pollyanna
Rosita
Skinner, Tessibel

Picon, Molly
Yente

Pidgeon, Walter
Curie, Pierre
Gruffydd, Mr.
Miniver, Clem

Pitts, Zasu
Trina

Place, Mary Kay
Meg

Poitier, Sidney
Cullen, Noah
Prentice, John
Ralfe, Gordon
Smith, Homer
Tibbs, Virgil

Polanski, Roman
Trelkovsky

Pollard, Michael J.
Moss, C.W.

Portman, Eric
Hirth

Powell, Jane
Milly

Powell, William
Charles, Nick
Father
Parke, Godfrey
Ziegfeld, Florenz, Jr.

Power, Tyrone, Sr.
Cobbler

Power, Tyrone
Darrell, Larry
Zorro

Preston, Robert
Hill, Harold
Toddy

Prevost, Marie
Stock, Mizzie

Pringle, Aileen
MacLean, Juneau

Quaid, Randy
Meadows

Quayle, Anthony
Wolsey

Quinn, Anthony
Eufemio
Gauguin, Paul
Gino
Zampano
Zorba, Alexis

Railsback, Steve
Cameron

Raimu
Baker
Pascal

Rainer, Luise
Held, Anna
O-Lan

Robinson, Edward G.
Keller, Joe
Larsen, Wolf
Little Caesar
Monetti, Gino
Morgan, Pete
Rocco, Johnny

Robson, Flora
Angelique

Robson, May
Apple Annie

Rogers, Charles
Powell, John

Rogers, Ginger
Applegate, Sue
Foyle, Kitty
Glossop, Mimi

Rogers, Will
Botts, Ezra

Rollins, Howard E.
Walker, Coalhouse, Jr.

Rooney, Mickey
Dailey, Henry
Dooley
Hardy, Andy
Macauley, Homer
Marsh, Whitey

Rosanova, Rosa
Hanneh

Ross, Diana
Holiday, Billie

Ross, Katherine
Place, Etta
Robinson, Elaine

Rowlands, Gena
Gloria
Longhetti, Mabel

Russell, Harold
Parrish, Homer

Russell, Kurt
Stephens, Drew

Russell, Rosalind
Grayne, Olivia
Jacoby, Bertha
Johnson, Hildy
Kenny, Elizabeth
Mame
Mannon, Lavinia
Sherwood, Ruth

Rutherford, Margaret
Duchess of Brighton

Ryan, Robert
Montgomery
Slade, Larry

Sabu
Abu

Saint, Eva Marie
Doyle, Edie

Samoilova, Tatiana
Veronica

Sampson, Will
Bromden, Chief

Sanders, George
DeWitt, Addison
Strickland, Charles

Sands, Diana
Fanny

Sarandon, Chris
Leon

Sarandon, Susan
Sally

Savalas, Telly
Gomez, Feto

Simmons, Jean
Jones, Ruth Gordon
Ophelia
Wilson, Mary

Simon, Michel
Hire, Monsieur

Simon, Simone
Dubrovna, Irena

Simpson, Russell
Garth, Hugh

Sinatra, Frank
Frankie
Maggio, Angelo

Skala, Lilia
Maria, Mother

Smith, Charles Martin
Nowat, Farley

Smith, Maggie
Augusta
Barrie, Diana
Brodie, Jean
Desdemona

Snodgress, Carrie
Balser, Tina

Sondergaard, Gale
Paleologus, Faith

Sordi, Alberto
Ferretti, Amadeo

Spacek, Sissy
Carrie
Horman, Beth
Lynn, Loretta
Pinky Rose

Stack, Robert
Hadley, Kyle

Staiola, Enzo
Bruno

Stallone, Sylvester
Rocky

Stamp, Terence
Budd, Billy
Clegg, Freddie

Stander, Lionel
Libby, Matt

Stanley, Kim
Farmer, Lillian
Myra

Stanwyck, Barbara
Dallas, Stella
Dietrichson, Phyllis
O'Shea, Sugarpuss
Stevenson, Leona

Stapleton, Maureen
Doyle, Fay
Goldman, Emma
Guerrero, Inez
Pearl

Steenburgen, Mary
Dummar, Lynda

Steiger, Rod
Gillespie, Bill
Malloy, Charley
Nazerman, Sol

Stephenson, James
Joyce, Howard

Sterling, Jan
McKee, Sally

Stevens, Rise
Actress

Todd, Richard
Lachie

Toler, Sidney
Chan, Charlie

Tomlin, Lily
Reese, Linnea

Tone, Franchot
Byam

Topol
Tevye

Tracy, Lee
Hockstader, Arthur

Tracy, Spencer
Banks, Stanley T.
Craig, Sam
Devereaux, Matt
Drayton, Matt
Drummond, Henry
Flanagan, Father
Haywood, Dan
Heisler, George
Jones, Clinton
Macreedy, John T.
Manuel
Mullin, Tim
Old Man
Wilson, Joe

Travers, Bill
Browning, Robert

Travers, Henry
Ballard

Travolta, John
Manero, Tony

Trevor, Claire
Dallas
Francey
Gaye

Trintignant, Jean-Louis
Judge

Tully, Tom
DeVriess

Turner, Lana
Constance
Lorrison, Georgia
Smith, Cora

Tushingham, Rita
Jo

Tyrrell, Susan
Oma

Tyson, Cicely
Morgan, Rebecca

Ullmann, Liv
Isaksson, Jenny
Kristine
Maria
Marianne
Rosenberg, Eva

Umeki, Miyoshi
Katsumi

Ure, Mary
Dawes, Clara

Ustinov, Peter
Batiatus
Nero
Simpson, Arthur

Vaccaro, Brenda
Linda
Shirley

Valentino, Rudolph
Gallardo, Juan
Sheik

Valli, Alida
Paradine, Maddelena

Van Fleet, Jo
Kate

Varsi, Diane
Allison

Vaughn, Robert
Gwyn, Chet

Veidt, Conrad
Cesare

Voight, Jon
Buck, Joe
Champ
Ed
Martin, Luke

Von Schreck, Max
Nosferatu

Von Stroheim, Erich
Karanzin
Von Mayerling, Max

Von Sydow, Max
Oskar, Karl

Walken, Christopher
Nick

Wallgren, Gunn
Ekdahl, Helena

Walters, Julie
Rita

Walthall, Henry B.
Cameron, Ben

Ward, Fannie
Hardy, Edith

Warden, Jack
Corkle, Max
Lester

Warner, David
Morgan

Warner, H.B.
Chang

Warren, Lesley Ann
Norma

Washbourne, Mona
Aunt

Waters, Ethel
Brown, Bernice Sadie
Granny

Watson, Lucille
Farrelly, Fanny

Wayne, John
Brittles, Nathan
Cogburn, Rooster
Dunsom, Tom
Edwards, Ethan
Hondo
Ringo Kid
Roman, Dan
Stryker
Thornton, Sean

Webb, Clifton
Belvedere, Lynn
Lydecker, Waldo
Templeton, Elliott

Wegener, Paul
Golem

Weissmuller, Johnny
Tarzan

Weld, Tuesday
Dunn, Katherine

Welles, Orson
Kane, Charles Foster
Lime, Harry
Rochester, Edward

Werner, Oskar
Fiedler
Happy
Schumann, Dr.

West, Mae
Lee, Flower Belle
Lou, Lady

White, Pearl
Gratia

Whitelaw, Billie
Lottie

Whiting, Leonard
Romeo

Whitman, Stuart
Fuller, Jim

Whitmore, James
Kinnie
Truman, Harry S

Whitty, Dame May
Beldon, Lady
Bramson, Mrs.

Widmark, Richard
Udo, Tommy

Wild, Jack
Artful Dodger

Wilder, Gene
Bloom, Leo

William, Warren
Dave, the Dude

Williams, Cara
Woman

Williams, Grant
Carey, Scott

Williams, John
Hubbard

Williams, Robin
Garp

Wilson, Dooley
Sam

Winfield, Paul
Morgan, Nathan Lee

Winger, Debra
Emma
Pokrifki, Paula

Winn, Kitty
Helen

Winters, Shelley
Belle
D'Arcey, Rose-Ann
Haze, Charlotte
Tripp, Alice

Wiseman, Joseph
Gennini, Charles

Withers, Googie
De Vries, Jo

Wood, Natalie
Angie
Carol
Judy
Loomis, Wilma Dean

Wood, Peggy
Mother Abbess

Woodward, Joanne
Beatrice
Boone, Leola
Cameron, Rachel
Eve
Walden, Rita

Woolley, Monte
Howard
Smollett, Colonel

Wright, Teresa
Beldon, Carol
Charlie

About the Compilers

SUSAN LIEBERMAN was a Reference Librarian at Pennsylvania State University.

FRANCES CABLE is a Reference Librarian at Pennsylvania State University.